IRON
JOHN

Addison-Wesley Publishing Company, Inc.

Reading, Massachusetts   Menlo Park, California   New York
Don Mills, Ontario   Wokingham, England   Amsterdam
Bonn   Sydney   Singapore   Tokyo   Madrid   San Juan

IRON JOHN

A Book About Men

ROBERT BLY

Acknowledgment of permissions granted to reprint previously published material appears on page 269.

Many of the designations used by manufacturers and sellers to distinguish their products are claimed as trademarks. Where those designations appear in this book and Addison-Wesley was aware of a trademark claim, the designations have been printed in initial capital letters (e.g., Windham Hill).

Library of Congress Cataloging-in-Publication Data

Bly, Robert.
   Iron John : a book about men / Robert Bly.
     p. cm.
    ISBN 0-201-51720-5
       0-201-57042-4 (limited edition)
    1. Men—United States. 2. Masculinity (Psychology) 3. Men—
United States—Psychology. I. Title.
HQ1090.3.B59 1990
305.31—dc20
                                     90-37877
                                        CIP

Jacket and text design by Copenhaver Cumpston
Jacket art © by Bruce Waldman
Set in 11½-point Galliard by DEKR Corporation, Woburn, MA

BCDEFGHIJ-MW-943210

For Noah, Micah, and Sam

Contents

Preface

We are living at an important and fruitful moment now, for it is clear to men that the images of adult manhood given by the popular culture are worn out; a man can no longer depend on them. By the time a man is thirty-five he knows that the images of the right man, the tough man, the true man which he received in high school do not work in life. Such a man is open to new visions of what a man is or could be.

The hearth and fairy stories have passed, as water through fifty feet of soil, through generations of men and women, and we can trust their images more than, say, those invented by Hans Christian Andersen. The images the old stories give—stealing the key from under the mother's pillow, picking up a golden feather fallen from the burning breast of the Firebird, finding the Wild Man under the lake water, following the tracks of one's own wound through the forest and finding that it resembles the tracks of a god—these are meant to be taken slowly into the body. They continue to unfold, once taken in.

It is in the old myths that we hear, for example, of Zeus energy, that positive leadership energy in men, which popular culture constantly declares does not exist; from King Arthur we learn the value of the male mentor in the lives of young men; we hear from the Iron John story the importance of moving from the mother's realm to the father's realm; and from all initiation stories we learn how essential it is to leave our parental expectations entirely and find a second father or "second King."

There is male initiation, female initiation, and human initiation. In this book I am talking about male initiation only. I want to make clear that this book does not seek to turn men against women, nor to return men to the domineering mode that has led to repression of women and their values for centuries. The thought in this book does not constitute a challenge to the women's movement. The two movements are related to each other, but each moves on a separate timetable. The grief in men has been increasing steadily since the start of the Industrial Revolution and the grief has reached a depth now that cannot be ignored.

The dark side of men is clear. Their mad exploitation of earth resources, devaluation and humiliation of women, and obsession with tribal warfare are undeniable. Genetic inheritance contributes to their obsessions, but also culture and environment. We have defective mythologies that ignore masculine depth of feeling, assign men a place in the sky instead of earth, teach obedience to the wrong powers, work to keep men boys, and entangle both men and women in systems of industrial domination that exclude both matriarchy and patriarchy.

Most of the language in this book speaks to heterosexual men but does not exclude homosexual men. It wasn't until the eighteenth century that people ever used the term homosexual; before that time gay men were understood simply as a part of the large community of men. The mythology as I see it does not make a big distinction between homosexual and heterosexual men.

I speak of the Wild Man in this book, and the distinction between the savage man and the Wild Man is crucial throughout. The savage mode does great damage to soul, earth, and humankind; we can say that though the savage man is wounded he prefers not to examine it. The Wild Man, who has examined his wound, resembles a Zen priest, a shaman, or a woodsman more than a savage.

The knowledge of how to build a nest in a bare tree, how to fly to the wintering place, how to perform the mating dance—all of this information is stored in the reservoirs of the bird's instinctual brain. But human beings, sensing how much flexibility they might need in meeting new situations, decided to store this sort of knowledge outside the instinctual system; they stored it in stories. Stories, then—fairy stories, legends, myths, hearth stories—amount to a reservoir where we keep new ways of responding that we can adopt when the conventional and current ways wear out.

Some of the great students of this reservoir in recent centuries have been George Groddeck, Gurdjieff, Carl Jung, Heinrich Zimmer, Joseph Campbell, and Georges Dumezil. My first teacher in unfolding the fairy story was Marie-Louise von Franz, and I have tried to be as true to the masculine stories as she has been to the feminine in her many books.

This book draws on a whole community of men, many of whom worked in this field long before I entered it. First among those is Alexander Mitscherlich, the German analyst, who died in 1981, and many fine thinkers in English as well. I am indebted deeply to the men with whom I have joyfully taught during the last eight years—Michael Meade, James Hillman, Terry Dobson, Robert Moore, and John Stokes, among many others. I thank Keith Thompson for his interest in the men's material; the first chapter is a rewriting of his interview with me. And I thank my editor, William Patrick, for his enthusiasm and insight.

I am grateful also to the many men who have trusted me enough to listen, and have honored me by telling me their own stories, or have simply sung, danced, or wept. Even though in this book I lay out an initiatory path in eight stages, other men may see a different order of those stages, or entirely different stages. We make the path by walking. Antonio Machado said:

You walker, there are no roads,
only wind trails on the sea.

Robert Bly

CHAPTER ONE

The Pillow and the Key

We talk a great deal about "the American man," as if there were some constant quality that remained stable over decades, or even within a single decade.

The men who live today have veered far away from the Saturnian, old-man-minded farmer, proud of his introversion, who arrived in New England in 1630, willing to sit through three services in an unheated church. In the South, an expansive, motherbound cavalier developed, and neither of these two "American men" resembled the greedy railroad entrepreneur that later developed in the Northeast, nor the reckless I-will-do-without culture settlers of the West.

Even in our own era the agreed-on model has changed dramatically. During the fifties, for example, an American character appeared with some consistency that became a model of manhood adopted by many men: the Fifties male.

He got to work early, labored responsibly, supported his wife and children, and admired discipline. Reagan is a sort of mummified version of this dogged type. This sort of man didn't see women's souls well, but he appreciated their bodies; and his view of culture and America's part in it was boyish and optimistic. Many of his qualities were strong and positive, but underneath the charm and bluff there was, and there remains, much isolation, deprivation, and passivity. Unless he has an enemy, he isn't sure that he is alive.

The Fifties man was supposed to like football, be aggressive, stick up for the United States, never cry, and always provide. But receptive space or intimate space was missing in this image of a man. The personality lacked some sense of flow. The psyche lacked compassion in a way that encouraged the unbalanced pursuit of the Vietnam war, just as, later, the lack of what we might call "garden" space inside Reagan's head led to his callousness and brutality toward the powerless in El Salvador, toward old people here, the unemployed, schoolchildren, and poor people in general.

The Fifties male had a clear vision of what a man was, and what male responsibilities were, but the isolation and one-sidedness of his vision were dangerous.

During the sixties, another sort of man appeared. The waste and violence of the Vietnam war made men question whether they knew what an adult male really was. If manhood meant Vietnam, did they want any part of it? Meanwhile, the feminist movement encouraged men to actually look at women, forcing them to become conscious of concerns and sufferings that the Fifties male labored to avoid. As men began to examine women's history and women's sensibility, some men began to notice what was called their *feminine* side and pay attention to it. This process continues to this day, and I would say that most contemporary men are involved in it in some way.

There's something wonderful about this development—I mean the practice of men welcoming their own "feminine" consciousness and nurturing it—this is important—and yet I have the sense that there is something wrong. The male in the past twenty years has become more thoughtful, more gentle. But by this process he has not become more free. He's a nice boy who pleases not only his mother but also the young woman he is living with.

In the seventies I began to see all over the country a phenomenon that we might call the "soft male." Sometimes even today when I look out at an audience, perhaps half the young males are what I'd call soft. They're lovely, valuable people—I like them—they're not interested in harming the earth or starting wars. There's a gentle attitude toward life in their whole being and style of living.

But many of these men are not happy. You quickly notice the lack of energy in them. They are life-preserving but not exactly life-giving. Ironically, you often see these men with strong women who positively radiate energy

Here we have a finely tuned young man, ecologically superior to his father, sympathetic to the whole harmony of the universe, yet he himself has little vitality to offer.

The strong or life-giving women who graduated from the sixties, so to speak, or who have inherited an older spirit, played an important part in producing this life-preserving, but not life-giving, man.

I remember a bumper sticker during the sixties that read "WOMEN SAY YES TO MEN WHO SAY NO." We recognize that it took a lot of courage to resist the draft, go to jail, or move to Canada, just as it took courage to accept the draft and go to Vietnam. But the women of twenty years ago were definitely saying that they preferred the softer receptive male.

So the development of men was affected a little in this preference. Nonreceptive maleness was equated with violence, and receptive maleness was rewarded.

Some energetic women, at that time and now in the nineties, chose and still choose soft men to be their lovers and, in a way, perhaps, to be their sons. The new distribution of "yang" energy among couples didn't happen by accident. Young men for various reasons wanted their harder women, and women began to desire softer men. It seemed like a nice arrangement for a while, but we've lived with it long enough now to see that it isn't working out.

I first learned about the anguish of "soft" men when they told their stories in early men's gatherings. In 1980, the Lama Community in New Mexico asked me to teach a conference for men only, their first, in which about forty men participated. Each day we concentrated on one Greek god and one old story, and then late in the afternoons we gathered to talk. When the younger men spoke it was not uncommon for them to be weeping within five minutes. The amount of grief and anguish in these younger men was astounding to me.

Part of their grief rose out of remoteness from their fathers, which they felt keenly, but partly, too, grief flowed from trouble in their marriages or relationships. They had learned to be receptive, but receptivity wasn't enough to carry their marriages through troubled times. In every relationship something *fierce* is needed once in a while: both the man and the woman need to have it. But at the point when it was needed, often the young man came up short. He was nurturing, but something else was required—for his relationship, and for his life.

The "soft" male was able to say, "I can feel your pain, and I consider your life as important as mine, and I will take care of you and comfort you." But he could not say what he wanted, and stick by it. *Resolve* of that kind was a different matter.

In *The Odyssey,* Hermes instructs Odysseus that when he approaches Circe, who stands for a certain kind of matriarchal energy, he is to lift or show his sword. In these early sessions it was difficult for many of the younger men to distinguish between showing the sword and hurting someone. One man, a kind of incarnation of certain spiritual attitudes of the sixties, a man who had actually lived in a tree for a year outside Santa Cruz, found himself unable to extend his arm when it held a sword. He had learned so well not to hurt anyone that he couldn't lift the steel, even to catch the light of the sun on it. But showing a sword doesn't necessarily mean fighting. It can also suggest a joyful decisiveness.

The journey many American men have taken into softness, or receptivity, or "development of the feminine side," has been an immensely valuable journey, but more travel lies ahead. No stage is the final stop.

Finding Iron John

One of the fairy tales that speak of a third possibility for men, a third mode, is a story called "Iron John" or "Iron Hans." Though it was first set down by the Grimm brothers around 1820, this story could be ten or twenty thousand years old.

As the story starts, we find out that something strange has been happening in a remote area of the forest near the king's castle. When hunters go into this area, they disappear and never come back. Twenty others go after the first group and do not come back. In time, people begin to get the feeling that there's something weird in that part of the forest, and they "don't go there anymore."

One day an unknown hunter shows up at the castle and says, "What can I do? Anything dangerous to do around here?"

The King says: "Well, I could mention the forest, but there's a problem. The people who go out there don't come back. The return rate is not good."

"That's just the sort of thing I like," the young man says. So he goes into the forest and, interestingly, he goes there *alone,* taking only his dog. The young man and his dog wander about in the forest and they go past a pond. Suddenly a hand reaches up from the water, grabs the dog, and pulls it down.

The young man doesn't respond by becoming hysterical. He merely says, "This must be the place."

Fond as he is of his dog and reluctant as he is to abandon him, the hunter goes back to the castle, rounds up three more men with buckets, and then comes back to the pond to bucket out the water. Anyone who's ever tried it will quickly note that such bucketing is very slow work.

In time, what they find, lying on the bottom of the pond, is a large man covered with hair from head to foot. The hair is reddish—it looks a little like rusty iron. They take the man back to the castle, and imprison him. The King puts him in an iron cage in the courtyard, calls him "Iron John," and gives the key into the keeping of the Queen.

———————

Let's stop the story here for a second.

When a contemporary man looks down into his psyche, he may, if conditions are right, find under the water of his soul, lying in an area no one has visited for a long time, an ancient hairy man.

The mythological systems associate hair with the instinctive and the sexual and the primitive. What I'm suggesting, then, is that every modern male has, lying at the bottom of his psyche, a large, primitive being covered with hair down to his feet. Making contact with this Wild Man is the step the Eighties male or the Nineties male has yet to take. That bucketing-out process has yet to begin in our contemporary culture.

As the story suggests very delicately, there's more than a little fear around this hairy man, as there is around all change. When a man begins to develop the receptive side of himself and gets over his initial skittishness, he usually finds the experience to be wonderful. He gets to write poetry and go out and sit by the ocean, he doesn't have to be on top all the time in sex anymore, he becomes empathetic—it's a new, humming, surprising world.

But going down through water to touch the Wild Man at the bottom of the pond is quite a different matter. The being who stands up is frightening, and seems even more so now, when the corporations do so much work to produce the sanitized, hairless, shallow man. When a man welcomes his responsiveness, or what we sometimes call his internal woman, he often feels warmer, more companionable, more alive. But when he approaches what I'll call the "deep male," he feels risk. Welcoming the Hairy Man *is* scary and risky, and it requires a different sort of courage. Contact with Iron John requires a willingness to descend into the male psyche and accept what's dark down there, including the *nourishing* dark.

For generations now, the industrial community has warned young businessmen to keep away from Iron John, and the Christian church is not too fond of him either.

Freud, Jung, and Wilhelm Reich are three investigators who had the courage to go down into the pond and to accept what they found there. The job of contemporary men is to follow them down.

Some men have already done this work, and the Hairy Man

has been brought up from the pond in their psyches, and lives in the courtyard. "In the courtyard" suggests that the individual or the culture has brought him into a sunlit place where all can see him. That is itself some advance over keeping the Hairy Man in a cellar, where many elements in every culture want him to be. But, of course, in either place, he's still in a cage.

The Loss of the Golden Ball

Now back to the story.

One day the King's eight-year-old son is playing in the courtyard with the golden ball he loves, and it rolls into the Wild Man's cage. If the young boy wants the ball back, he's going to have to approach the Hairy Man and ask him for it. But this is going to be a problem.

The golden ball reminds us of that unity of personality we had as children—a kind of radiance, or wholeness, before we split into male and female, rich and poor, bad and good. The ball is golden, as the sun is, and round. Like the sun, it gives off a radiant energy from the inside.

We notice that the boy is eight. All of us, whether boys or girls, lose something around the age of eight. If we still have the golden ball in kindergarten, we lose it in grade school. Whatever is still left we lose in high school. In "The Frog Prince," the princess's ball fell into a well. Whether we are male or female, once the golden ball is gone, we spend the rest of our lives trying to get it back.

The first stage in retrieving the ball, I think, is to accept—firmly, definitely—that the ball has been lost. Freud said: "What a distressing contrast there is between the radiant intelligence of the child and the feeble mentality of the average adult."

So where is the golden ball? Speaking metaphorically, we could say that the sixties culture told men they would find their golden ball in sensitivity, receptivity, cooperation, and nonaggressiveness. But many men gave up all aggressiveness and still did not find the golden ball.

The Iron John story says that a man can't expect to find the golden ball in the feminine realm, because that's not where the ball is. A bridegroom secretly asks his wife to give him back the golden ball. I think she'd give it to him if she could, because most women in my experience do not try to block men's growth. But she can't give it to him, because she doesn't have it. What's more, she's lost her own golden ball and can't find that either.

Oversimplifying, we could say that the Fifties male always wants a woman to return his golden ball. The Sixties and Seventies man, with equal lack of success, asks his interior feminine to return it.

The Iron John story proposes that the golden ball lies within the magnetic field of the Wild Man, which is a very hard concept for us to grasp. We have to accept the possibility that the true radiant energy in the male does not hide in, reside in, or wait for us in the feminine realm, nor in the macho/John Wayne realm, but in the magnetic field of the deep masculine. It is protected by the *instinctive* one who's underwater and who has been there we don't know how long.

In "The Frog Prince" it's the frog, the un-nice one, the one that everyone says "Ick!" to, who brings the golden ball back. And in the Grimm brothers version the frog himself turns into the prince only when a hand throws him against the wall.

Most men want some nice person to bring the ball back, but the story hints that we won't find the golden ball in the force field of an Asian guru or even the force field of gentle Jesus. Our story is not anti-Christian but pre-Christian by a thousand years or so, and its message is still true—getting the golden ball back is incompatible with certain kinds of conventional tameness and niceness.

The kind of wildness, or un-niceness, implied by the Wild Man image is not the same as macho energy, which men already know enough about. Wild Man energy, by contrast, leads to forceful action undertaken, not with cruelty, but with resolve.

The Wild Man is not opposed to civilization; but he's not completely contained by it either. The ethical superstructure of popular Christianity does not support the Wild Man, though there is some suggestion that Christ himself did. At the beginning of his ministry, a hairy John, after all, baptized him.

When it comes time for a young male to talk with the Wild Man he will find the conversation quite distinct from a talk with a minister, a rabbi, or a guru. Conversing with the Wild Man is not talking about bliss or mind or spirit or "higher consciousness," but about something wet, dark, and low—what James Hillman would call "soul."

The first step amounts to approaching the cage and asking for the golden ball back. Some men are ready to take that step, while others haven't yet bucketed the water out of the pond—they haven't left the collective male identity and gone out into the unknown area alone, or gone with only their dog.

The story says that after the dog "goes down" one has to start to work with buckets. No giant is going to come along and suck out all the water for you: that magic stuff is not going to help. And a weekend at Esalen won't do it. Acid or cocaine won't do it. The man has to do it bucket by bucket. This resembles the slow discipline of art: it's the work that Rembrandt did, that Picasso and Yeats and Rilke and Bach did. Bucket work implies much more discipline than most men realize.

The Wild Man, as the writer Keith Thompson mentioned to me, is not simply going to hand over the golden ball either. What kind of story would it be if the Wild Man said: "Well, okay, here's your ball"?

Jung remarked that all successful requests to the psyche involve deals. The psyche likes to make deals. If part of you, for example, is immensely lazy and doesn't want to do any work, a flat-out New Year's resolution won't do any good. The whole thing will go better if you say to the lazy part: "You let me work for an hour, then I'll let you be a slob for an hour—deal?" So in "Iron John," a deal is made: the Wild Man agrees to give the golden ball back if the boy opens the cage.

The boy, apparently frightened, runs off. He doesn't even answer. Isn't that what happens? We have been told so often by parents, ministers, grade-school teachers, and high-school principals that we should have nothing to do with the Wild Man that when he says "I'll return the ball if you let me out of the cage," we don't even reply.

Maybe ten years pass now. On "the second day" the man could be twenty-five. He goes back to the Wild Man and says, "Could I have my ball back?" The Wild Man says, "Yes, if you let me out of the cage."

Actually, just returning to the Wild Man a second time is a marvelous thing; some men never come back at all. The twenty-five-year-old man hears the sentence all right, but by now he has two Toyotas and a mortgage, maybe a wife and a child. How can he let the Wild Man out of the cage? A man usually walks away the second time also without saying a word.

Now ten more years pass. Let's say the man is now thirty-five . . . have you ever seen the look of dismay on the face of a thirty-five-year-old man? Feeling overworked, alienated, empty, he asks the Wild Man with full heart this time: "Could I have my golden ball back?"

"Yes," the Wild Man says, "If you let me out of my cage."

Now something marvelous happens in the story. The boy speaks to the Wild Man, and continues the conversation. He says, "Even if I wanted to let you out, I couldn't, because I don't know where the key is."

That's so good. By the time we are thirty-five we don't know where the key is. It isn't exactly that we have forgotten—we never knew where it was in the first place.

The story says that when the King locked up the Wild Man, "he gave the key into the keeping of the Queen," but we were only about seven then, and in any case our father never told us what he had done with it. So where is the key?

I've heard audiences try to answer that one:

"It's around the boy's neck."

No.

"It's hidden in Iron John's cage."

No.

"It's inside the golden ball."

No.

"It's inside the castle . . . on a hook inside the Treasure Room."

No.

"It's in the Tower. It's on a hook high up on the wall!"

No.

The Wild Man replies, "The key is under your mother's pillow."

The key is not inside the ball, nor in the golden chest, nor in the safe . . . the key is under our mother's pillow—just where Freud said it would be.

Getting the key back from under the mother's pillow is a troublesome task. Freud, taking advice from a Greek play, says that a man should not skip over the mutual attraction between himself and his mother if he wants a long life. The mother's pillow, after all, lies in the bed near where she makes love to your father. Moreover, there's another implication attached to the pillow.

Michael Meade, the myth teller, once remarked to me that the pillow is also the place where the mother stores all her expectations for you. She dreams: "My son the doctor." "My son the Jungian analyst." "My son the Wall Street genius." But very few mothers dream: "My son the Wild Man."

On the son's side, he isn't sure he wants to take the key. Simply transferring the key from the mother's to a guru's pillow won't help. Forgetting that the mother possesses it is a bad mistake. A mother's job is, after all, to civilize the boy, and so it is natural for her to keep the key. All families behave alike: on this planet, "The King gives the key into the keeping of the Queen."

Attacking the mother, confronting her, shouting at her, which some Freudians are prone to urge on us, probably does not accomplish much—she may just smile and talk to you with her elbow on the pillow. Oedipus' conversations with Jocasta never did much good, nor did Hamlet's shouting.

A friend mentioned that it's wise to steal the key some day when your mother and father are gone. "My father and mother are away today" implies a day when the head is free of parental inhibitions. That's the day to steal the key. Gioia Timpanelli, the writer and storyteller, remarked that, mythologically, the theft of the key belongs to the world of Hermes.

And the key has to be *stolen*. I recall talking to an audience of men and women once about this problem of stealing the key. A young man, obviously well trained in New Age modes of operation, said, "Robert, I'm disturbed by this idea of stealing the key. Stealing isn't right. Couldn't a group of us just go to the mother and say, 'Mom, could I have the key back?'?"

His model was probably consensus, the way the staff at the health food store settles things. I felt the souls of all the women in the room rise up in the air to kill him. Men like that are as dangerous to women as they are to men.

No mother worth her salt would give the key anyway. If a son can't steal it, he doesn't deserve it.

"I want to let the Wild Man out!"

"Come over and give Mommy a kiss."

Mothers are intuitively aware of what would happen if he got the key: they would lose their boys. The possessiveness that mothers typically exercise on sons—not to mention the possessiveness that fathers typically exercise on daughters—can never be underestimated.

The means of getting the key back varies with each man, but suffice it to say that democratic or nonlinear approaches will not carry the day.

One rather stiff young man danced one night for about six hours, vigorously, and in the morning remarked, "I got some of the key back last night."

Another man regained the key when he acted like a wholehearted Trickster for the first time in his life, remaining fully conscious of the tricksterism. Another man stole the key when he confronted his family and refused to carry any longer the shame for the whole family.

We could spend days talking of how to steal the key in a practical way. The story itself leaves everything open, and simply says, "One day he stole the key, brought it to the Wild Man's cage, and opened the lock. As he did so, he pinched one of his fingers." (That detail will become important in the next part of the story.) The Wild Man is then free at last, and it's clear that he will go back to his own forest, far from "the castle."

What Does the Boy Do?

At this point a number of things could happen. If the Wild Man returns to his forest while the boy remains in the castle, the fundamental historical split in the psyche between primitive man and the civilized man would reestablish itself in the boy. The boy, on his side, could mourn the loss of the Wild Man forever. Or he could replace the key under the pillow before his parents got home, then say he knows nothing about the Wild Man's escape. After that subterfuge, he could become a corporate executive, a fundamentalist minister, a tenured professor, someone his parents could be proud of, who "has never seen the Wild Man."

We've all replaced the key many times and lied about it. Then the solitary hunter inside us has to enter into the woods once more with his body dog accompanying him, and then the dog gets pulled down again. We lose a lot of "dogs" that way.

We could also imagine a different scenario. The boy convinces, or imagines he could convince, the Wild Man to stay in the courtyard. If that happened, he and the Wild Man could carry on civilized conversations with each other in the tea garden, and this conversation would go on for years. But the story suggests that Iron John and the boy cannot be united—that is, cannot experience their initial union—in the castle courtyard. It's probably too close to the mother's pillow and the father's book of rules.

We recall that the boy in our story, when he spoke to the Wild Man, told him he didn't know where the key was. That's brave. Some men never address a sentence to the Wild Man.

When the boy opened the cage, the Wild Man started back to his forest. The boy in our story, or the thirty-five-year-old man in our mind—however you want to look at it—now does something marvelous. He speaks to the Wild Man once more and says, "Wait a minute! If my parents come home and find you gone, they will beat me." That sentence makes the heart sink, particularly if we know something about child-rearing practices that have prevailed for a long time in northern Europe.

As Alice Miller reminds us in her book *For Your Own Good*, child psychologists in nineteenth-century Germany warned parents especially about *exuberance*. Exuberance in a child is bad, and at the first sign of it, parents should be severe. Exuberance implies that the wild boy or girl is no longer locked up. Puritan parents in New England often punished children severely if they acted in a restless way during the long church services.

"If they come home and find you gone, they will beat me."

The Wild Man says, in effect, "That's good thinking. You'd better come with me."

So the Wild Man lifts the boy up on his shoulders and together they go off into the woods. That's decisive. We should all be so lucky.

As the boy leaves for the forest, he has to overcome, at least for the moment, his fear of wildness, irrationality, hairiness, intuition, emotion, the body, and nature. Iron John is not as primitive as the boy imagines, but the boy—or the mind—doesn't know that yet.

Still, the clean break with the mother and father, which the old initiators call for, now has taken place. Iron John says to the boy, "You'll never see your mother and father again. But I have treasures, more than you'll ever need." So that is that.

Going Off on the Wild Man's Shoulders

The moment the boy leaves with Iron John is the moment in ancient Greek life when the priest of Dionysus accepted a young man as a student, or the moment in Eskimo life today when the shaman, sometimes entirely covered with the fur of wild animals, and wearing wolverine claws and snake vertebrae around his neck, and a bear-head cap, appears in the village and takes a boy away for spirit instruction.

In our culture there is no such moment. The boys in our culture have a continuing need for initiation into male spirit, but old men in general don't offer it. The priest sometimes tries, but he is too much a part of the corporate village these days.

Among the Hopis and other native Americans of the Southwest, the old men take the boy away at the age of twelve and bring him *down* into the all-male area of the kiva. He stays *down* there for six weeks, and does not see his mother again for a year and a half.

The fault of the nuclear family today isn't so much that it's crazy and full of double binds (that's true in communes and corporate offices too—in fact, in any group). The fault is that the old men outside the nuclear family no longer offer an effective way for the son to break his link with his parents without doing harm to himself.

The ancient societies believed that a boy becomes a man only through ritual and effort—only through the "active intervention of the older men."

It's becoming clear to us that manhood doesn't happen by itself; it doesn't happen just because we eat Wheaties. The active intervention of the older men means that older men welcome the younger man into the ancient, mythologized, instinctive male world.

One of the best stories I've heard about this kind of welcoming is one that takes place each year among the Kikuyu in Africa. When a boy is old enough for initiation, he is taken away from his mother and brought to a special place the men have set up some distance from the village. He fasts for three days. The third night he finds himself sitting in a circle around the fire with the older men. He is hungry, thirsty, alert, and terrified. One of the older men takes up a knife, opens a vein in his own arm, and lets a little of his blood flow into a gourd or bowl. Each older man in the circle opens his arm with the same knife, as the bowl goes around, and lets some blood flow in. When the bowl arrives at the young man, he is invited to take nourishment from it.

In this ritual the boy learns a number of things. He learns that nourishment does not come only from his mother, but also from men. And he learns that the knife can be used for many purposes besides wounding others. Can he have any doubt now that he is welcome among the other males?

Once that welcoming has been done, the older men teach him the myths, stories, and songs that embody distinctively male values: I mean not competitive values only, but spiritual values. Once these "moistening" myths are learned, the myths themselves lead the young male far beyond his personal father and into the moistness of the swampy fathers who stretch back century after century.

In the absence of old men's labor consciously done, what happens? Initiation of Western men has continued for some time in an altered form even after fanatics destroyed the Greek initiatory schools. During the nineteenth century, grandfathers and uncles lived in the house, and older men mingled a great deal. Through hunting parties, in work that men did together in farms and cottages, and through local sports, older men spent much time with younger men and brought knowledge of male spirit and soul to them.

Wordsworth, in the beginning of "The Excursion," describes the old man who sat day after day under a tree and befriended Wordsworth when he was a boy:

> *He loved me; from a swarm of rosy boys*
> *Singled me out, as he in sport would say,*
> *For my grave looks, too thoughtful for my years.*
> *As I grew up, it was my best delight*
> *To be his chosen comrade. Many a time*
> *On holidays, we wandered through the woods . . .*

Much of that chance or incidental mingling has ended. Men's clubs and societies have steadily disappeared. Grandfathers live in Phoenix or the old people's home, and many boys experience only the companionship of other boys their age who, from the point of view of the old initiators, know nothing at all.

During the sixties, some young men drew strength from women who in turn had received some of their strength from the women's movement. One could say that many young men in the sixties tried to accept initiation from women. But only men can initiate men, as only women can initiate women. Women can change the embryo to a boy, but only men can change the boy to a man. Initiators say that boys need a second birth, this time a birth from men.

Keith Thompson, in one of his essays, described himself at

twenty as a typical young man "initiated" by women. His parents divorced when Keith was about twelve, and he lived with his mother while his father moved into an apartment nearby.

Throughout high school Keith was closer to women than to other men, and that situation continued into college years, when his main friends were feminists whom he described as marvelous, knowledgeable, and generous, and from whom he learned an enormous amount. He then took a job in Ohio state politics, working with women and alert to the concerns of women.

About that time he had a dream. He and a clan of she-wolves were running in the forest. Wolves suggested to him primarily independence and vigor. The clan of wolves moved fast through the forest, in formation, and eventually they all arrived at a riverbank. Each she-wolf looked into the water and saw her own face there. But when Keith looked in the water, he saw no face at all.

Dreams are subtle and complicated, and it is reckless to draw any rapid conclusion. The last image, however, suggests a disturbing idea. When women, even women with the best intentions, bring up a boy alone, he may in some way have no male face, or he may have no face at all.

The old men initiators, by contrast, conveyed to boys some assurance that is invisible and nonverbal; it helped the boys to see their genuine face or being.

So what can be done? Thousands and thousands of women, being single parents, are raising boys with no adult man in the house. The difficulties inherent in that situation came up one day in Evanston when I was giving a talk on initiation of men to a group made up mostly of women.

Women who were raising sons alone were extremely alert to the dangers of no male model. One woman declared that she realized about the time her son got to high-school age that he needed more hardness than she could naturally give. But, she said, if she made herself harder to meet that need, she would lose touch with her own femininity. I mentioned the classic solution in many traditional cultures, which is to send the boy to his father when he is twelve. Several women said flatly, "No, men aren't nurturing;

they wouldn't take care of him." Many men, however—and I am one of them—have found inside an ability to nurture that didn't appear until it was called for.

Even when a father is living in the house there still may be a strong covert bond between mother and son to evict the father, which amounts to a conspiracy, and conspiracies are difficult to break. One woman with two sons had enjoyed going each year to a convention in San Francisco with her husband, the boys being left at home. But one spring, having just returned from a women's retreat, she felt like being private and said to her husband: "Why don't you take the boys this year?" So the father did.

The boys, around ten and twelve, had never, as it turned out, experienced their father's company without the mother's presence. After that experience, they asked for more time with their dad.

When the convention time rolled around the following spring, the mother once more decided on privacy, and the boys once more went off with their father. The moment they arrived back home, the mother happened to be standing in the kitchen with her back to the door, and the older of the two boys walked over and put his arms around her from the back. Without even intending it, her body reacted explosively, and the boy flew across the room and bounced off the wall. When he picked himself up, she said, their relationship had changed. Something irrevocable had happened. She was glad about the change, and the boy seemed surprised and a little relieved that he apparently wasn't needed by her in the old way.

This story suggests that the work of separation can be done even if the old man initiators do not create the break. The mother can make the break herself. We see that it requires a great deal of intensity, and we notice that it was the woman's body somehow, not her mind, that accomplished the labor.

Another woman told a story in which the mother-son conspiracy was broken from the boy's side. She was the single parent of a son and two daughters, and the girls were doing well but the boy was not. At fourteen, the boy went to live with his father, but he stayed only a month or so and then came back. When he returned, the mother realized that three women in the house amounted to an overbalance of feminine energy for the son, but what could she do? A week or two went by. One night she said to her son, "John, it's time to come to dinner." She touched him on the arm and *he* exploded and *she* flew against the wall—the same sort of explosion as in the earlier story. We notice no intent of abuse either time, and no evidence that the event was repeated. In each case the psyche or body knew what the mind didn't. When the mother picked herself off the floor, she said, "It's time for you to go back to your father," and the boy said, "You're right."

The traditional initiation break clearly is preferable, and side-steps the violence. But all over the country now one sees hulking sons acting ugly in the kitchen and talking rudely to their mothers, and I think it's an attempt to make themselves unattractive. If the old men haven't done their work to interrupt the mother-son unity, what else can the boys do to extricate themselves but to talk ugly? It's quite unconscious and there's no elegance in it at all.

A clean break from the mother is crucial, but it's simply not happening. This doesn't mean that the women are doing something wrong: I think the problem is more that the older men are not really doing their job.

The traditional way of raising sons, which lasted for thousands and thousands of years, amounted to fathers and sons living in close—murderously close—proximity, while the father taught the son a trade: perhaps farming or carpentry or blacksmithing or tailoring. As I've suggested elsewhere, the love unit most damaged by the Industrial Revolution has been the father-son bond.

There's no sense in idealizing preindustrial culture, yet we know that today many fathers now work thirty or fifty miles from the house, and by the time they return at night the children are often in bed, and they themselves are too tired to do active fathering.

The Industrial Revolution, in its need for office and factory workers, pulled fathers away from their sons and, moreover, placed the sons in compulsory schools where the teachers are mostly women. D. H. Lawrence described what this was like in his essay

"Men Must Work and Women as Well." His generation in the coal-mining areas of Britain felt the full force of that change, and the new attitude centered on one idea: that physical labor is bad.

Lawrence recalls that his father, who had never heard this theory, worked daily in the mines, enjoyed the camaraderie with the other men, came home in good spirits, and took his bath in the kitchen. But around that time the new schoolteachers arrived from London to teach Lawrence and his classmates that physical labor is low and unworthy and that men and women should strive to move upward to a more "spiritual" level—higher work, mental work. The children of his generation deduced that their fathers had been doing something wrong all along, that men's physical work is wrong and that those sensitive mothers who prefer white curtains and an elevated life are right and always have been.

During Lawrence's teenage years, which he described in *Sons and Lovers,* he clearly believed the new teachers. He wanted the "higher" life, and took his mother's side. It wasn't until two years before he died, already ill with tuberculosis in Italy, that Lawrence began to notice the vitality of the Italian workingmen, and to feel a deep longing for his own father. He realized then that his mother's ascensionism had been wrong for him, and had encouraged him to separate from his father and from his body in an unfruitful way.

A single clear idea, well fed, moves like a contagious disease: "Physical work is wrong." Many people besides Lawrence took up that idea, and in the next generation that split between fathers and sons deepened. A man takes up desk work in an office, becomes a father himself, but has no work to share with his son and cannot explain to the son what he's doing. Lawrence's father was able to take his son down into the mines, just as my own father, who was a farmer, could take me out on the tractor, and show me around. I knew what he was doing all day and in all seasons of the year.

When the office work and the "information revolution" begin to dominate, the father-son bond disintegrates. If the father inhabits the house only for an hour or two in the evenings, then women's values, marvelous as they are, will be the only values in the house. One could say that the father now loses his son five minutes after birth.

When we walk into a contemporary house, it is often the mother who comes forward confidently. The father is somewhere else in the back, being inarticulate. This is a poem of mine called "Finding the Father":

> *My friend, this body offers to carry us for nothing—as the ocean carries logs. So on some days the body wails with its great energy; it smashes up the boulders, lifting small crabs, that flow around the sides.*
>
> *Someone knocks on the door. We do not have time to dress. He wants us to go with him through the blowing and rainy streets, to the dark house.*
>
> *We will go there, the body says, and there find the father whom we have never met, who wandered out in a snowstorm the night we were born, and who then lost his memory, and has lived since longing for his child, whom he saw only once . . . while he worked as a shoemaker, as a cattle herder in Australia, as a restaurant cook who painted at night.*
>
> *When you light the lamp you will see him. He sits there behind the door . . . the eyebrows so heavy, the forehead so light . . . lonely in his whole body, waiting for you.*

The Remote Father

The German psychologist Alexander Mitscherlich writes about this father-son crisis in his book called *Society Without the Father*. The gist of his idea is that if the son does not actually see what his father does during the day and through all the seasons of the year, a hole will appear in the son's psyche, and the hole will fill with demons who tell him that his father's work is evil and that the father is evil.

The son's fear that the absent father is evil contributed to student takeovers in the sixties. Rebellious students at Columbia University took over the president's office looking for evidence of

CIA involvement with the university. The students' fear that their own fathers were evil was transferred to all male figures in authority. A university, like a father, looks upright and decent on the outside, but underneath, somewhere, you have the feeling that it and he are doing something demonic. That feeling becomes intolerable because the son's inner intuitions become incongruous with outer appearances. The unconscious intuitions come in, not because the father is wicked, but because the father is remote.

Young people go to the trouble of invading the president's office to bridge this incongruity. The country being what it is, occasionally they do find letters from the CIA, but this doesn't satisfy the deeper longing—the need of the son's body to be closer to the father's body. "Where is my father . . . why doesn't he love me? What is going on?"

The movie called *The Marathon Man* concentrates on the young American male's suspicion of older men. The main character, played by Dustin Hoffman, loses his father, a leftist driven to suicide in the McCarthy era. The plot puts the young man in dangerous contact with a former concentration camp doctor, whom Hoffman must confront and defeat before he can have any peace with his own dead father.

When the demons are so suspicious, how can the son later make any good connection with adult male energy, especially the energy of an adult man in a position of authority or leadership? As a musician he will smash handcrafted guitars made by old men, or as a teacher suspicious of older writers he will "deconstruct" them. As a citizen he will take part in therapy rather than politics. He will feel purer when not in authority. He will go to northern California and raise marijuana, or ride three-wheelers in Maine.

There's a general assumption now that every man in a position of power is or will soon be corrupt and oppressive. Yet the Greeks understood and praised a positive male energy that has accepted authority. They called it Zeus energy, which encompasses intelligence, robust health, compassionate decisiveness, good will, generous leadership. Zeus energy is male authority accepted for the sake of the community.

The native Americans believe in that healthful male power. Among the Senecas, the chief—a man, but chosen by the women— accepts power for the sake of the community. He himself owns virtually nothing. All the great cultures except ours preserve and have lived with images of this positive male energy.

Zeus energy has been steadily disintegrating decade after decade in the United States. Popular culture has been determined to destroy respect for it, beginning with the "Maggie and Jiggs" and "Blondie and Dagwood" comics of the 1920s and 1930s, in which the man is always weak and foolish. From there the image of the weak adult man went into animated cartoons.

The father in contemporary TV ads never knows what cold medicine to take. And in situation comedies, "The Cosby Show" notwithstanding, men are devious, bumbling, or easy to outwit. It is the women who outwit them, and teach them a lesson, or hold the whole town together all by themselves. This is not exactly "what people want." Many young Hollywood writers, rather than confront their fathers in Kansas, take revenge on the remote father by making all adult men look like fools.

They attack the respect for masculine integrity that every father, underneath, wants to pass on to his grandchildren and great-grandchildren. By contrast, in traditional cultures, the older men and the older women often are the first to speak in public gatherings; younger men may say nothing but still aim to maintain contact with the older men. Now we have twenty-seven-year-olds engaged in hostile takeovers who will buy out a publishing house and dismantle in six months what an older man has created over a period of thirty years.

I offered my help in undermining Zeus energy during my twenties and thirties. I attacked every older man in the literary community who was within arrow range, and enjoyed seeing the arrows pass through his body, arrows impelled by the tense energy bottled in my psyche. I saw many parts of my father's daytime life, his work habits, and his generous attitude toward working men; but he was inaccessible in some other way, and the hole in me filled with demons, as Mitscherlich predicted. Older men whom I hardly knew received the anger.

When a son acts on that fear of demonism it makes him flat, stale, isolated, and dry. He doesn't know how to recover his wet and muddy portion. A few years ago, I began to feel my diminishment, not so much on my "feminine" side as on my masculine side. I found myself missing contact with men—or should I say my father?

I began to think of him not as someone who had deprived me of love or attention or companionship, but as someone who himself had been deprived, by his father and his mother and by the culture. This rethinking is still going on.

Every time I see my father I have new and complicated feelings about how much of the deprivation I felt with him came willingly and how much came against his will—how much he was aware of and unaware of.

Jung said something disturbing about this complication. He said that when the son is introduced primarily by the mother to feeling, he will learn the female attitude toward masculinity and take a female view of his own father and of his own masculinity. He will see his father through his mother's eyes. Since the father and the mother are in competition for the affection of the son, you're not going to get a straight picture of your father out of your mother, nor will one get a straight picture of the mother out of the father.

Some mothers send out messages that civilization and culture and feeling and relationships are things which the mother and the daughter, or the mother and the sensitive son, share in common, whereas the father stands for and embodies what is stiff, maybe brutal, what is unfeeling, obsessed, rationalistic: money-mad, uncompassionate. "Your father can't help it." So the son often grows up with a wounded image of his father—not brought about necessarily by the father's actions, or words, but based on the mother's observation of these words or actions.

I know that in my own case I made my first connection with feeling through my mother. She provided me my first sense of discrimination of feeling. "Are you feeling sad?" But the connection entailed picking up a negative view of my father, who didn't talk very much about feelings.

It takes a while for a son to overcome these early negative views of the father. The psyche holds on tenaciously to these early perceptions. Idealization of the mother or obsession with her, liking her or hating her, may last until the son is thirty, or thirty-five, forty. Somewhere around forty or forty-five a movement toward the father takes place naturally—a desire to see him more clearly and to draw closer to him. This happens unexplainably, almost as if on a biological timetable.

A friend told me how that movement took place in his life. At about thirty-five, he began to wonder who his father really was. He hadn't seen his father in about ten years. He flew out to Seattle, where his father was living, knocked on the door, and when his father opened the door, said, "I want you to understand one thing. I don't accept my mother's view of you any longer."

"What happened?" I asked.

"My father broke into tears, and said, 'Now I can die.'" Fathers wait. What else can they do?

I am not saying that all fathers are good; mothers can be right about the father's negative side, but the woman also can be judgmental about masculine traits that are merely different or unexpected.

If the son learns feeling primarily from the mother, then he will probably see his own masculinity from the feminine point of view as well. He may be fascinated with it, but he will be afraid of it. He may pity it and want to reform it, or he may be suspicious of it and want to kill it. He may admire it, but he will never feel at home with it.

Eventually a man needs to throw off all indoctrination and begin to discover for himself what the father is and what masculinity is. For that task, ancient stories are a good help, because they are free of modern psychological prejudices, because they have endured the scrutiny of generations of women and men, and because they give both the light and dark sides of manhood, the admirable and the dangerous. Their model is not a perfect man, nor an overly spiritual man.

In the Greek myths, Apollo is visualized as a golden man standing on an enormous accumulation of the dark, alert, dangerous energy called Dionysus. The Wild Man in our story includes some of both kinds of energy, both Apollo and Dionysus.

The Bhutanese make masks of a bird-headed man with dog's teeth. That suggests a good double energy. We all know the temple guardians set before Oriental temple doors. A guardian is a man with bulging brows and fierce will, foot raised as if to dance, who lifts a club made of a flower. The Hindus offer as an image of masculinity Shiva, who is both an ascetic and a good lover, a madman and a husband. He has a fanged form called Bhairava, and in that aspect he is far from the niceness suggested by the conventional Jesus.

There's a hint of this Bhairava energy when Christ goes wild in the temple and starts whipping the moneychangers. The Celtic tradition offers as a male image Cuchulain—when he gets hot, his shin muscles switch around to the front and smoke comes out of the top of his head.

These powerful energies inside men are lying, like Iron John, in ponds we haven't walked past yet. It is good that the divine is associated with the Virgin Mary and a blissful Jesus, but we can sense how different it would be for young men if we lived in a culture where the divine also was associated with mad dancers, fierce fanged men, and a being entirely underwater, covered with hair.

All of us, men and women both, feel some fear as we approach these images. We have been trying for several decades, rightly, to understand the drawbacks of the destructive, macho personality type, and in that regard I think it is helpful to keep in mind the distinctions between the Wild Man and the savage man.

When a man gets in touch with the Wild Man, a true strength may be added. He's able to shout and say what he wants in a way that the Sixties-Seventies man is not able to. The approach to, or embodying of, receptive space that the Sixties-Seventies man has achieved is infinitely valuable, and not to be given up. But as I wrote in a poem called "A Meditation on Philosophy":

When you shout at them, they don't reply.
They turn their face toward the crib wall, and die.

The ability of a male to shout and to be fierce does not imply domination, treating people as if they were objects, demanding land or empire, holding on to the Cold War—the whole model of machismo.

Women in the 1970s needed to develop what is known in the Indian tradition as Kali energy—the ability really to say what they want, to dance with skulls around their neck, to cut relationships when they need to.

Men need to make a parallel connection with the harsh Dionysus energy that the Hindus call Kala. Our story says that the first step is to find the Wild Man lying at the bottom of the pond. Some men are able to descend to that place through accumulated grief. However, connecting with this Kala energy will have the effect also of meeting that same energy in women. If men don't do that, they won't survive.

Men are suffering right now—young men especially. Now that so many men have gotten in touch with their grief, their longing for father and mentor connections, we are more ready to start seeing the Wild Man and to look again at initiation. But I feel very hopeful.

At this point, many things can happen.

CHAPTER TWO

When One Hair
Turns Gold

We could ask: "Why not stop here?" We have a young man who has stolen the key from under his mother's pillow. He has escaped from mother and father, and he is in touch with the Wild Man and, through him, the wilderness. Like Huck Finn, he has started "down the Mississippi" on a raft with a companion from a different world. But if our story describes initiation, we know we will have to deal soon with some sort of wound, the breaking of a bone, a puncture to the skin, a making of wound patterns on the body. That is all part of it.

Mircea Eliade, in his reports of initiation experiences in dozens of cultures all over the world, mentions that initiation of boys begins with two events: the first is a clean break with the parents, after which the novice goes to the forest, desert, or wilderness. The second is a wound that the older men give the boy, which could be scarring of the skin, a cut with a knife, a brushing with nettles, a tooth knocked out. But we mustn't leap to the assumption that the injuries are given sadistically. Initiators of young men in most cultures make sure that the injuries they give do not lead to meaningless pain, but reverberate out from a rich center of meaning. An initiatory practice the aborigines of Australia followed is a good example. The old men, having brought the young boys away from the community, tell the boys the story of the first man, Darwalla. The boys listen intently to this tale of the original man, their Adam. It turns out that Darwalla is sitting in that tree over there. While the boys try to see Darwalla in the tree, an old man comes down the line, and knocks out a tooth from each boy's mouth. The old men then remind the boys that something similar happened to Darwalla. He lost a tooth. Their tongues for the rest of their lives associate the broken tooth with a living connection to Darwalla. Most of us would give up a tooth for a living connection to Adam.

Early adolescence is the time traditionally chosen for initiation to begin, and we all recall how many injuries we received at that age. Adolescence is the time of risk for boys, and that risk-taking is also a yearning for initiation.

The number of injuries a typical man has endured is astounding. This became visibly clear to me one day in San Francisco, when several hundred men were gathered in a large room. One of the teachers, Doug van Koss, handed out two or three thousand strips of red cloth, and asked each man to fasten or tie a red strip over any part of his body that had been wounded in some way— a cut, a broken bone, a knife wound, a scar.

Many men needed ten or more strips. For some men the entire right side of the body, head to ankle, was brilliant red; on others the red almost covered the head; for some, both arms and legs. When the exercise was over, the room was a sea of red.

Something in the adolescent male wants risk, courts danger, goes out to the edge—even to the edge of death.

In our story then, the boy's finger hints of wounds each of us have already received in our attempts to let the "Wild Man" out of the cage. Old men don't give us the wound. We do it ourselves. Whether the old men of the past scar us with a seashell, or tattoo us painfully, or we do it ourselves, the scar stands for a wound that is already there, some missing tooth that we have each felt with our tongues. The wounded finger in our story stands for a wound most young men in our culture have already received. Let's go back to the story:

The Story: The First Day at the Pond

When the Wild Man had reached the dark forest once more, he took the boy from his shoulders, put him down on the earth, and said, "You will never see your mother and father again, but I will keep you with me, for you have set me free, and I feel compassion for you. If you do everything as I tell you, all will go well. I have much gold and treasure, more than anyone else in the world."

The Wild Man prepared a bed of moss for the boy to sleep on, and in the morning took him to a spring. "Do you see this golden spring? It is clear as crystal, and full of light. I want you to sit beside it and make sure that nothing falls into it, because if that happens, it will wrong the spring. I'll return each evening to see if you've obeyed my order."

The boy sat down at the spring's edge. Occasionally he glimpsed a golden fish or a gold snake, and he took care to let nothing fall in. But as he sat there, his wounded finger was so painful that, without intending to, he dipped it into the water. He pulled it out instantly, but he saw that the finger had turned to gold, and no matter how much he washed it, the washing did no good.

Iron John came back that evening and said, "Anything happen with the spring today?"

The boy held his finger behind his back to keep Iron John from seeing it, and said, "No, nothing at all."

"Ah, you've dipped your finger in the spring!" said the Wild Man. "We can let it pass this once, but don't let that happen again."

We will talk of the gold attaching itself to the fingertip in a moment, but for now we'll stay a little longer with the wound. The wound hurt so much that the boy dipped it involuntarily into the pond. That is basically what the story says.

If we are to live in this story, rather than merely observe it, we have to ask ourselves, "What wound do we have that hurts so much we have to dip it in water?" Initiation, then, for young men amounts to helping them remember the wound, and by that we mean the soul wounds, or injuries to the emotional body. Sometimes the outward scars exist to remind us of inward scars.

Let's list some inward injuries, as we listed some outward injuries above. Not receiving any blessing from your father is an injury. Robert Moore said, "If you're a young man and you're not being admired by an older man, you're being hurt." How many men have said to me, "I waited for two days with my father when he was dying, and wanted him to tell me that he loved me." What happened? "He never did."

Not seeing your father when you are small, never being with him, having a remote father, an absent father, a workaholic father, is an injury. Having a critical, judgmental father amounts to being one of Cronos' sons, whom Cronos ate. Some blow usually comes from the father, one way or another.

Michael Meade found an African story in which the hunter father takes his boy hunting with him one day. Having killed a small rat, he asks the son to keep it. "The son, thinking it was nothing, threw it in the bush," the story says.

No more game comes along that day, and at dusk the father asks the boy for the rat so they can cook it and have something to eat. The boy tells the father, "I threw it in the bush." Then, according to the story, "The father took up his axe, and hit his son, who was knocked unconscious; and the father then left the boy lying where he was."

Men who hear the story know in the most astonishing detail exactly where that axe blow fell. One says the axe hit the left side of his head. Another said it landed in the chest area. Another said, "On my shoulder." Another, "On the back of my head." Another, "Right down the center of my skull." Another, "On my stomach." Another, "In my groin," and so on and so on. Almost every man remembers that blow coming in. So this event seems to be a part of father-son material: the father gives a blow, and the son gets it. And it's a wound the boy remembers for years.

And what of the blows from the mother? "You are very frail,

you know; you shouldn't play with those boys." "How could you kill such a beautiful little bird?" "If you don't stop that, I'll send you to a foster home! See how you like that!" "You're too big for your britches." "Now you're acting just like your father." The father gives a son a vivid and unforgettable blow with an axe, which has the hint of murder in it; many a mother makes sure the son receives a baptism of shame. She keeps pouring the water of shame over his head to make sure.

One man said, "My mother had tripod rage—the irresistible urge to kick anything with three legs."

Sometimes that shaming produces a long-lasting wound that won't heal. The Greeks going to the Trojan War left Philoctetes behind on an island because his wound smelled so bad. Later, they had to go back and find him when the oracle said that retrieving him was the only way to win the war. The wounded man knows something, or is something.

Beatings, slaps in the face, verbal batterings are injuries. Blows that lacerate self-esteem, puncture our sense of grandeur, pollute enthusiasm, poison and desolate confidence, give the soul black-and-blue marks, undermining and degrading the body image . . . these all make a defilement. They damage and do harm.

Being lied to by older men amounts to a broken leg. When the young men arrived in Vietnam and found that they had been lied to, they received immeasurably deep wounds.

Never being welcomed into the male world by older men is a wound in the chest. The police chief of Detroit remarked that the young men he arrests not only don't have any responsible older man in the house, they have never met one. When you look at a gang, you are looking, as Michael Meade remarked, at young men who have no older men around them at all. Gang members try desperately to learn courage, family loyalty, and discipline from each other. It works for a few, but for most it doesn't.

To judge by men's lives in New Guinea, Kenya, North Africa, the pygmy territories, Zulu lands, and in the Arab and Persian culture flavored by Sufi communities, men have lived together in heart unions and soul connections for hundreds of thousands of years.

Contemporary business life allows competitive relationships only, in which the major emotions are anxiety, tension, loneliness, rivalry, and fear. After work what do men do? Collect in a bar to hold light conversations over light beer, unities which are broken off whenever a young woman comes by or touches the brim of someone's cowboy hat. Having no soul union with other men can be the most damaging wound of all.

These wounds come into us whether we honor our parents or not, whether we are good or bad. Most of them we can describe as wounds to our grandiosity. When we are tiny we have the feeling that we are God. Our kingly life in the womb pointed to some such possibility, and if anyone, once we are out, tries to tell us we are not God, we don't hear it. This early sense of our Godliness we could call Infantile Grandiosity, and we need to distinguish that from greatness or True Grandiosity, which is a part of us also. At any rate, as adolescents we still have enough infantile grandiosity so we imagine we can decide whether the rat is big enough to keep or not. Then, when the father hits us with an axe and leaves us lying on the ground, we find our condition—wounded, on the ground—difficult to reconcile with our fantasy of princehood.

All wounds threaten our princehood. The shame blows, "Who do you think you are? You're just a snotty-nosed kid like all the rest," are like blows to the prince's stomach. And there is always something wrong with us. One boy feels too thin, or too short, or too stringy; another has a stutter or a limp. One is too shy; another is "not athletic" or can't dance, or has a bad complexion. Another has big ears, or a birthmark, or is "dumb," can't hit the ball, and so on. We usually solve the problem by inflating ourselves further. A little ascension takes us above it all.

Perhaps some grandiosity or godlikeness is useful in protecting ourselves when we are very young. Alice Miller remarks that when abuse enters, when the parents do cruelties the child cannot imagine any parent doing, it takes either a grandiose road or a depressed road. If we take the grandiose road, we climb up above the wound and the shame. Perhaps we get good grades, become the one in the family hired to be cheerful, become a sort of doctor of our own suffering, take care of others. Something prodigious carries us away. We can be cheerful but not very human.

If we take the depressed road, we live inside the wound and the shame. We are actually closer to the wound than those on the grandiose path, but we are not necessarily more human. The victim is an imposing person, too. The victim accepts the crown of victimhood, becomes a prince or a princess in another way. Sometimes men with no fathers take this road.

Each of us takes both of these roads, though we use one on Sundays and holidays, and the other on weekdays. Some take a third road: it is the road of paralysis, robot behavior, seriously pursued numbness—a hollow at the center, no affect, no emotion upward or downward, automaton life.

Ancient initiation practice would affect all these responses, since it gives a new wound, or gives a calculated wound sufficiently pungent and vivid—though minor—so that the young man remembers his inner wounds. The initiation then tells the young man what to do with wounds, the new and the old.

The old men tell the boys stories as soon as they enter the men's world. If we have no story, we cannot take hold of the wound. We either climb above it, so far up that we can't reach down to take hold of it, or we become the wound, get stepped on by something so huge we see only the ground below us.

Letting the boy's injured finger stand then for a variety of childhood wounds, let's go back to the story and imagine how the wound happened. We tried to let the "Wild Man," who here represents our own brilliance, bounty, wildness, greatness, and spontaneity, out of the cage, at which point the wound arrived.

In our families, we can rise above the shame of having an alcoholic father by adding fuel secretly to our grandiose rocket, pulling away from the family, riding upward on that fuel. Or we can sink down into the shamed child, become him, be no one else, live in our secret unworthiness, lose our king, and become a slave. There is a pleasure in becoming a slave. Then we can turn into an addict, and never be in charge of our own life, and shame ourselves further.

The addictive state is the fastest growing state in the United

States, outstripping California and Hawaii. In this way of dealing with the axe wound, we say "I am that child." As we know from Philippe Aries's *Centuries of Childhood*, before the nineteenth century or so there were no clothes designed especially for children. During and after the Middle Ages the child said, "I am a small-sized adult," and he or she wore clothes similar to those the adults wore. That practice had some drawbacks, but the reversal has been catastrophic. When people identify themselves with their wounded child, or remain children, the whole culture goes to pieces. We learn from teenage pregnancies that children cannot mother their own children or father their own children. People lead lives that radiate destruction to the immediate family as well as to the neighborhood. Everyone is in the emergency ward.

The recovery of some form of initiation is essential to the culture. The United States has undergone an unmistakable decline since 1950, and I believe that if we do not find a third road besides the two mentioned here, the decline will continue. We have the grandiose road, taken by junk-bond dealers, high rollers, and the owners of private jets; and we have the depressed road, taken by some long-term alcoholics, single mothers below the poverty line, crack addicts, and fatherless men.

Ascending into excitement and ecstasy does not give us the key either. The key remains hidden.

Ecstasy too early—or generalized excitement—may be, as James Hillman has remarked, just another way the Great Mother has of keeping the man from developing any discipline. When the key remains under the mother's pillow, we will end up in a treatment center sooner or later. The counselors and the therapists will do their best to free us, but we usually stuff the key under their pillow when they aren't watching.

Suppose we do succeed in stealing the key from under the mother's pillow, and we relieve a finger wound, then what? Would we go off with the Wild Man at that point? Probably not. We might spend ten years feeling the wounded finger, blaming our parents and the patriarchy for it. We would probably sue the Wild Man for having a rusty lock, and sue our mother for not protecting her key better. The story of the Wild Man ends abruptly if one decides one is the Wild Man (the grandiose path) or if one agrees one is the victimized helpless child (the depressed path).

The people who are wholeheartedly devoted to infantile grandiosity—the Wall Street man, the New Age harp player—why should they go with the Wild Man? They imagine themselves to be the Wild Man already—they are the latest thing in wildness, able to stay up all night playing with their computers, or able to think nonpolluting thoughts for four days running.

Few American men in the last decades get past the detail of the key.

If a man imagines that he is either the Wild Man or a victim child, the adoption of a mentor is out of the question. We can each ask ourselves: is there anyone we know or have heard of who possesses a true greatness? If so, we should leave with him or with her.

We need to understand the Wild Man is not "inside" us. The story suggests that the Wild Man is actually a being who can exist and thrive for centuries outside the human psyche. He can be compared on the human plane to a mentor, who will continue to live and grow whether he takes us as a student or not.

The ancient practice of initiation then—still very much alive in our genetic structure—offers a third way through, between the two "natural" roads of manic excitement and victim excitement. A mentor or "male mother" enters the landscape. Behind him, a being of impersonal intensity stands, which in our story is the Wild Man, or Iron John. The young man investigates or experiences his wound—father wound, mother wound, or shaming-wound—in the presence of this independent, timeless, mythological initiatory being.

If the young man steals the key and climbs on the shoulders of this being, three things will change: the wound, rather than being regarded as bad luck, will be seen as a gift. Second, the sacred or secret water—whatever that is—will appear. Finally, the energy of the sun will somehow be carried into the man's body. We will repeat that part of the story.

When the Wild Man had reached the dark forest once more, he took the boy from his shoulders, put him down on the earth, and said, "You will never see your mother and father again, but I will keep you with me, for you have set me free, and I feel compassion for you. If you do everything as I tell you, all will go well. I have much gold and treasure, more than anyone else in the world."

The Wild Man prepared a bed of moss for the boy to sleep on, and in the morning took him to a spring. "Do you see this golden spring? It is clear as crystal, and full of light. I want you to sit beside it and make sure that nothing falls into it, because if that happens, it will wrong the spring. I'll return each evening to see if you've obeyed my order."

The boy sat down at the spring's edge. Occasionally he glimpsed a golden fish or a gold snake, and he took care to let nothing fall in. But as he sat there, his wounded finger was so painful that, without intending to, he dipped it into the water. He pulled it out instantly, but he saw that the finger had turned to gold, and no matter how much he washed it, the washing did no good.

Iron John came back that evening and said, "Anything happen with the spring today?"

The boy held his finger behind his back to keep Iron John from seeing it, and said, "No, nothing at all."

"Ah, you've dipped your finger in the spring!" said the Wild Man. "We can let it pass this once, but don't let that happen again."

The Wild Man takes the boy to a Sacred Spring, to water. We note that golden fish and gold snakes swim in this water. Mythologically, this is the old sacred spring guarded by the Wild Man and sometimes the Wild Woman as well. If this spring is ever polluted, the old Celtic knowers say, then everything on the earth will die. So the water is an important place. It is a traditional place for the Wild Man to carry on his brooding, and we know from the *Vita Merlini* that Merlin brooded there during his madness. They were also places where the ordinary person went for inspiration, spiritual food, and wisdom. Travelers received nourishment for centuries at the holy well at Logres. At Connla's Well the great holy salmon swam, waiting for the overhanging trees to drop the hazelnuts of inspired madness once every year.

Psychologically, this is the water of soul life, but only for those ready to go in. Mircea Eliade says of male initiation: "The puberty initiation represents above all the revelation of the sacred . . . before initiation, [boys] do not yet fully share in the human condition precisely because they do not yet have access to the religious life."

Religion here does not mean doctrine, or piety, or purity, or "faith," or "belief," or my life given to God. It means a willingness to be a fish in the holy water, to be fished for by Dionysus or one of the other fishermen, to bow the head and take hints from one's own dreams, to live a secret life, praying in a closet, to be lowly, to eat grief as the fish gulps water and lives. It means being both fisherman and fish, not to be the wound but to take hold of the wound. Being a fish is to be active; not with cars or footballs, but with soul.

Those working with alcoholic families in the last ten years have made much of the word denial, and it is a good word. Denial stands for amnesia, forgetfulness, oblivion. An ocean of oblivion sweeps over a child when it is shamed. A woman is sexually abused at four and forgets the event entirely until she is thirty-eight—and there is no blame for the oblivion. Denial means we have been entranced; we live for years in a trance.

In "The Raven" (Grimm brothers) a young girl changes into a raven when her mother objects to her behavior, and remains so enchanted for years; in the "Six Swans," six young boys turn into swans when the father, through his cowardice, opens the house to evil, and the boys remain enchanted for years.

I wrote in a poem called "Fifty Males Sitting Together" concerning a young man about to go into trance:

The woman stays in the kitchen, and does not want
to waste fuel by lighting a lamp,
as she waits
for the drunk husband to come home.
Then she serves him
food in silence.
What does the son do?
He turns away,
loses courage,
goes outdoors to feed with wild
things, lives among dens
and huts, eats distance and silence;
he grows long wings, enters the spiral, ascends.

Being brought to the water by a mentor means the end of enchantment. The Wild Man's water does not itself heal the wound that led to the escape or ascension; but it gives strength to the part of us that wants to continue the effort to gain courage and be human.

When Iron John takes the boy to the water, the energy of the sun is somehow carried into the young man's body. The story says it this way:

> Without intending to, he dipped it into the water. He pulled it out instantly, but he saw that the finger had turned to gold.

Gold all over the world symbolizes sun-glory, royal power, self-generating radiance, freedom from decay, immortality, spiritual luminosity, and it is that gold which has come to the boy's finger. By arranging the surprise of the golden fingertip, the Wild Man, acting as a spiritual guide here, gives the promise.

The promise is a rediscovery, we could say, a rediscovery of a gold that was always there. We do not laboriously, by hard labor in grade school, accumulate a story of sun energy in the spirit warehouse. The gold was in us while we were in the womb.

The child is born, as Wordsworth said, "trailing clouds of

glory." The child is the inheritor of millennia of spiritual and imaginative labor. Kabir says:

> *We sense there is some sort of spirit that loves birds*
> *   and the animals and the ants—*
> *Perhaps the same one who gave a radiance to you in*
> *   your mother's womb.*
> *Is it logical you would be walking around entirely*
> *   orphaned now?*
> *The truth is you turned away yourself,*
> *And decided to go into the dark alone.*

We know from a famous papyrus describing mummification that the Egyptian priests applied gold to the fingernails of the dead man or woman. As they did so, they spoke these words: "Now the gold which belongs to Horus comes to your fingernails and makes you immortal."

The image of the gold fingertip in our story, then, is very old, and may come down all the way from the second or third millennium B.C. But instead of the Egyptian temples with their solid-gold statues of the gods, we have the golden fish and snakes swimming in the pond.

We can pick up from Greco-Roman life one more detail that helps us to grasp the meaning of the gold that will not wash away. The Romans believed that each human being had inside him or her an angel or "daimon," which came down through the family line and was the seed of the individual good fortune in that person. They called this seed or spark or lucky star the "genius" when noticed in a man, and the "juno" when noticed in a woman.

The Romans imagined the daimon as a guide, halfway between human and divine, a messenger from the holy world, a kind of guardian angel, or what the Norwegian poet Rolf Jacobsen calls "the white shadow." We notice that the gold appears on the very same finger that dared to open the Wild Man's cage, so the boy's fate is intimately bound to the use he made of the key.

So much for the mythological way of seeing things. Psychologically, what is the gold on the finger? When does it show up in ordinary life?

The story says that when we are in the presence of either a mentor or the "Wild Man" a hint will come to us as to where our genius lies.

Sometimes in a love affair, the lovers make love with the Wild Man—and Wild Woman—right in the room; and if we are those lovers, we may feel certain body cells turn gold that we thought were made entirely of lead. Lovers and saints feel their fingertips are golden, all right; they may sense in themselves a freedom from ordinary limits for days or months.

An artist feels a curious mood of intensity when he or she is working on an art object, a poem or a painting or a sculpture; we could say that the sacred pond is right there in the studio; and the artist becomes capable of thoughts and feelings much wilder than he or she ever experiences in shut-down days. The fingers holding the pen or brush turn gold, and we suddenly see amazing images, and realize what we are really good at.

The Wild Man here amounts to an invisible presence, the companionship of the ancestors and the great artists among the dead. A love poem or an ecstatic meditation poem is really an ingenious way to preserve memory of the moment when the fingertip turns gold.

The young runner crosses the finish line in the presence of her coach: the tips of her toes are gold. The physicist working with his mentor at Princeton suddenly writes an equation on the board with his golden chalk. Good gardeners have golden thumbs, not green thumbs; and sometimes the mentor or teacher, sitting with a student, slips into soul water and the tongue turns to gold.

I think we can regard therapy, when it is good, as a waiting by the pond. Each time we dip our wound into that water, we get nourishment, and the strength to go on further in the process. Initiation, then, does not mean ascending above the wound, nor remaining numbly inside it; but the process lies in knowing how or when, in the presence of the mentor, to dip it in the water.

The wound that hurts us so much we "involuntarily" dip it in water, we have to regard as a gift. How would the boy in our story have found out about his genius if he had not been wounded? Those with no wounds are the unluckiest of all. (Of course one

can't think that, because no such person has ever been found.)
Men are taught over and over when they are boys that a wound
that hurts is shameful. A wound that stops you from continuing
to play is a girlish wound. He who is truly a man keeps walking,
dragging his guts behind.

Our story gives a teaching diametrically opposite. It says that
where a man's wound is, that is where his genius will be. Wherever
the wound appears in our psyches, whether from alcoholic father,
shaming mother, shaming father, abusing mother, whether it stems
from isolation, disability, or disease, that is precisely the place for
which we will give our major gift to the community.

The Norwegian artist Eduard Munch clearly gave his immense gift out of his disabling anxiety. We feel such a gift-giving
in Franz Kafka also, in Charles Dickens, in Emily Dickinson, in
Anna Akhmatova, in César Vallejo.

Before we finish this discussion of the wound and the genius,
we must ask the question: what gender might the water be? Is it
masculine or feminine?

It's both—but in this century we are unlikely to give that
answer very quickly. A strange thing has happened. In our society,
the earth and all the water in it is considered to be feminine, and
by extension, it belongs to women. In the West, the sky belongs
to men, and the earth to women; there is a "sky-father" and an
"earth-mother." There's nothing wrong with those phrases, but
two other phrases have fallen into oblivion: sky-mother and the
earth-father.

The Egyptians, when Plato visited them, remarked that the
Greeks were only children; and the Egyptians did have the older
mythological and religious base. They well knew Ra, the sky-father,
and Isis, the earth-mother. But prominent in every Egyptian moment were two other gods, Nut and Geb. Nut, the sky-mother,
was painted on the inside of every coffin or mummy-lid, so that
the dead person looking up saw a being bending down from the
stars. Stars were shown on her body and around her body. Her
hands and feet touched the earth, and the rest arched among the
heavens. "I came out of the mother naked, and I will be naked

when I return," the dead man or woman said. "The mother gave and the mother takes away. Blessed be the name of the mother."

Then there was Geb, the earth-father. Libby and Arthur Coleman, in their book *The Father*, reproduce fine paintings of Geb, who lies with his back to the earth, his stomach and erect phallus, earth-colored, reaching up toward the woman in the sky, or longing for the stars. The Greeks, and the Europeans after them, lost track of the full complement of four gods and preserved memory of only two. When we remember only two gods, the sexes polarize and begin to seem opposite. Each gender becomes identified, men with sky, women with earth. Men become identified with sky-fire, women with earth-water.

Many women today say, "The earth is female." A man told me that when he hears that, he feels he has lost the right to breathe. And when a man says, "God is male," women have said that they feel they have no right to pray. Mythology is important. The polarization coming from our fragmentary Greek mythology has already caused immense harm.

Today when a man or woman dreams of a lake, the therapist assumes that water refers to the feminine. For those who know Latin, *mare* (the sea) associates with Mary, and pretty soon the sea is female, and since the sea is the unconscious, the unconscious is female as well, and so on.

The Iron John story, which is pre-Greek, does not polarize earth and sky. Iron John lives in the water, under the water. He also lives wholeheartedly on earth; his wildness and hairiness in fact belong to earth and its animals. Neither earth nor water seems exclusively feminine or masculine.

The old Celts had a male god called Dommu, or "Depth of the Waters," and it is possible this god has been living in the spring to which the Wild Man has just introduced the boy. Because the Wild Man and the Wild Woman both guard the pond in some Celtic stories, it is more appropriate to say that the water is soul water, and as such, both masculine and feminine.

Water in symbolic systems does not stand for spiritual or metaphysical impulses (which are better suggested by air or fire) but earthy and natural life. Water belongs to lowly circumstances, ground life, birth from the womb, descent from the eternal realm to the watery earth, where we take on a body composed mostly of water. When our mythology opens again to welcome women into sky-heaven and men into earth-water, then the genders will not seem so far apart. White men will feel it more natural, then, for them to protect earth, as the native American men have always felt it right to do.

As we end our discussion of the first day, we must notice that not all young men who put their hand in the water see the fingertip turn gold. The analyst Alexander Mitscherlich retells the dream of a young German man he once treated. This young man, from illegitimate birth, abandoned by his father, was held to his mother "by both spoiling and punishments." In his dream an old man in a car with a skull for a head drove straight at him. Later, he said, "I walked a long way, went into a park, and saw some goldfish in a fountain. At the bottom of the fountain I saw a town and heard bells ringing. I put my hand in the water, but was terribly frightened, for when I withdrew my arm, my hand was missing. I ran away and saw that the old man was following me, pointing a pistol at me. I saw a flash and lost consciousness" (*Society Without the Father*). No positive mentor or Iron John appears. An evil old man tries to kill him twice. The pond with its goldfish has an astonishing resemblance to the spring in our story, but this isolated pond takes his whole hand. What we see today in street gangs are many handless boys.

The Story: The Second Day

Early the next morning, the boy sat again at the spring watching over it. His finger still hurt and after a while, he ran his hand up through his hair. One hair, alas, came loose from his head and fell into the spring. He immediately reached down and pulled it out, but the hair had already turned to gold.

The moment Iron John returned, he knew what had happened. "You've let a hair fall into the spring. I'll allow it this time, but if it happens a third time it will dishonor the spring, and you will not be able to stay with me any longer."

We could say that the boy has elevated his wounded finger this time, and that is a little different from dipping it. First a man dips his wound, one could say, into psychological water, and then he elevates it into mythological space. All stories of the blacksmith with a wound—the Fisher King, the man whose wound won't heal—help us to see our own wounds in an impersonal way. And we know from the shaman stories that their wounds were impersonal. Wounds need to be expanded into air, lifted up on ideas our ancestors knew, so that the wound ascends through the roof of our parents' house and we suddenly see how our wound (seemingly so private) fits into a great and impersonal story.

Mythology helps to give weight to our private wounds. To feel the wound in a particular part of our body gives the wound weight, and to understand it as a part of an ancient story gives it weight. Without the weight given by a wound consciously realized, the man will lead a provisional life.

The wounded finger this time gets associated with hair. Hair covers the Wild Man and the Wild Woman, as we know from many sources. The question of hair comes up a lot in this story.

When we look for cultural associations with the word hair, we notice at least four linkages. The first is to sexual energy. When a young Roman woman joined the Vestal Virgins, the other women ritually shaved her head. Monks during the Middle Ages were tonsured, and Orthodox Jewish women to this day wear wigs to hide their own hair.

Because animals exhibit hair in profusion and because we see our own sexuality as animal, the linkage is unavoidable.

A man's moustache may stand for his pubic hair. A friend once grew a moustache when he was around thirty. The next time he visited his mother, she looked into the corners of the room as she talked to him, and would not look at his face, no matter what they talked about. Hair, then, can represent sexual energy.

Hunters traditionally wear long hair, as do the animals that they hunt. Hair, then, can stand for animal life in general, particularly the life of wild animals. Many boys become fascinated with hunting, and make small bows and arrows, form hunting bands, and shoot rabbits or birds. It doesn't always turn out well. The boy enthusiastically brings home a dead cottontail or a killed robin, but many women, and some men, feel that a boy's hunting instinct is deplorable and he should be educated out of it. New Age parents usually want the boy to bypass hunting and go directly to ethics. The trouble with such a bypass is that the boy is mythologically living through the past history of man, which includes century after century of joyful hunting which we would guess the women of that time relished as well.

During the hunting era the man's emotional life, and even his religious life, resonated to the empty spaces of forest and plain, and he learned about God through hunting animals, as the drawings in the Dordogne caves make clear. If a shaming mother or father blocks a boy from living that time through, he will never arrive at contemporary time. He will still be bringing a deer back to Detroit on the top of his car when he is fifty.

Hair suggests not only closeness to animals, through hunting or domestication, but it suggests all forms of animal hot-bloodedness. Reptiles—cold-blooded—lack hair, and so hair comes to represent that passionate flaring nature peculiar to mammals: hot tempers (redheads), fiery temperaments, passionate impulsiveness, spontaneity, explosive emotions, leonine fierceness, tigerish jealousy.

But whether the haired people are symphony conductors with flowing hair, or corporate men with medium-cut, gray flannel hair, so to speak, or the real pruners of extravagance, the fundamentalists who favor crewcuts or shaved heads, the amount of hair allowed suggests how far the instincts are curtailed and the spontaneity curbed.

Some people make no distinction between the instinct for fierceness and the instinct for aggression. In recent decades, the separatist wing of the feminist movement, in a justified fear of brutality, has labored to breed fierceness out of men.

Finally, hair suggests excess. The hairiness of Enkidu, the Babylonian Wild Man, or Pan, the goat-man, suggests that hair stands for what is beyond the boundaries of all middle-of-the-road civilization. Pan is outside the enclosure. When a woman's hair tumbles down, abundantly and richly, we hear the hair saying words about the value of excess.

Blake says, "The road of excess leads to the palace of wisdom." He associates hair with earth. "The eyes of fire, the nostrils of air, the mouth of water, the beard of earth."

When the boy in our story then inadvertently dislodges one hair that falls into the spring, and it turns to gold, we could say he learns these things: that sexual energy is good; that the hunting instinct, which mammals possess without shame, is good; that animal heat, fierceness, and passionate spontaneity is good; and that excess, extravagance, and going with Pan out beyond the castle boundaries is good too.

Hair also suggests thoughts. Hair keeps coming out of the head day and night, so hairs resemble thoughts that come out even when we are sleeping. Even when the conscious system is shut down at night, thoughts keep coming out: some of them are called dreams.

We know that the hormonal and digestive systems go on working below any conscious control of the ego. "Can you, by thinking, add an inch to your height?" Growth, oxygen replenishment, bloodcleaning, cell replacement, all go on when no one is watching.

So much happens when
no one is watching,
perhaps because
no one is watching. . .

Pirates bring their ship in
when night has come;
the dancer perfects her art
after she performs
no more . . .

. . . The planet turns, and cows
wait for the grassblades
to come rushing to their mouths.
    —R.B.

Hair, then, stands for all those intuitions that appear out of nowhere, following channels we cannot observe; a scientist glimpses the solution to a problem he or she has worked on with no success for weeks. Friedrich Kekulé, for example, saw in a dream a formation of snakes, and one snake caught hold of its own tail. Through that image he suddenly saw the structure of the benzene ring.

When an artist is at work on a painting, images he or she had never thought of arrive instead of the images the artist had planned to set down. Some psychics receive knowledge of strangers through pictures that appear in their mind's eye, arriving particularly if they do not strive to know. Yeats has a crane say:

It's certain there are trout somewhere
And maybe I shall take a trout
If but I do not seem to care.

Hair is intuition. Hair is the abundance of perceptions, insights, thoughts, resentments, images, fantasies waiting and ready to come out whenever we are thinking of something else. Marian Woodman retold, one day, a dream a client of hers had who had been working for months against great inner resistance. The woman dreamt she had been walking through cluttered and swampy forest for days or weeks, and just when she thought she was nearly out of it came down to a wide and dangerous river. Horrified and discouraged, she glanced up toward the forested mountain on the other side of the river. She saw that far up on the mountain someone had been creating a path that led down toward the river.

If a human being takes an action, the soul takes an action. When a hair enters the water, the soul adds gold to it. That is what the soul is like, apparently. This spring water, with gold snakes and fish in it, is the soul itself which does nothing if you do nothing; but if you light a fire, it chops wood; if you make a boat, it becomes the ocean.

It is possible that a dream comes forward at night in response to some verbal arrow or bodily gesture that came out of us in daylight. The water understands a blow or a kiss to be a movement toward it, and it responds with an image or a narrative, perhaps an entire dream as elaborate as Hamlet. Rainer Maria Rilke says:

> *My eyes already touch the sunny hill,*
> *going far ahead of the road I have begun.*
> *So we are grasped by what we cannot grasp;*
> *it has its inner light, even from a distance—*
>
> *and changes us, even if we do not reach it,*
> *into something else, which, hardly sensing it, we*
> *   already are;*
> *a gesture waves us on, answering our own wave . . .*
> *but what we feel is the wind in our faces.*

But the generous response made by the sacred pond spring depends on a serious decisive effort made by a man or woman. In our story that would be the boy's stealing the key from under his mother's pillow, his decision to let the Wild Man out of the cage and go with him, and his agreement to sit by the spring and try to do the Wild Man's tasks.

We could say that the boy has learned the difference between secular space and ritual space. Ritual space gives something back to the man or woman who, prepared by discipline and quiet, enters it.

The Story: The Third Day

The third day, as the boy sat by the spring, he was determined, no matter how much his finger hurt him, not to let it move. Time passed slowly, and he began gazing at the reflection of his face in the water. He got the desire to look straight into his own eyes, and in doing this, he leaned over farther and farther. All at once his long hair fell down over his forehead and into the water. He threw his head back but now all his hair, every bit, had turned gold, and it shone as if it were the sun itself. Now the boy was frightened! He took out a kerchief and covered his head so that the Wild Man wouldn't know what had happened. But when Iron John arrived home, he knew immediately. "Take that kerchief off your head," he said. The golden hair then came tumbling down over the boy's shoulders, and the boy had to be silent.

The boy's hands now remain behind his back. It isn't the hands that reach out now, but the eyes. The eyes begin to search around him, their curiosity perhaps intensified by the intimation that gold is everywhere, mysteriously present even in clear water. He focuses on his own face, finally on his own eyes. We know that shame often keeps us from meeting other people's eyes—or our own. But when we do look into our own eyes, whether we do that staring into a mirror, or into a pond surface—we have the inescapable impression, so powerful and astonishing, that someone is looking back at us.

Rilke said about his own face in the mirror:

In the arch of eyebrows some firmness remains
From long-disciplined and large-browed ancestors.
Inside the eyes the fearfulness of childhood persists
And some blue also, and some lowliness, not a
     laborer's,
but the humbleness of a serving man and of
     woman. . . .

The face carries so far only a suggestion of unity.
It has never gathered itself up, either in grief
or in ecstasy, for any permanent task.
And yet, with all its scattered things, it feels
As if someone there were planning a serious labor.

     —"Self-Portrait from the Year 1906"
     Translated by R.B.

That experience of being looked back at sobers us up immediately. If, as human beings, we have any doubts about the existence of the interior soul, we give up those doubts instantly. When we look in the mirror, someone looks back questioning, serious, alert, and without intent to comfort; and we feel more depth in the eyes looking at us than we ordinarily sense in our own eyes as we stare out at the world. How strange! Who could it be that is looking at us? We conclude that it is another part of us, the half that we don't allow to pass out of our eyes when we glance at others—and that darker and more serious half looks back at us only at rare times. Antonio Machado said:

> *Look for your other half*
> *who walks always next to you*
> *and tends to be who you aren't.*
> > *Translated by R.B.*

The person who gazes in the mirror receives an awareness of his other half, his shadow, or hidden man; awareness of that hidden man is a proper aim for all initiation. The experience teaches him that the eyes he sees are not just "him," but some other man, not included very well under the name his parents gave him, Edward or Lance or Kerry. These eyes belong to some other being whom we have never met. Juan Ramon Jiménez said:

> *I am not I.*
> > *I am this one*
> *Walking beside me, whom I do not see,*
> *Whom at times I manage to visit,*
> *And at other times I forget.*
> *The one who forgives, sweet, when I hate,*
> *The one who remains silent when I talk,*
> *The one who takes a walk when I am indoors,*
> *The one who will remain standing when I die.*
> > *Translated by R.B.*

The one we see in the mirror is complicated, and the glance that takes one moment in the tale could take several years in life.

The one looking back is at the same time a man's shadow, or dark side, and also his spiritual twin, his white shadow. Rolf Jacobsen, the Norwegian poet, calls him

> *your shadow, the white one,*
> *whom you cannot accept,*
> *and who will never forget you.*
>   *Translated by R.B.*

The Gnostics spoke a great deal about the twin, whom they imagine to have been separated from us at birth. The twin retains the spiritual knowledge given us before birth. The twin, when he or she reenters the psyche, insists on intensity and seriousness.

An adult, for example, might dream that an unknown person has entered his or her apartment, moved things about, taken a jewel away or left one. One man whom I know saw one day, while meditating, a man of light at the end of the corridor, nine feet tall with a spear. The man of light approached and said, "If you don't make something of your life, I will take it from you." My friend was then thirty-eight years old.

We have been talking of "the other one" whom we sometimes see when looking into a mirror. In our story, there is no mirror; the mirror is made by nature or, more exactly, it is nature. We could say that the boy in our story has seen eyes looking back at him from nature.

The story implies that we, as human beings, are not the only source of ordered intelligence and conscious awareness. "The eyes in the water" can be regarded as an emblem of the consciousness in nature, the intelligence "out there." We know that neither consciousness nor "intelligence" is quite the right word. Human beings invented the word "consciousness" to describe their own particular sentience, but nature's awareness is not exactly intelligence nor sentience, nor consciousness, nor awareness. It falls between all the words. Blake said:

> *How do you know but that ev'ry Bird that cuts the*
> *airy way*

Is an immense world of delight, clos'd by your senses
five?

I like the phrasing "How do you know but that. . . ."

Now we need to take one more step. Suppose that, rather than describing the intelligence in nature by using an abstract word such as consciousness, or even a phrase such as an immense world of delight, we were to imagine it as a personality?

Some anthropologists speculate that the early hunters did just that.

The native American culture is full of stories that describe exactly the glimpse of such a personality. The human tribe and the buffalo tribe get connected through a buffalo chief, or a holy white buffalo declares himself to be both a buffalo and a god. When the hunters do their share of the ritual, or task, the buffalo tribe participates in the hunt.

We presume that the native American hunters saw this being, part animal, part god, part human, with their inner eyes; and it seems clear that the artists of the Dordogne caves had also seen him.

Women saw with their inner eyes another being, whom they have called The Great Mother, and we guess that women for thousands of years held small statues of her in their closed palms during childbirth.

We can consider the possibility that the boy in our story sees some personality in nature looking back at him, and that is why his head turns gold. We don't know. All the story leaves us with is the image of the boy looking into the water, and we can make of it what we can.

It's an odd image. A boy sits by a pond. Most of us recall from Greek mythology the better-known scene in which Narcissus sits by his pond. Narcissus has already become separated from his male hunting companions as the story opens. That is interesting in itself. It turns out that Hera is also angry at him, and has sent a nymph called Echo who repeats each of his words as soon as he speaks them. Narcissus is bottled up inside his own circuits. When he looks down he falls in love with his own face. The boy in Iron

John's pond, guided or protected by the Wild Man, does not fall in love with his own face, but sees through the eyes to the consciousness in nature itself. He breaks free, so to speak, from his own circuits, and that is an important difference between the stories.

Going Out into the World

We could sum up by saying that when a man has received a glimpse of his own psychic twin, and when he has seen the intelligence in nature, its consciousness or intent, then that man's hair turns gold—he has a "golden head." We note that the boy in our story seems very young to have a golden head. We gather from the way he hides it under the kerchief that he feels it is not proper and right to show it.

Three days have passed in ritual time. These three days could be fifteen years in our time. The initiator gave him a task and he failed at it three times. But he receives a gift anyway each time. The failures rose from the pain he felt and from his human inability to keep attention. But the gift came from the water, with whom he had somehow established a relationship. We deduce that accepting an initiatory task is more important than succeeding or failing at it. We guess that the boy has done all right.

Iron John says to him:

> "You can't stay here any longer because you didn't make it through the trial. Go out into the world now and there you will learn what poverty is. I see no evil in your heart, however, and I wish you well, so I'll give you this gift: whenever you are in trouble, come to the edge of the forest and shout, 'Iron John, Iron John!' I'll come to the edge of the forest and help you. My power is great, greater than you believe, and I have gold and silver in abundance."

We've seen something of how the Wild Man behaves in these three days by the spring. When we hear the phrase, "the Wild Man," our fantasies move toward a monster, or savage, but it is clear now that the Wild Man is closer to a meditation instructor than to a savage. In part he resembles a rabbi teaching the Kabala; in part, he resembles a holder of a mystery tradition; in part, he resembles a hunting god.

We sometimes assume that contemporary initiation is accomplished by being confirmed, or receiving the Bar Mitzvah ceremony, or getting a driver's license. To receive initiation truly means to expand sideways into the glory of oaks, mountains, glaciers, horses, lions, grasses, waterfalls, deer. We need wilderness and extravagance. Whatever shuts a human being away from the waterfall and the tiger will kill him.

The Iron John story retains memories of initiation ceremonies for men that go back ten or twenty thousand years in northern Europe. The Wild Man's job is to teach the young man how abundant, various, and many-sided his manhood is. The boy's body inherits physical abilities developed by long-dead ancestors, and his mind inherits spiritual and soul powers developed centuries ago.

The job of the initiator, whether the initiator is a man or woman, is to prove to the boy or girl that he or she is more than mere flesh and blood. A man is not a machine only for protecting, hunting, and reproduction; a woman is not a machine only for protecting, gathering, and reproduction, but each carries desires far beyond what is needed for physical survival. William James praises "the number and fantastic and unnecessary character" of the human being's wants.

The metaphors in the Iron John story refer to all human life, but are tuned to the psyches of men. A young man is asked to descend into his own wounds, to climb up into the realm of "the twin," and to expand sideways into the consciousness that is in trees, water, animals, and "the ten thousand things." When a young man has achieved these three realizations, or completed these three journeys, his hair turns gold. That doesn't solve all his problems; on the contrary it brings new ones, and that golden head is going to be a problem.

CHAPTER THREE

The Road of Ashes,
Descent, and Grief

We've come to a new section of the story now, and we might look back on the boy's progress so far. The king's son, in following the Wild Man, has not gone the way of delinquency, drug addiction, and self-shaming; on the contrary he has been lifted up to what is great in him. It is as if his teacher in high school had been Pablo Casals, who taught him what genius is, and by commenting on the gold tip of his finger, convinced him that he had some. He also learned to trust his instinctual body or "hair," and finally he sees eyes looking back at him from the water, and by extension, looking at him from the grass, the trees, the mountains. He learned that the whole world is on fire. "Everything is intelligent!" All of his hair turns gold.

Such teaching can have strange effects. If such good luck happened to one of us, a friend would probably warn us that we were in danger of becoming overly grand. These teachings moreover got laid on the boy quite young—that is one problem in going to a sacred spring with a wild man. And yet, most of us, even though the lessons may have arrived in a fragmentary form, one bit now and one bit then, scattered through months or years, received a similar teaching.

For some, the teaching about eyes arrived in early childhood, when we were amazed by woods and gardens, and knew they were "alive." The gold-hair teaching appeared at twelve or fourteen, when, fueled by sexual instinct, we rose or fell deeply in love, and knew that it was good, very good. Later, when our teens came, we felt mental or physical abilities in us that we had never even imagined.

Each of us had already guessed that we were sons of kings and queens, and somehow had landed mistakenly in our prosaic and dumb family. Our grandiosity then was already in us, even if no visible wild man took us to his magical pond. We know the feeling of grandeur, and we want to have it all the time.

In order to keep the grandeur feeling a child may refuse to remember ugly facts of childhood, may look away from disorganization, abuse, abandonment, lack of protection, and skip over our parents' indifference, addictions, or dark side. Animals apparently don't have to worry so much about inflation, but we are human beings, and a little bit of gold—or genius feeling—can send us into high altitudes, from which we don't want to descend. It was Robinson Jeffers, who, in speaking of mankind's scientific knowledge and the subsequent grandiosity, said:

> *A little knowledge, a pebble from the shingle,*
> *A drop from the oceans; who would have dreamed*
> *this infinitely little too much?*

What Happens

Young men when lifted up may become white swans, grandiose ascenders, "flying boys," just as young women similarly lifted up may become flying girls, and both make love with invisible people at high altitudes. The Jungian thinkers have done well in noticing and describing this phenomenon, and the phrase *puer aeternus* (holy or eternal boy) and *puella aeterna* (holy or eternal girl) are phrases familiar to many. The Jungians have evoked the eternal boy in great detail; Marie-Louise von Franz's *Puer Aeternus* is the classic book.

In any case these flying people, giddily spiritual, do not inhabit their own bodies well, and are open to terrible shocks of abandonment; they are unable to accept limitations, and are averse to a certain boring quality native to human life. Marie-Louise von

Franz named *The Little Prince* as the generic story. It was written by Antoine de Saint-Exupery, who was literally a pilot-hero, always longing for pure life on other planets, but whose "Little Prince" died when bitten by a snake on this one.

Peter Pan belongs among the flyers, as do most ashram habitués, devotees of "higher consciousness," determined to avoid earthly food, platonic lovers and celibates, and some Don Juans, who want such heavenly perfection in women that they are obliged to leave each one in whom they fail to find the missing pearl.

Grandiose ascenders sometimes dream of rising in an elevator that is attached to the outside of a building, but when they get to an upper floor, they often find themselves with no entrance to the building. The flying man usually likes women, but may shrink a woman to keep her in a bottle so that he can carry her in his pocket. The young *puer aeternus* men are by no means negative; they love spirit and embody much of the spiritual energy in the nation. Their ascensions bring many blessings to the culture. Without them the American culture would probably thicken and harden into concrete. So the grandiose ascender is a complicated person.

Grandiose ascenders—I was and am a good example—come out of all sorts of families, and sometimes the ascension is taken on as an intelligent survival method. I gave these lines earlier:

> *What does the son do?*
> *He turns away,*
> *loses courage,*
> *goes outdoors to feed with wild*
> *things, lives among dens*
> *and huts, eats distance and silence;*
> *he grows long wings, enters the spiral, ascends.*

That scene already took place when I was twelve or so. When I was twenty-eight I still had the longing for purity, "to be above it all," not to be involved.

Marie-Louise von Franz concluded from her experience with these heavenly flyers or flying splinters that they choose ascent as a revolt against maternal earthiness and female conservatism. They fly upward, she believes, out of fear of the magnets that she says some women hide in the ground in the hope of luring light-headed men down to the ground of marriages, jobs, and long-range commitment.

The evolution of the boy into a birdlike creature is a natural movement; he looks up at the light when he wants to escape, as do birds. Imprisoned birds flutter up the wall toward any cracks of light. So the young ascenders often find themselves achieving spirit, but at the expense of life or their own grounding in masculine life.

How far he is from working men when he is forty!
From all men. . . .

I am not saying that spiritual work in itself is wrong, not at all; but it's important to consider when in a person's life it should take place. We remember the Baal Shem Tov, that genius of the spirit in the early eighteenth century in Poland, would not let his young men read certain spiritual texts until they were thirty-five. Some say that the man's task in the first half of his life is to become bonded to matter: to learn a craft, become friends with wood, earth, wind, or fire. When Jung established a training center in Zurich, he would not accept a person who was not already a success in some other career. It was a way of saying thirty-five or older.

We need to add that not all young men are ascenders. Some are earthbound, take on responsibility too early, commit themselves to supporting others; they walk slowly, move close to the ground, carry enormous burdens, feel they have no right to look at slivers of sunlight. Their family tradition is that the son's grandiosity is to be wiped out early; sometimes in those families the women are the inflated ones, and the men are not; men take the depressed road. They do not become artists or musicians; their life takes place where the soles of their shoes touch the ground. Some fairy tales call them "shoemakers," and note the tension between them and the higher-hearted "tailors."

The scarcity culture of the European Middle Ages—to name only one scarcity culture—did not allow the young men many possibilities of ascension; our culture of abundance, or entitlement, sets very few limitations; and for many college students the goddess of necessity is almost unknown.

The boy in our story is at the moment of ascension now. As such, he is similar, for better or worse, to millions of people in American culture now. We have to look very carefully at these ascenders, these tailors or flyers, if we are going to make any change in men's and women's lives, and we might look at them in the light of three words: passivity, naïveté, and numbness.

We all know that women's ascensionism is very intense and widespread; but I think a woman could talk with much more accuracy than I could about its nature, and I think it is appropriate for women to describe it. So we will confine ourselves here to men's ascensionism.

We know that for hundreds of thousands of years men have admired each other, and been admired by women, in particular for their activity. Men and women alike once called on men to pierce the dangerous places, carry handfuls of courage to the waterfalls, dust the tails of the wild boars. All knew that if men did that well the women and children could sleep safely. Now the boars have turned to pigs in the stockyard, and the rushing rivers to the waterfall in the Museum of Modern Art courtyard. The activity men were once loved for is not required.

Men dared to enter the realm of animals, engage them, fight them, wrestle with the soul of the animal, learned their dances, crossed through the veil to them. Some men, called shamans, entered into the realm of the spirits as well, wrestled with them, outwitted them, and saved people who had become ill through the mischievous activities of those spirits. Men have been loved for their astonishing initiative: embarking on wide oceans, starting a farm in rocky country from scratch, imagining a new business, doing it skillfully, working with beginnings, doing what has never been done. Young Viking men sometimes trained themselves by walking on the ends of the oars while the rowers continued rowing.

Women, until recent times, have not been praised for their activity. They have been asked for centuries to live in an enforced passivity, demanded of them by monks, doctors, philosophers, moralists, theologians, and judges. Women are coming out into activity just as the men are passing them going the other way, into passivity. (The passivity of the "soft male" of the first chapter is often a great surprise to women.)

During the last thirty years men have been asked to learn how to go with the flow, how to follow rather than lead, how to live in a nonhierarchical way, how to be vulnerable, how to adopt consensus decision-making. Some women want a passive man if they want a man at all; the church wants a tamed man—they are called priests; the university wants a domesticated man—they are called tenure-track people; the corporation wants a team-worker, and so on. In Blake's time the corporations were called charter companies, and he said:

> *I wander thro' each charter'd street*
> *Near where the charter'd Thames does flow,*
> *And mark in every face I meet*
> *Marks of weakness, marks of woe.*

Passivity increases exponentially as the educational system turns out "products."

The average American child by eighteen has seen four thousand hours of commercials, yet very few televisions have been smashed by axes, very few presidential debates interrupted by "activists," very few increases in the military budgets stopped by mass protests. Blake roots passivity in earliest childhood:

> *Struggling in my father's hands,*
> *Striving against my swaddling bands,*
> *Bound and weary I thought best*
> *To sulk upon my mother's breast.*

The infant boy struggles against the father's hands, fighting the narcissistic father's desire to bind or murder him; and he struggles against swaddling bands, fighting the narcissistic mother's desire to change him to what she wants. When the boy fails to get free, then, Blake says he learns to sulk. How often every adult man has felt himself, when baffled by a woman's peculiar interpretation of his behavior—so different from his own—go into a sulk. In our twenties we may stay a week in a sulk of that sort—

it doesn't feel too long at all—and during that time we will probably refuse to speak about our hurt feelings, and may not speak at
all. In such a mood screaming, shouting, kvetching never appear—
these are too active. When a man sulks, he becomes passive to his
own hurts.

When no old men appear to break the hold of the sulking
infant, the habit of passivity spreads to other parts of his life.

The passive man, for example, may ask the woman to do his
loving for him. Talking is not everything, but it is a part of loving,
as are buying gifts, getting to "completion" in a conversation,
praising the other person, keeping the thread of intimacy unbro-
ken. Maggy Scarf remarks in *Intimate Partners* that three-quarters
or so of American marriages follow a curious scenario: the woman
wants more intimacy and the man flees from that; she runs after,
but not quite fast enough to catch him, and he flees but not quite
fast enough to get away. This game can go on for years.

The passive man may not say what he wants, and the girlfriend
or wife has to guess it. As a compensation for passivity at home,
he may go into robot production at work, but that isn't really
what he wants either.

We can go farther. The passive man may ask his children to
do his loving for him. Children often observe the parents with
great acuteness. The family therapists around Murray Bowman,
working on anxiety in families, study how much anxiety there is
and who carries it. They conclude that an adolescent "in trouble"
who is "acting out" may in fact be transferring some of the anxiety
between mother and father to himself, and in that sense carrying
it. Children are active in loving to the point of sacrificing themselves.

The passive man may skip over parenting. Parenting means
feeling, but it also means doing all sorts of boring tasks, taking
children to school, buying them jackets, attending band concerts,
dealing with curfews, setting rules of behavior, deciding on responses when these rules are broken, checking on who a child's
friends are, listening to the child's talk in an active way, et cetera.
The passive man leaves his wife to do that.

A Swedish man, when I asked him what complaints the

women in Sweden had about men, told me recently that his women friends complain that the Swedish man has no overview of the relationship. The man knows what he wants today or tomorrow, but does not know how he wants the relationship to be two years or ten years from now. We could call that a sort of passivity of vision.

Finally, a husband or lover may avoid being active in the woman's life.

> *Bound and weary I thought best*
> *To rest upon a woman's breast.*

A woman does not want a man to tell her what to do, but other forces may have turned her away from a fruitful action or act. If her husband sees this happening, he should tell her about it. A man hopes a woman will tell him as well, if she sees him accepting the direction of invisible forces.

Naïveté

We see more and more passivity in men, but also more and more naïveté. The naïve man feels a pride in being attacked. If his wife or girlfriend, furious, shouts that he is "chauvinist," a "sexist," a "man," he doesn't fight back, but just takes it. He opens his shirt so that she can see more clearly where to put the lances. He ends with three or four javelins sticking out of his body, and blood running all over the floor. If he were a bullfighter, he would remain where he was when the bull charges, would not even wave his shirt or turn his body, and the horn would go directly in. After each fight friends have to carry him on their shoulders to the hospital.

He feels, as he absorbs attacks, that he is doing the brave and advanced thing; he will surely be able to recover somewhere in isolation. A woman, so mysterious and superior, has given him some attention. To be attacked by someone you love—what could be more wonderful? Perhaps the wounds may pay for some chauvinistic act, and so allow him to remain special still longer.

The naïve man will also be proud that he can pick up the pain of others. He particularly picks up women's pain. When at five years old he sat at the kitchen table, his mother may have confided her suffering to him, and he felt flattered to be told of such things by a grown-up, even if it showed his father up poorly. He becomes attracted later to women who "share their pain." His specialness makes him, in his own eyes, something of a doctor. He is often more in touch with women's pain than with his own, and he will offer to carry a woman's pain before he checks with his own heart to see if this labor is proper in the situation. In general, I think each gender drops its own pain when it tries to carry the pain of the other gender. I don't mean that men shouldn't listen. But hearing a woman's pain and carrying it are two different things. Women have tried for centuries to carry men's pain, and it hasn't worked well.

The word special is important to the naïve man, and he has special relationships with certain people. We all have some special relationships, but he surrounds the special person with a cloying kind of goodwill. The relationship is so special that he never examines the dark side of the person, which could be a son, a daughter, a wife, a male friend, a girlfriend. He accepts responses that are way off, conspires somehow with their dark side. "Some people are special," he says.

We might say that if he doesn't investigate his son's or daughter's dark side, perhaps they will not investigate his. He may also have a secret and special relationship with a wounded little boy inside himself. If so, he won't challenge the little boy, nor will he point out his self-pity, nor actually listen to the boy either. He will simply let the boy run his life.

Sincerity is a big thing with him. He assumes that the person, stranger, or lover he talks with is straightforward, goodwilled, and speaking from the heart. He agrees with Rousseau and Whitman that each person is basically noble by nature, and only twisted a little by institutions. He puts a lot of stock in his own sincerity. He believes in it, as if it were a horse or a city wall. He assumes that it will, and should, protect him from consequences that fall to less open people. He may say, "It's true that I betrayed you with your best friend while you were away, and even after you were back, but I was frank with you and told about it. So why should you be angry with me?"

A naïve man acts out strange plays of self-isolation. For example, when an angry woman is criticizing him, he may say, quite sensibly, "You're right. I had no right to do that." If her anger turns to rage, he bends his head and says, "I've always been this way." In the third act, he may implicate his father. "He was never there; he never gave me any support." Her rage continues and he bends over still farther. He is losing ground rapidly, and in the fourth act he may say: "All men are shits." He is now many more times isolated than he was a few minutes ago. He feels rejected by the woman and he is now isolated from all other men as well. One man I knew went through this play every time he had a serious fight with a woman, about once a week.

The naïve man will lose what is most precious to him because of a lack of boundaries. This is particularly true of the New Age man, or the man seeking "higher consciousness." Thieves walk in and out of his house, carrying large bags, and he doesn't seem to notice them. He tells his "white light" experiences at parties; he confides the contents of last night's dream to a total stranger. Mythologically, when he meets the giant he tells him all his plans. He rarely fights for what is his; he gives away his eggs, and other people raise the chicks. We could say that, unaware of boundaries, he does not develop a good container for his soul, nor a good container for two people. There's a leak in it somewhere. He may break the container himself when he sees an attractive face. As an artist he improvises; as a poet his work lacks meter and shape. Improvisation is not all wrong, but he tends to be proud of his lack of form because he feels suspicious of boundaries. The lack of boundaries will eventually damage him.

The naïve man tends to have an inappropriate relation to ecstasy. He longs for ecstasy at the wrong time or in the wrong place, and ignores all masculine sources of it. He wants ecstasy through the feminine, through the Great Mother, through the goddess, even though what may be grounding for the woman ungrounds him. He uses ecstasy to be separated from grounding or discipline.

The naïve man will sink into a mood as if into a big hole. Some women, we notice, are able to get around a mood. If a woman has a bad mood before a party, for example, she may walk around the mood, detach it, and get rid of it, at least for a time. But the naïve man's mood seems attached as if to a mountain. He can't separate it. If he feels hurt, or in a low mood, he identifies with the mood, and everyone around him has to go down into the hole. In his mood-trance, he is not present to wife, children, friends.

The man without limitations may also specialize in not telling. If, for example, he and others decide that some chairs should be arranged before a performance, and he is assigned to do that, he will probably not tell anyone that he has decided to leave the chairs as they are. The people involved, usually older, immediately get mad and shout. Basically he has tricked them into carrying the anger, and its heaviness. He is clean and light, and wonders why other people get angry so often.

The naïve man often doesn't know that there is a being in him that wants to remain sick. Inside each man or woman there is a sick person and a well person: and one needs to know which one is talking at any moment. But awareness of the sick being, and knowledge of how strong he is, is not part of the naïve man's field of perceptions.

The naïve man often lacks what James Hillman has called "natural brutality." The mother hawk pushes the younglings out of the nest one day; we notice the father fox drives the cubs away in early October. But the ascender lets things go on too long. At the start of a relationship, a few harsh words of truth would have been helpful. Instead he waits and waits, and then a major wounding happens farther down the line.

His timing is off. We notice that there will often be a missing beat a second or so after he takes a blow, verbal or physical. He will go directly from the pain of receiving the blow to an empathetic grasp of the reason why it came, skipping over the anger entirely. Misusing Jesus' remark, he turns the missing cheek.

As a final remark about naïveté, we might mention that there is something in naïveté that demands betrayal. The naïve man will have a curious link to betrayal, deceit, and lies. Not only will he betray others easily, being convinced his motives are always good, but when a woman lives with a truly naïve man for a while, she feels impersonally impelled to betray him. When there is too much naïveté around, the universe has no choice but to crystallize out some betrayal.

Numbness

A spiritual man may love light, and yet be entirely numb in the chest area. It's hard to say this right, and it's not clear where the numbness comes from. I'll set down a personal fable.

> When I was two or three years old, I went to my father and asked him for protection. But he was an intense man, and being with him felt more dangerous than being out on the street. I then went to my mother, and asked her for protection. At the instant she said yes, I went numb from my neck down to my lower belly.

That's the fable. It may not be true. I don't know at what age the numbness came. Perhaps I had a genetic expectation that my father would protect me, and when that didn't happen, I went numb from the shock of it. It's also possible that I knew, or thought I knew, that if I accepted my mother's protection, I would have to learn to feel as a woman feels. But I was a man, and so I decided to have no feelings at all.

The fable does suggest that a mother's protection, no matter how well intentioned, will not do as a substitute for the father's protection.

My chest area remained numb up to and through high school. My head was fiery and full of blood, and my genitals were fiery and curious too. The area in between was the problem.

In high school a girl might ask, "Do you love me?" I couldn't answer. If I asked her the same question, she might reply, "Well, I respect you, and I admire you, and I'm fond of you, and I'm even *interested* in you, but I don't love you." Apparently when she looked into her chest, she saw a spectrum of affections, a whole procession of feelings, and she could easily tell them all apart. If I looked down into my chest, I saw nothing at all. I had then either to remain silent or fake it.

Some women feel hurt when a man will not "express his feelings," and they conclude that he is holding back, or "telling them something" by such withholding; but it's more likely that when such a man asks a question of his chest, he gets no answer at all.

Some of that numbness is gone now. I can answer questions about my feelings, and I can see people down there with different colored robes, walking around, and tell one from the other. It's possible that as a man gets older, certain numb parts of his body naturally begin to come to life. It's also possible that the numbness moves away as we learn to go to other people besides our parents for protection. Men my own age protect me, or so I feel, and a few feisty and loving women, and a few determined younger men.

The Story: Taking Kitchen Work

If the golden boy in our story is an ascender and a flyer after he leaves the spring, then Iron John is quite correct when he says to the boy in essence: "You know a great deal about gold now, but nothing about poverty." In effect he says, "You know a lot about going up, and nothing about going down." This is the way the story says it:

> "Go out into the world now and there you will learn what poverty is. I see no evil in your heart, however, and I wish you well, so I'll give you this gift: whenever you are in trouble, come to the edge of the forest and shout, 'Iron John, Iron John!' I'll come to the edge of

the forest and help you. My power is great, greater than you believe, and I have gold and silver in abundance."

Then the King's son left the forest, and walked by beaten and unbeaten paths ever onwards until at length he reached a great city. There he looked for work, but could find none, and he had learnt nothing by which he could help himself. At length, he went to the palace, and asked if they would take him in. The people about court did not at all know what use they could make of him, but they liked him, and told him to stay. At length the cook took him into his service, and said he might carry wood and water, and rake the cinders together.

To fall from being a king's son to being a cook is the step the story asks for. Carrying wood and water, working in the basement of the castle—where the kitchen is—stands for the Drop Through the Floor, the Descent, the humiliation, the "way down and out." We find that phrase in George Orwell's title: *Down and Out in Paris and London.* When Orwell decided to go beyond the naïveté he inherited with his middle-class upbringing, he too got a job in the basement, and his novel is full of the underground life of the kitchen help in big hotels. For young men who have graduated from privileged colleges, or who have been lifted upward by the expensive entitlement culture, their soul life often begins with this basement work in the kitchen.

Katabasis

The mark of Descent, whether undertaken consciously or unconsciously, is a newly arrived-at lowliness, associated with water and soul, as height is associated with spirit. "Water prefers low places." The lowliness happens particularly to men who are initially high, lucky, elevated.

The way down and out usually separates the young man from his companion flyers and from their support, and it makes him aware of a depression that may have been living unnoticed in him for years. A mean life of ordinariness, heaviness, silences, cracks in the road, weightiness, and soberness begins.

Our story simply says that after wandering around a while, having no "craft," the young man at last got a job in the kitchen—which is traditionally in the basement—of a castle. The story says that after all the gold fingertips and hair, what is proper next for the man is the whirlpool, the sinking through the floor, the Drop, what the ancient Greeks called *katabasis*.

There is something more than a little frightening about this Drop. Our ego doesn't want to do it and even if we drop, the ego doesn't want to see it. The sounds in "katabasis," harsh and abrupt, feel right for this trip.

What I am saying, then, is that the next step in initiation for men is finding the rat's hole. The rat's hole is the "dark way," the one that Williams or Haverford doesn't prepare one for, the trip that the upwardly mobile man imagines that only lower-class men take, the way down and out.

When "katabasis" happens, a man no longer feels like a special person. He is not. One day he is in college, being fed and housed—often on someone else's money—protected by brick walls men long dead have built, and the next day he is homeless, walking the streets, looking for some way to get a meal and a bed. People know immediately when you are falling or have fallen: doormen turn their backs, waiters sneer, no one holds the subway car door for you.

Your inner psychology changes as an old shame surfaces, one walks with head down and feels it's all inevitable. The inner masculine self changes. While one is still grandiose and naïve, a young man lives inside, shiny-faced, expectant, hopeful, dandified, a prince. After the Descent begins, an old man takes the place of the prince. To one's amazement a helpless, anti-social, brittle, isolated derelict takes over.

We remember Oedipus in his katabasis: one day an arrogant, demanding king, the next a blind man led around by others. These days, katabasis comes about through addiction—alcohol, cocaine, crack. The man loses his health and ends up with thin legs, flat energy, deprived of wife and children, deprived of friends, house, money. He loses his job, self-respect, "and every mark of his former art and life."

To a man deeply involved in his work, the katabasis can appear without either addiction or ill health. A man does well in his business, lives a sweet life with home and family, enjoys his weekends at Lake Tahoe, and one Sunday morning finds himself on the lawn with a loaded shotgun, and about to pull the trigger. He lives, but loses "every shred of his former art and life."

We remember that Joseph's brothers put him down into a gravel pit—the Arab version says into a deep dry well. A few days later they sell him to the slave traders, who in turn take him still farther downward into Egypt, where he makes a third Descent into a dungeon after offending the commandant's wife.

It is as if life itself somehow "discharges" him. There are many ways of being "discharged": a serious accident, the loss of a job, the breaking of a long-standing friendship, a divorce, a "breakdown," an illness.

It is said that whenever a friend reported enthusiastically, "I have just been promoted!" Jung would say, "I'm very sorry to hear that; but if we all stick together, I think we will get through it." If a friend arrived depressed and ashamed, saying, "I've just been fired," Jung would say, "Let's open a bottle of wine; this is wonderful news; something good will happen now."

The young man in "The Devil's Sooty Brother" (the Grimm brothers story) meets a dark man while wandering in the woods just after having been discharged from the army. He accepts a job boiling pots in a place underground, uniting in this image the kitchen and the Descent. We can say that the state of being "discharged" is a good and holy state that prepares for the Descent. Iron John, we could say, discharges the boy after his three days at the spring.

We know that nineteenth-century men characteristically failed to notice female suffering. *The Madwoman in the Attic,* by Sandra Gilbert and Susan Gubar, describes how strong that suffering was. In this century, men have added another inattention: they characteristically failed to notice their own suffering.

The wound a man receives from his father, or from life, or

from contact with the Wild Man, first turned up in our story when the boy pinched his finger. Through that hurt, his way of dealing with the world was damaged.

Some parents administer the wound to us by being indifferent or cold, by beating, by verbal abuse, by sexual abuse, by regarding us as nothing, or providing us with a fundamentalist shaming. As we mentioned in the last chapter, a son can dip the wound into therapeutic or ritual water to make the particular wound conscious, to feel its injustice, its enormity, its harmful effect on his spontaneity and joy, its connection to his open or covert rage.

Kitchen work means intensification of the dipping. The descender makes an exit—from ordinary and respectable life—through the wound. The wound now is thought of as a door. If his father abandoned him, he now truly becomes abandoned; during this time he has no house, no mother, no woman. If shame wounded him, through sexual abuse, physical beating, or by ingesting a shame-filled parent, this time he lives the shaming out—he associates with men and women who are chronically shamed, puts himself down and out where he will be shamed fifty times a day.

If the mother wounded him through her possessiveness, making him feel inadequate and too small, this time he becomes really helpless, has no status, no "contacts." He's confirmed in the knowledge of that smallness.

If some parental event or cultural pressure separated his "head" from his "body," got him stuck in the position of the observer, this time in his katabasis he becomes really stuck. The Peruvian poet César Vallejo, who spent ten years in Paris, utterly down-and-out, catches the mood of stuckness:

> *It is a huge spider, which can no longer move;*
> *a spider which is colorless, whose body,*
> *a head and an abdomen, is bleeding.*

> *Today I watched it with great care. With what*
> *tremendous energy*
> *to every side*
> *it was stretching out its many feet.*

And I have been thinking of its invisible eyes,
the death-bringing pilots of the spider.

It is a spider which was shivering, fixed
on the sharp ridge of a stone;
the abdomen on one side, and on the other the
    head.

With so many feet the poor thing, and still it
    cannot solve it!
And seeing it
confused in such great danger,
what a strange pain that traveler has given me
    today!

It is a huge spider, whose abdomen
prevents him from following his head.
And I have been thinking of his eyes
and of his many, many feet . . .
And what a strange pain that traveler has given
    me!

    Translated by R.B.

Vallejo's mode has been called "a heroic exit through the wound." He does not exit, as the hero does, through his heroism, nor through his invincibility, as the warrior does, but he exits through his wound. Vallejo said in another poem,

Well, on the day I was born,
God was sick.

The way down and out doesn't require poverty, homelessness, physical deprivation, dishwasher work, necessarily, but it does seem to require a fall from status, from a human being to a spider, from a middle-class person to a derelict. The emphasis is on the consciousness of the fall.

In divorce, when a man's emotional safety may disintegrate, he can either walk backward through the door while looking at funny movies, or he can try to take in the true darkness of the door as he faces it. The divorce itself may have come about because of some particular childhood wound a man had—or perhaps the marriage may have come about because of that particular wound— but in either case, the marriage's breakup or breakdown revives the wound.

Divorce feels for most men like a discharge, as if one had been fired from a task taken on the day of the wedding. And the agony of separation from a substitute mother figure, the sense of inadequacy among demands for more money, the lack of warmth or grace in the new apartment or house, the felt rejection and isolation as the community withdraws some of its approval and support, the self-doubt the change evokes—all these add up to a new sort of loneliness. If the man refuses to be cheered up, and considers all of the discomforts to be cunning expressions of an isolating wound received in early childhood, then the man can use the divorce—like any other serious collapse—as an invitation to go through the door, accept katabasis, immerse himself in the wound, and exit from his old life through it.

Often the moment of katabasis is not without its own dark humor. A spiritual teacher whom I knew came to a fork in the road while driving home one night from a lecture on enlightenment. The way to the left led to a motel where friends were, and where he knew there would be some liquor and women, and the road to the right led to the ascetic meditation center that he administered. He couldn't decide and the car went straight ahead into a yellow brick wall on which was painted in large letters an advertisement for THE JOKE SHOP. The result wasn't humorous. He came out of the hospital partly paralyzed on one side and remained so for the rest of his life.

I remember these stories with a sense of awe. The energies who ask for katabasis have immense powers at their control. The mood is that of Christ's remark, "You shall not get out until you have paid the last penny."

Katabasis also carries with it the whole concept of disaster, perhaps bringing it into the man's life for the first time. Another man, lively in his spiritual discipline, a flyer but a hard worker, always ready to help the community, saw a grass fire in a ditch. He stopped his car, ran down to help put out the grass fire, and then became aware of something large looming over his left shoulder. A second later a car flying through the air pinned him to the earth. He ended up in a hospital also, ribs and pelvis broken, flat on his back. Up till now, the boat of his life has retained its buoyancy. Most of us, as Tomas Tranströmer mentions, transfer weights from one pocket to the other in order to keep the boat balanced. Suddenly, the boat turns over. As the descender hits the water, he remembers the people who went down on the *Titanic* in the dark, into freezing water, the big ice mountain floating nearby. Antonio Machado said:

Mankind owns four things
That are no good at sea—
Rudder, anchor, oars,
And the fear of going down.

A Lutheran minister in our small town in Minnesota had always been able to keep his boat balanced even in the jealous choppy waters of the congregation. He acts firmly; and he uses the firm approach on his son of sixteen, who still demands to use the family car, even after the father has said no. The boy steals it. The father, finding it gone, calls the police, who locate the car, chase it, and stop it. Then the boy pulls a .22 rifle out of the back seat and kills the state patrolmen. So here the boat goes down for both of them.

One has the sense that some power in the psyche arranges a severe katabasis if the man does not know enough to go down on his own. Depression is a small katabasis, and something other than us arranges it. Depression usually surprises us by its arrival and its departure. In depression, we refuse to go down, and so a hand comes up and pulls him down. In grief we choose to go down.

With initiators gone from our culture, we do not receive instruction on how to go down on our own. We could use the phrase going into grief for the conscious act of descent, but one sometimes feels that in the United States a man is supposed to feel grief only at a funeral.

Some Turkish Sufi groups begin their night-work with a repeated word reminding them of the grief of what they have not done the past year. The emotion is not around sin, guilt, or shame; but around what one has not done. The soul itself asks us to go down. D. H. Lawrence said:

> I am not a mechanism, an assembly of various
>   sections.
> And it is not because the mechanism is working
>   wrongly, that I am ill.
> I am ill because of wounds to the soul, to the deep
>   emotional self—
> and the wounds to the soul take a long, long time,
>   only time can help
> and patience, and a certain difficult repentance
> long difficult repentance, realization of life's
>   mistake, and the freeing oneself
> from the endless repetition of the mistake
> which mankind at large has chosen to sanctify.

The "long difficult repentance" is a way of saying descent, though I prefer the verticality of katabasis and the image of a door. Drinking is a door that opens for some. Instead of repeating, "I can handle it," and "I'm never out of control," such a man says, "I'm an alcoholic—that's obvious." The Twelve Steps of AA take him down.

Earlier in this chapter we spoke of some characteristics of the naïve man, among them the agreement not to look at the dark side, the assumption that everyone speaks from the heart, an inappropriate relation to ecstasy, the failure to notice that some part of him wants to remain sick, and so on. My guess is that at every point where we have one of those naïvetés, we will eventually find a katabasis to correspond with it.

Seeing the dark side of a person close to us is a discipline the descender accepts. I ask a friend about a mutual chum; he says, "I trust him for the most part." That's right—"for the most part."

So-called street people learn the idea of partial trust early. And one looks at oneself the same way, partially trusting. It is said that in marriage, the man and woman give each other "his or her nethermost beast" to hold. Each holds the leash for the "nethermost beast" of the other. It's a wonderful phrase.

The naïve man who flies directly toward the sun will not be able to see his own shadow. It is far behind him. In katabasis, it catches up.

> *Well, on the day I was born,*
> *God was sick . . .*
> *They all know that I'm alive,*
> *that I chew my food . . . and they don't know*
> *why harsh winds whistle in my poems,*
> *the narrow uneasiness of a coffin,*
> *winds untangled from the sphinx*
> *who holds the desert for routine questioning . . .*
>
> *On the day I was born,*
> *God was sick,*
> *gravely.*
>
> —César Vallejo
> *Translated by James Wright*

On the way down, one receives a little instruction about the dark side of God.

The naïve man may receive a little instruction also about the dark side of the Great Mother. Sooner or later, also, the dark side of the Great Mother crystallizes out of the universe; the black darling has to appear, the one with boar tusks coming down from her lips. Perhaps she will appear in ordinary life as an enraged woman, a woman astounded by inconsistency or betrayal.

The man experiences an angry woman; but something in the angry woman's malice introduces him perhaps for the first time to the Rageful One, the Dark Side of the Moon, the Ogre who lives on the back side of the moon with bat wings and ripped-apart birds. Experiencing the Malicious One is a compensation for the earlier life "above the ground," being fed with fish and fowl, and dainty things.

When we are betrayed the toothed side of the universe shows

its mouth: black dogs run behind the carriage, the pitiless cook kills the daughter and buries her in the garden; the misguided groom cuts off the head of the magic horse, and the princess is sent out to take care of the pigs.

The black side of the Great Mother in India is called Kali. The flowers around her neck can change to skulls and back again in a fraction of a second. Only Shiva, one of the forms of the Wild Man, can stand up to her, and that gives a hint as to why in our story it is the Wild Man who guides the initiation of the young boy.

Pwyll, Prince of Dyved, whose story appears in *The Mabinogion*, does not become king until he has exchanged places for a year with the King of the Underworld. Practically, that means that for a year he feels next to him in the bed all night the body of the Black Darling, the Queen of the Underworld.

So we do not descend to the bottom of the hill merely by seeing the dark side of ourself, or our friends, difficult as that is. Baba Yaga, in Russian tales, asks: Are you here to pursue a good deed or to shirk it? We reach the bottom when Baba Yaga's hostile boar energy has completely replaced—for a time—the childlike eros which each of us felt when our mother set a breast to our mouth, or later set a cup of milk down for us at the table, or when our first marvelous girlfriend beckoned us to bed. These loves are all well; but descent is complete when both have been replaced by the boar-tusked, hog-bristled, big-mouthed, skull-necklaced, insanely high-spirited energy of Baba Yaga.

Something wants us there, wants the meeting with the Dark Queen, wants the boar to open his mouth, wants Grendel's pool to fill with blood, wants the swords to melt, wants the Giantess to put the boy in her sack.

Young men in our culture often imagine, when they look forward to meeting Baba Yaga, that they can "kill" her. They imagine annihilation, total victory; but the stories make clear that such fantasies belong to the uninitiated men. The only solution to the power of the witch is for the young man to develop energy as great as hers, as harsh, as wild, as shrewd, as clear in its desire.

When a young man arrives at her house, proves himself to be up to her level of intensity, purpose, and respect for the truth, she will sometimes say, "Okay, what do you want to know?"

Taking the Road of Ashes

Descent or "kitchen work" can take three other forms. We'll name these as Taking the Road of Ashes, Learning to Shudder, and Moving from the Mother's World to the Father's World.

"The cook took him into his service, and said he might carry wood and water, and rake the cinders together." This is a reference to the cinders boy in Norwegian fairy tales, named Askaladden (Ash-Boy), and to Cinderella (Cinder Girl) in the fairy tales of many countries. Ashes do not belong to the sunlit crown of the tree, nor to its strong roots. Ash is literally the death of the trunk.

"Ashes" and "cinders" in fairy tales are code words for the ashy, sooty, depressed, "out of it" time. We imagine in our day that to be assigned to the hearth is some sort of punishment, but in the fairy stories that assignment goes to the lucky third son, who is the magical ashy fool, and to the lucky third daughter, Cinderella, the magical suffering child of the mother. For those two children, tending the hearth is the right task.

We know what it is like to take ashes in our hands. How light they are! The fingertips experience them as a kind of powder. Ashes are sometimes tan in color, sometimes pale gray, or white as lace, delicate as unfolding insect wings. Ashes, we note, find their way into the whorls of our fingertips, cling there, make the whorls more noticeable, more visible, more clear to us. We can take our own fingerprints with ashes.

To live the life of ashes is very different from dropping into katabasis. It doesn't require a fall in social status. It is not so explosive; there is something about ashes that is steady, even lethargic.

Young men in Viking times, according to the Norwegian scholar R. Keyser, were allowed sometimes two or three years of ashes.

Norwegians at that time lived in long communal houses, not unlike the long houses of the West Coast Indians. In his book on the old Norsemen, Keyser described how thirty or forty people slept in the beds along the walls. Down the center of the hall they laid out a pavement which acted as the fireplace. Smoke went up through holes in the roof. Ashes lay in long heaps two or three feet from the pavement between it and the beds. It turned out that young men sometimes would lie down in that space between the fire and the ash pile, and stay there two or three years. "Such as these might constantly be seen crouching over the fire, rolling themselves in the ashes, eating ashes, and neither caring to employ themselves in anything useful, nor to keep themselves in a state of cleanliness." Apparently some also chewed cinders. They were called Cinder-Biters. It's clear that the young men were going through some kind of hibernation or ritual lethargy, and the older men and women allowed it. If a young man now feels the need to drop out of school, there is no ritual for that, and he may easily end up shamed, or worse, in prison.

Keyser mentions a Cinder-Biter in the eleventh century named Starkad, who remained in the ashes several years, until his foster father invited him to go on an expedition. At that point he stood up, shaved, and dressed and became one of the best warriors on the expedition, and later became a distinguished poet as well, remembered in the sagas.

We remember the Catholic church's emphasis on Ash Wednesday, of ashes on the forehead.

Mircea Eliade recounts in his books the brilliant use of ashes made by old men initiators in Australia, Africa, the Near East, South America, the Pacific. Initiation says that before a boy can become a man, some infantile being in him must die. Ashes Time is a time set aside for the death of that ego-bound boy. The boy between eight and twelve years of age, having been taken away from the mother, passes into the hands of the old men guides who cover his face and sometimes his whole body with ashes to make him the color of dead people and to remind him of the inner death about to come. He may be put into the dark for hours or maybe days, introduced to spirits of dead ancestors. Then he may crawl through a tunnel—or vagina—made of brush and branches. The old men are waiting for him at the other end, only now he has a new name. The mothers in some cultures feel so strongly about the importance of the ritual that when reunited to their sons, they pretend not to recognize them and have to be reintroduced. The mothers participate joyfully in this initiation.

The gold-obsessed man, whether a New Age man or a Dow Jones man, can be said to be the man who hasn't yet handled ashes.

The word ashes contains in it a dark feeling for death; ashes when put on the face whiten it as death does. Job covered himself with ashes to say that the earlier comfortable Job was dead; and that the living Job mourned the dead Job. But, for us, how can we get a look at the cinders side of things when the society is determined to create a world of shopping malls and entertainment complexes in which we are made to believe that there is no death, disfigurement, illness, insanity, poverty, lethargy, or misery? Disneyland means "no ashes."

Despite our Disneyland culture, some men around thirty-five or forty will begin to experience ashes privately, without ritual, even without old men. They begin to notice how many of their dreams have turned to ashes. A young man in high school dreams that he will be a race driver, a mountain climber, he will marry Miss America, he will be a millionaire by thirty, he will get a Nobel Prize in physics by thirty-five, he will be an architect and build the tallest building ever. He will get out of his hick town and live in Paris. He will have fabulous friends . . . and by thirty-five, all these dreams are ashes.

At thirty-five his inner stove begins to produce ashes as well. All through his twenties, his stove burned with such a good draft that he threw in whole nights until dawn, drinking parties, sexual extravagance, enthusiasm, madness, excitement. Then one day he notices that his stove doesn't take such big chunks anymore. He opens the stove door and ashes fall out on the floor. It's time for him to buy a small black shovel at the hardware store and get down on his knees. The ashes fall off the shovel and onto the floor, and he can see the print of our bootsoles in the ashes.

Robert Frost said of the "Oven Bird":

The question that he frames in all but words
is what to make of a diminished thing.

New diets, new pop singers, new authors, all ashes by the time you are thirty-five.
When I was about thirty-eight I wrote this poem:

Those great sweeps of snow that stop suddenly six
*   feet from the house . . .*
Thoughts that go so far.
The boy gets out of high school and reads no more
*   books;*
The son stops calling home.
The mother puts down her rolling pin and makes
*   no more bread.*
And the wife looks at her husband one night at a
*   party, and loves him no more.*
The energy leaves the wine, and the minister falls
*   leaving the church.*
It will not come closer—
The one inside moves back, and the hands touch
*   nothing, and are safe.*
The father grieves for his son, and will not leave the
*   room where the coffin stands.*
He turns away from his wife, and she sleeps alone.

And the sea lifts and falls all night, the moon goes
*   on through the unattached heavens alone.*
The toe of the shoe pivots
in the dust . . .
And the man in the black coat turns, and goes back
*   down the hill.*
No one knows why he came, or why he turned away,
*   and did not climb the hill.*
             —"Snowbanks North of the House"

Some habitual error we keep making in our relationships produces more ash than heat. A number of men around thirty-five have told me that they are afraid to go into a new relationship for fear it will end as the last ten or twelve have ended, in "ashes." But young men can't get enough ashes. Enlightenment addicts think they want ecstasy from their association with their guru, but they may really want the ashes. Having no kitchen fire to sit beside, and no Wild Man to send us there, the young man smears soot on his face and hopes that his own mother will not recognize him.

Pablo Neruda says:

Out of everything I've done, everything I've lost,
everything I've gotten unexpectedly,
I can give you a little in leaves, in sour iron . . .
here I am with the thing that loses stars,
like a vegetable, alone.

> —from "Brussels"
> *Translated by R.B.*

Ashes present a great diminishment away from the living tree with its huge crown and its abundant shade. The recognition of this diminishment is a proper experience for men who are over thirty. If the man doesn't experience that diminishment sharply, he will retain his inflation, and continue to identify himself with all in him that can fly: his sexual drive, his mind, his refusal to commit himself, his addiction, his transcendence, his coolness. The coolness of some American men means that they have skipped ashes.

Franklin Roosevelt found his ashes in his polio; Anwar Sadat in his prison; Solzhenitsyn in the gulag. Some of our liveliest writers— John Steinbeck, William Faulkner, Thomas McGrath, Tillie Olson, David Ignatow, Kenneth Rexroth—found their ashes in the poverty of the Depression.

Katabasis and ashes are a little different. We could say that a man finds katabasis only through dropping, poverty, abrupt change in social class; and prison is a traditional place to experience both katabasis and ashes. But a man may keep his job and family and still experience ashes if he knows what he is doing.

Murray Stein, in his book *In Midlife*, suggests that what I've called Ashes Time may be thought of as a search for the corpse. Somewhere in our past life there is a dead body. It could be a career mislaid; it could be a relationship gone into the river; it could be the corpse of a shamed boy.

After Achilles killed Hector, his father, Priam, longed to get Hector's body back to Troy for a proper funeral. Priam, with the help of Hermes, "He of the Invisible Cap," guides Priam, Stein notes, "through the night stealthily past the lines of the Greeks into the heart of their camp."

So we have to slip at night "through the lines" to find the corpse. That is ashes work. It requires cunning and stealth. It requires the help of a god.

Learning to Shudder

The descent has a third face, what we will call "learning to shudder." In the early Grimm brothers collection there is a story about a young man who seemed normal in every way except that he couldn't shudder. All sorts of shocks were prepared for him: ghosts, hanged men, demon cats, bodies in coffins—nothing did any good.

Children are able to shudder easily, and a child will often break into tears when he or she sees a wounded animal. But later the domination system enters, and some boys begin to torture and kill insects and animals to perfume their own insignificance.

Boys at that point become Titans. We recall that the Titans were in the world before the gods. It was a Titan—Cronos—who castrated his father Uranus, and later ate each of his own children as they were born, except Zeus. Eventually, Zeus defeated the Titans decisively, and put them below the earth, but they remained around somehow, and later they "accidentally" ate Dionysus, their grandson, the shudderer, the one who could feel grief. In his anger, Zeus burned the Titans to ashes. But human beings, the story says, were made from those ashes. Dionysus himself was reconstituted from his heart, which the Titans didn't get.

It is such a marvelous mythological idea to have human beings created out of the Titans' ashes; it helps explain our own cruelty and coldness. Of course, we also received in the ashes Dionysus' body, but not the heart, alas. We can say then that it is Dionysus, the last of the Greek gods to be developed, who guides that secret process in which the young man—or young woman—learns to shudder. After adolescence, a young man needs to learn precisely what the Titans never did learn. That is a legitimate aim of initiation.

The recent movie *Casualties of War* makes a brilliant statement about the difficulty of this initiation. The movie recounts an actual incident during the Vietnam war in which four men in a platoon of five capture, then rape, then finally kill a Vietnamese woman. From the initiator's point of view, none of the four is properly a man at all, but they are brutal boys, stuck in some stage before ashes and descent. They are undone, unfinished men, dangerous in their inability to shudder.

Michael J. Fox plays the fifth man, who refuses to take part in the rape, later tries to save the woman's life, and still later reports the brutal rape and death at the risk of his life. The horror at what these "Titans" can do makes him shudder. His ability to shudder is his most adult aspect.

Most of us remember from our childhood how much the non-shudderers hate the boys who can shudder. The four men in this movie threaten to isolate Fox, to put him out in the cold beyond the community of men, and to do that by raping him if they feel like it.

Gaining the ability to shudder means feeling how frail human beings are, and how awful it is to be a Titan. When one is shuddering, the shudder helps to take away the numbness we spoke of. When a man possesses empathy, it does not mean that he has developed the feminine feeling only; of course he has, and it is good to develop the feminine. But when he learns to shudder, he is developing a part of the masculine emotional body as well. Just as Hermes helps him "through the lines" on the road to retain the corpse, he is helped to shudder by the god Dionysus, the grandson of the Titans.

Going from the Mother's House to the Father's House

When initiation is in place, the old men help the boys to move from the mother's world to the father's world. Boys have lived happily since birth in the mother's world, and the father's world naturally seems to them dangerous, unsteady, and full of unknowns.

We recall that most cultures describe the first stage of initiation as a sharp and clean break with the mother. Old men simply go into the women's compounds with spears one day when the boys are between eight and twelve and take the boys away. Up to that point, the boys have lived exclusively with the women. In New Guinea, to take one example, the initiated men live together in houses at the edge of the village. Mothers in New Guinea carefully refrain from telling the boys anything about the impending events, retaining the element of surprise. As the men lead them away, the boys may be crying out, "Save me, Momma, save me!" The mother's world looks wonderful all at once. The women put up a resistance, but it does no good. The old men start to take the boys to, say, an island where the initiator's hut has been built. The mothers of the boys being abducted appear on the bridge with spears. "Here I am, Momma! Save me!" the boys say, but the old men drive the mothers back. The mothers go home, have coffee, meet the other women and say things like, "How did I do? Did I look fierce enough?" "You were great."

When "gender issues," as we call them, are well understood, the women do not oppose the initiatory work with the boys, nor helplessly yearn for it but participate enthusiastically and sadly in the drama of it. The relevant sentence is the one accepted in New Guinea by men and women of eighty or so tribes: "A boy cannot change into a man without the active intervention of the older men." A girl changes into a woman on her own, with the bodily developments marking the change; old women tell her stories and chants, and do celebrations. But with the boys, no old men, no change.

So the first stage then is a clean break with the mother. That happens in our story when the Wild Man takes the boy on his shoulders. But a break is only a break, and it doesn't imply any internal movement inside the boy. All that is still to happen; with most of us, it is still happening.

Simply put, the boy needs to move from the mother's house to the father's house. Shakespeare's *Hamlet* describes with fantastic wit and in heartbreaking detail the difficulty of this move. The ghost gives Hamlet a clear order: "Shudder over my death, look at the ashes of my kingship, give up your studious life." But Hamlet has not yet taken work "in the kitchen." He knows about his genius all right, but he is stuck somewhere. Perhaps he has carefully put the key back underneath his mother's pillow. Throughout the entire play, he struggles to move away from her realm. We sense that he makes too much of his mother's sexual life; and he is obsessed there. He doesn't regard her as an "other," with the awe and respect proper to a grown person. The father has to come back from the grave again and again to keep things moving, to prevent Hamlet from being drawn entirely back into his old stuck place.

If no old man or competent initiator is present at this stage— and Polonius certainly is not such a man—all moves slowly. We learn one valuable thing as we watch: a young man cannot make the move to the father's world alone without taking on the Trickster and particularly the dark side of the Trickster. The good side won't do it. The Grimm brothers story "The Raven" says it clearly: the mother's boy there has to learn to *rob the robbers*, or he can't get to the end of the story. Hamlet's Trickster rewrote some lines in the little play, and then got the actors to perform it. The same Dark Trickster also kills Polonius after Polonius has overheard a conversation. On board the ship, when Hamlet discovers that his old friends Rosencrantz and Guildenstern are carrying Claudius' letter to the king of England, requesting the king to kill Hamlet on arrival, he could simply have been firm; what he does is to forge another letter, ordering the king of England to kill them. We notice that he returns to Denmark with the help of pirates, another nod to the Dark Trickster.

Hamlet tries and tries to make the decisive move to the father's world but the move seems too drastic for him. Meanwhile, Ophelia dies—the young feminine suffers when the man cannot get to the father's world. We could also say that some sentimental girl inside Hamlet, here called Ophelia, has gone mad at this clumsily performed move and will "die." We recall that Parsifal, another man without an older mentor, who had lived with his mother all through his childhood and youth, met knights one day, thought they were "angels," and felt an instant desire to go with them. When his mother saw him leave, she died on the spot. Some deaths stand for the naïveté that dies when the son accepts the father's world.

Hamlet ends with a highly intricate scene of double and triple trickery. In the course of the last scene, a duel, Hamlet arrives at last at the father's house; his own mother dies, and he kills his father's murderer. Almost immediately he dies himself, but nothing is perfect. Shakespeare allows the stage to be occupied at the final moment by Fortinbras and his men, who do not know how to shudder. That is an unsentimental moment.

A man's effort to move to the father's house takes a long time; it's difficult, and each man has to do it for himself. For Hamlet it meant giving up the immortality or the safe life promised to the faithful mother's son, and accepting the risk of death always imminent in the father's realm.

The story of Pwyll, which we've mentioned above, describes the move as an exchange of houses for one year with the Lord of the Dead. Among a man's jobs is to reclaim his own grief. When a man has reclaimed his grief and investigated his wound, he may find that they resemble the grief and the wound his father had, and the reclaiming puts him in touch with his father's soul. Once his senses are sharpened, he will be able to smell the father's wound. One could say that the son smells his father as one smells a serpent, who sheds skins and lives.

Moving to the father's world does not necessarily mean rejecting the mother or shouting at her—Hamlet is off in that respect—but rather the movement involves convincing the naïve boy or the comfort-loving boy, to die. Other interior boys remain alive; this one dies. Fish and turtles are independent of the mother on their first day. But independence from the mother's womb world goes in agonizingly slow motion for developing men. One wants to run, but the legs will not move. We wake exhausted.

The image of the snake leads us to one final image around this complicated matter of the move to the father's house. In his *Occidental Mythology*, Joseph Campbell notes that we observe a certain scene over and over, with variations, on numerous Babylonian seals. We see a male figure standing, and nearby we see a female figure, usually seated, probably a goddess or the goddess's priestess, and we see a third figure—a large snake. It is possible that such a seal amounts to a meditation object for men who have been brought up in a culture strengthened by, or ruled by, or moistened by the Great Mother.

We assume that the man's personal mother in such a culture would be strong as well. The young man, if he is to live, will have to detach himself from both mothers. He either does that or he doesn't escape from the Great Mother's field. Campbell's speculation goes as follows: the male figure we see standing there is a man's male body which he received from his mother in the womb. To hate her, conquer her, destroy her—all those fantasies are off. Instead the man, meditating, attaches himself in imagination to the serpent father. We must remember that the ancient world did not consider the serpent to be evil. On the contrary, it was a holy animal. This serpent lives under the roots of the World Tree—in earth—even though we know snakes climb to the branches of the tree as well.

Attaching himself to the serpent father reminds us of Hamlet. We recall that in the opening scenes Hamlet at one point calls his father's voice a "mole" because it moves under the ground, and speaks now here, now there. It is possible that identification with the serpent father was a characteristic male meditation of the second and third millennia B.C. Other meditations have been created by men in later centuries, and we might glance at the Jesuit meditations of the late seventeenth century. In these Jesuit meditations, the man disidentifies with the matter-loving side of the Great Mother, and with all paganism. (He keeps some identification with the Virgin.) He disidentifies with his own body by calling it names, punishing it with sleeplessness, fasts, and occasionally whipping. He identifies, however, with a spirit who is heavenly, bodiless, celestial, golden, eternal, above it all. The serpent as a force is not mentioned. That is a great change from the earlier meditation.

In the earlier meditation, still practiced in essence in India, Africa, New Guinea, and aboriginal Australia, the young man moves to join the Beneath Father. The Beneath Father retains his shape through many changes as snakes do. The Beneath Father, moreover, being a snake, associates with the spinal cord. It is said that a powerful snake of some kind lives in us at the bottom of the spinal cord, at the survival house.

The man today, as he embarks toward the father's house, is in between these two mythologies. If he is an ascender, he flees from earth, water, dust, and flesh, and effectively asks women to take care of the earth. By contrast, the old men in traditional initiation lead the young man to the Beneath Father, near where the ancestors live and where snakes are. That voyage does not exile him from heaven, for snakes can be found even in the crown of the tree. The snake swims in water, as well. The snake is the Lord of the Waters. Mythologically then, the snake resembles the Wild Man, the King, and other beings who lie in the water at the bottom of our psyches.

We surmise, then, that when a man accepts the Descent as a way to move to the father's house, he learns to look at the death side of things, he glances down to the rat's hole, which is also the snake's hole, and he accepts the snake rather than the bird as his animal. The father in the middle-class household may own the car and the credit cards, but the mother lives longer, and comes back from the cemetery after the father is buried. The son feels a pull to identify with the mother's sturdiness and, beyond that, with the vibrant energy of the Great Mother.

Initiation asks the son to move his love energy away from the attractive mother to the relatively unattractive serpent father. All that is ashes work. When a man enters this stage he regards Descent as a holy thing, he increases his tolerance for ashes, eats dust as snakes do, increases his stomach for terrifying insights, deepens his ability to digest the evil facts of history, accepts the job of working seven years under the ground, leaves the granary at will through the rat's hole, bites on cinders, learns to shudder, and follows the voice of the old mole below the ground.

During each stage of Iron John's initiation process, a masculine god has taken part. Apollo was present at the spring. And we could say that concealed in the ashes work there is the old Mediterranean god Saturn, the natural container of restraint, melancholy, vast systems, disciplined repetition, mentor standards, and heavy grieving. When Saturn is present, the failure just sits there solidly and is not to be explained away.

Saturn, then, helps men to get heavy with the full weight of their wound, and the full power of their failures. After Saturn introduces a man to the Lord of Melancholy, that man begins the black courtship of the soul which eventually leads the man to the Garden.

CHAPTER FOUR

The Hunger for the King in a Time with No Father

Disturbances in Sonhood

As I've participated in men's gatherings since the early 1980s, I've heard one statement over and over from American males, which has been phrased in a hundred different ways: "There is not enough father." The sentence implies that father is a substance like salt, which in earlier times was occasionally in short supply, or like groundwater, which in some areas now has simply disappeared.

Geoffrey Gorer remarked in his book *The American People* that for a boy to become a man in the United States in 1940 only one thing was required: namely, that he reject his father. He noticed, moreover, that American fathers expect to be rejected. Young men in Europe, by contrast, have traditionally imagined the father to be a demonic being whom they must wrestle with (and the son in Kafka's "The Judgment" does wrestle his father to the death and loses). Many sons in the United States, however, visualize the father as a simple object of ridicule to be made fun of, as, in fact, he is so often in comic strips and television commercials. One young man summed it up: "A father is a person who rustles newspapers in the living room."

Clearly, "father water" in the home has sunk below the reach of most wells.

TOO LITTLE FATHER

When the father-table, the groundwater, drops, so to speak, and there is too little father, instead of too much father, the sons find themselves in a new situation. What do they do: drill for new father water, ration the father water, hoard it, distill mother water into father water?

Traditional cultures still in existence seem to have plenty of father. In so-called traditional cultures, many substitute fathers work with the young man. Uncles loosen the son up, or tell him about women. Grandfathers give him stories. Warrior types teach weaponry and discipline, old men teach ritual and soul—all of them honorary fathers.

Bruno Bettelheim noticed, too, that in most traditional cultures Freud's version of father-son hatred doesn't hold. The wordless tension between fathers and sons in Vienna, which he assumed to be universal and based on sexual jealousy, was, in Bettelheim's opinion, true mostly in Vienna in the late nineteenth century.

Fathers and sons in most tribal cultures live in an amused tolerance of each other. The son has a lot to learn, and so the father and son spend hours trying and failing together to make arrowheads or to repair a spear or track a clever animal. When a father and son do spend long hours together, which some fathers and sons still do, we could say that a substance almost like food passes from the older body to the younger.

The contemporary mind might want to describe the exchange between father and son as a likening of attitude, a miming, but I think a physical exchange takes place, as if some substance was passing directly to the cells. The son's body—not his mind—receives and the father gives this food at a level far below consciousness. The son does not receive a hands-on healing, but a body-on healing. His cells receive some knowledge of what an adult masculine body is. The younger body learns at what frequency the masculine body vibrates. It begins to grasp the song that adult male cells sing, and how the charming, elegant, lonely, courageous, half-shamed male molecules dance.

During the long months the son spent in the mother's body,

his body got well tuned to female frequencies: it learned how a woman's cells broadcast, who bows to whom in that resonant field, what animals run across the grassy clearing, what the body listens for at night, what the upper and lower fears are. How firmly the son's body becomes, before birth and after, a good receiver for the upper and lower frequencies of the mother's voice! The son either tunes to that frequency or he dies.

Now, standing next to the father, as they repair arrowheads, or repair plows, or wash pistons in gasoline, or care for birthing animals, the son's body has the chance to retune. Slowly, over months or years, that son's body-strings begin to resonate to the harsh, sometimes demanding, testily humorous, irreverent, impatient, opinionated, forward-driving, silence-loving older masculine body. Both male and female cells carry marvelous music, but the son needs to resonate to the masculine frequency as well as to the female frequency.

Sons who have not received this retuning will have father-hunger all their lives. I think calling the longing "hunger" is accurate: the young man's body lacks salt, water, or protein, just as a starving person's body and lower digestive tract lack protein. If it finds none, the stomach will eventually eat up the muscles themselves. Such hungry sons hang around older men like the homeless do around a soup kitchen. Like the homeless, they feel shame over their condition, and it is nameless, bitter, unexpungeable shame.

Women cannot, no matter how much they sympathize with their starving sons, replace that particular missing substance. The son later may try to get it from a woman his own age, but that doesn't work either.

DISTRUST OF OLDER MEN

Only one hundred and forty years have passed since factory work began in earnest in the West, and we see in each generation poorer bonding between father and son, with catastrophic results. A close study of the Enclosure Act of England shows that the English government, toward the end of that long legislative process, denied the landless father access to free pasture and common land with the precise aim of forcing him, with or without his family, to travel to the factory. The South Africans still do that to black fathers today.

By the middle of the twentieth century in Europe and North America a massive change had taken place: the father was working, but the son could not see him working.

Throughout the ancient hunter societies, which apparently lasted thousands of years—perhaps hundreds of thousands—and throughout the hunter-gatherer societies that followed them, and the subsequent agricultural and craft societies, fathers and sons worked and lived together. As late as 1900 in the United States about ninety percent of fathers were engaged in agriculture. In all these societies the son characteristically saw his father working at all times of the day and all seasons of the year.

When the son no longer sees that, what happens? After thirty years of working with young German men, as fatherless in their industrial society as young American men today, Alexander Mitscherlich, whom we spoke of in the first chapter, developed a metaphor: a hole appears in the son's psyche. When the son does not see his father's workplace, or what he produces, does he imagine his father to be a hero, a fighter for good, a saint, or a white knight? Mitscherlich's answer is sad: demons move into that empty place—demons of suspicion.

The demons, invisible but talkative, encourage suspicion of all older men. Such suspicion effects a breaking of the community of old and young men. One could feel this distrust deepen in the sixties: "Never trust anyone over thirty."

The older men in the American military establishment and government did betray the younger men in Vietnam, lying about the nature of the war, remaining in safe places themselves, after having asked the young men to be warriors and then in effect sending them out to be ordinary murderers. And so the demons have had a lot to work with in recent American history. The demons urge all young men to see *Lawrence of Arabia* and *Dead Poets Society* because they remind us how corrupt all men in authority are and how thoroughly they betray the young male idealist. Mentorship becomes difficult to sustain; initiation is rejected.

Anthropologists affected by those demons suggest that elders in primitive cultures always perform sadistic and humiliating acts on young men under cover of initiatory ritual. A young architect controlled by the demons secretly rejoices when a Louis Sullivan building gets knocked down; and the rock musician plays with a touch of malice the music that his grandfather could never understand.

This distrust is not good for the son's stability either. The son, having used up much of his critical, cynical energy suspecting old men, may compensate by being naïve about women—or men—his own age. A contemporary man often assumes that a woman knows more about a relationship than he does, allows a woman's moods to run the house, assumes that when she attacks him, she is doing it "for his own good." Many marriages are lost that way. He may be unsuspecting in business also: he may allow a man his own age to steal all his money, or he may accept humiliation from another man under cover of friendship or teaching. Having all the suspicion in one place—toward older men—often leads to disaster in relationships and great isolation in spirit and soul.

In the next decade we can expect these demons of suspicion to cause more and more damage to men's vision of what a man is, or what the masculine is. Between twenty and thirty percent of American boys now live in a house with no father present, and the demons there have full permission to rage.

It seems possible, too, that as more and more mothers work out of the house, and cannot show their daughters what they produce, similar emotions may develop in the daughter's psyche, with a consequent suspicion of grown women. But that remains to be seen.

TEMPERAMENT WITHOUT TEACHING

When a father, absent during the day, returns home at six, his children receive only his temperament, and not his teaching. If the father is working for a corporation, what is there to teach? He is reluctant to tell his son what is really going on. The fragmentation of decision making in corporate life, the massive effort that produces the corporate willingness to destroy the environment for the sake of profit, the prudence, even cowardice, that one learns in bureaucracy—who wants to teach that?

We know of rare cases in which the father takes sons or daughters into his factory, judge's chambers, used-car lot, or insurance building, and those efforts at teaching do reap some of the rewards of teaching in craft cultures. But in most families today, the sons and daughters receive, when the father returns home at six, only his disposition, or his temperament, which is usually irritable and remote.

What the father brings home today is usually a touchy mood, springing from powerlessness and despair mingled with longstanding shame and the numbness peculiar to those who hate their jobs. Fathers in earlier times could often break through their own humanly inadequate temperaments by teaching rope-making, fishing, posthole digging, grain cutting, drumming, harness making, animal care, even singing and storytelling. That teaching sweetened the effect of the temperament.

The longing for the father's blessing through teaching is still present, if a little fossilized; but the children do not receive that blessing. The son particularly receives instead the nonblesser, the threatened, jealous "Nobodaddy," as Blake calls him: "No One's Father"—the male principle that lives in the Kingdom of Jealousy.

A father's remoteness may severely damage the daughter's ability to participate good-heartedly in later relationships with men. Much of the rage that some women direct to the patriarchy stems from a vast disappointment over this lack of teaching from their own fathers.

We have said that the father as a living force in the home disappeared when those forces demanding industry sent him on various railroads out of his various villages.

No historical models prepare us for the contemporary son's psychic condition. To understand the son's psyche we have to imagine new furniture, new psychic figures, new demon possessions, new terrors, new incapacities, new flights.

Enormous changes have appeared at the last minute; few of us—fathers or sons—are prepared for such vast changes. I have mentioned so far the young men's father-hunger and the starving bodies of the sons; also the demons of suspicion who have invaded the psyches of young men; and the son's dissatisfaction when he receives only temperament and no teaching. We might look now at the disappearance of positive kings.

The Darkened Father

The patriarchy is a complicated structure. Mythologically, it is matriarchal on the inside, and a matriarchy is equally complicated, being patriarchal on the inside. The political structure has to resemble our interior structure. And we know each man has a woman inside him, and each woman has a man inside her.

The genuine patriarchy brings down the sun through the Sacred King, into every man and woman in the culture; and the genuine matriarchy brings down the moon, through the Sacred Queen, to every woman and every man in the culture. The death of the Sacred King and Queen means that we live now in a system of industrial domination, which is not patriarchy. The system we live in gives no honor to the male mode of feeling nor to the female mode of feeling. The system of industrial domination determines how things go with us in the world of resources, values, and allegiances; what animals live and what animals die; how children are treated. And in the mode of industrial domination there is neither king nor queen.

The death of the Sacred King, and the disappearance of the Group King, means that the father shortage becomes still more acute. When a father now sits down at the table, he seems weak and insignificant, and we all sense that fathers no longer fill as large a space in the room as nineteenth-century fathers did. Some welcome this, but without understanding all its implications.

These events have worked to hedge the father around with his own paltriness. D. H. Lawrence said: "Men have been depressed now for many years in their male and resplendent selves, depressed into dejection and almost abjection. Is that not evil?"

As the father seems more and more enfeebled, dejected, paltry, he also appears to be the tool of dark forces. We remember that in *Star Wars* we are given the image of "Darth Vader," a pun on dark father. He is wholeheartedly on the side of the dark forces. As political and mythological kings die, the father loses the radiance he once absorbed from the sun, or from the hierarchy of solar beings; he strikes society as being endarkened.

The demons who have set up a propaganda shop in the son's psyche convince him that his father's darkness is deeper than the son ever imagined. What can be done about that? The son finds out early that his mother cannot redeem his father; moreover, in most cases, she doesn't want to. The only one left to do it is the son.

As long as the political kings remained strong, the father picked up radiance from above; and the son tried to emulate the father, to become as bright as he is, to reach to his height. The son perceives the father as bright. Though this may not have been true in reality, we notice that literature as late as the eighteenth century is full of this sort of deference, this reverence for the father, and emulation.

In our time, when the father shows up as an object of ridicule (as he does, as we've noted, on television), or a fit field for suspicion (as he does in *Star Wars*), or a bad-tempered fool (when he comes home from the office with no teaching), or a weak puddle of indecision (as he stops inheriting kingly radiance), the son has a problem. How does he imagine his own life as a man?

Some sons fall into a secret despair. They have probably adopted, by the time they are six, their mother's view of their father, and by twenty will have adopted society's critical view of fathers, which amounts to a dismissal. What can they do but ask women for help?

That request is not all bad. But even the best-intentioned women cannot give what is needed. Some father-hungry sons embody a secret despair they do not even mention to women. Without actually investigating their own personal father and why he is as he is, they fall into a fearful hopelessness, having fully accepted the generic, diminished idea of father. "I am the son of defective male material, and I'll probably be the same as he is." Then, with this secret they give up, collapse, live with a numb place inside, feel compelled to be dark because the father is dark. They lose the vigorous participation in political battles, so characteristic of nineteenth-century men in the United States, feel their opinions do not matter, become secret underground people, and sometimes drown themselves in alcohol while living in a burrow under the earth.

Other sons respond by leaping up and flying into the air. The deeper the father sinks in their view, the longer their flights become. More and more evidence comes out in newspapers and books each day about sexual abuse perpetrated by fathers, inability of fathers to relate in a human way, the rigid promilitary stance of many fathers, the workaholism of fathers, their alcoholism, wife-beating, and abandonment. All of this news intensifies the brightness that some sons feel compelled to achieve because the father is dark.

We can sense in this situation one answer to the question "Why are there more and more naïve men in the world?" Whether the fathers are actually darker than they were in the past, they are perceived so, and a son assigns himself the task of redeeming the dark father.

We can look once more at the phenomenon we talked of earlier, the phenomenon of the ascending son, the "eternal boy," the moth mad for the light, the "*puer*," or "constant boy," as some people call him. Marie-Louise von Franz, in *Puer Aeternus*, understands his flight upward as a revolt against the earthly, conservative, possessive, clinging part of the maternal feminine.

James Hillman in his essay "The Great Mother, Her Son, Her Hero, and the Puer" sees it all differently. He relates the phenomenon to the father. It is characteristic of contemporary psychology that it has so far related everything to the mother. Both Freud and Jung were mothers' men, and our psychology comes out of them.

We have suggested that a young man in our times may sense that his father is somehow immersed in demonic darkness, the sort of darkness suggested by the words *workaholism, weakness, submission, isolation, alcoholism, addiction, abusiveness, evasion,* or *cowardice.*

Many contemporary sons, then, do not fight the father as in earlier eras, or figure out strategies to defeat him, but instead ascend above him, beyond him. We have Transcendental Psychology, the psychology of men like Thoreau determined to have a higher consciousness than their fathers. That is not wrong at all; but it is flying.

I count myself among the sons who have endured years of deprivation, disconnection from earth, thin air, the loneliness of the long-distance runner, in order to go high in the air and be seen. Such a son attempts to redeem the "endarkened father" by becoming "enlightened."

This is not entirely new; it is new only in degree. James Hillman has suggested that we can find a model for the redeeming in the Egyptian god Horus, the son of Osiris. He is a hawk and falcon god, and magnificent statues have survived, depicting him in his falcon form with his far-seeing eyes.

We all remember that Osiris went into darkness. His brother Set tricked him into lying in a coffin; the lid was nailed down, and the coffin was thrown into the Nile. There, enclosed in darkness, Osiris eventually drifted across the Mediterranean to Byblos, where he became incorporated into a second darkness inside a tree trunk. Osiris remained so endarkened for years. The soaring of Horus' falcon can be thought of as a response to the father's imprisonment.

Horus says of himself that he intends to fly farther than any of the other gods. One script says:

> Horus soars up into the sky beyond the flight of the original god's soul, and beyond the divinities of former times . . . I have gone beyond the bounds of Set. I am unique in my flight.

We can do a great deal with this image. We have mentioned that the son, flying toward the sun, will not see his own shadow, for his shadow falls behind him as he flies. He has seen his father's shadow, but his own remains hidden.

Flying of that sort does not *rescue* the father either. The ascensionist son is flying away from the father, not toward him. The son, by ascending into the light, rising higher on the corporate ladder and achieving enlightenment, to some extent redeems the father's name.

This explanation of the drive for ascension moves me, because it suggests that not all this labor gets done out of fear of the possessive mother, but that some gets done out of love of the endarkened father.

Some sons have always been ascenders, but never so many as now. A man may of course pursue spirituality too early in his life. The ascension, then, I add to our list of imbalances brought about by the diminishment and belittlement of the father.

Society without the father produces these birdlike men, so intense, so charming, so open to addiction, so sincere, as those great bays of the Hellespont produced the cranes Homer noticed that flew in millions toward the sun.

The Story: Visiting the King

The boy in our story rose when the Wild Man carried him off on his shoulders. Then he went down along with his damaged finger into the water, then rose steeply when his whole head turned gold, then descended again deeper when he experienced his Ashes Time in the kitchen.

This inbreathing and outbreathing seems a right sort of breathing, and since the boy has learned that sort of breathing, perhaps we could leave him here and end the story. Every man who has taken the way down and out has become a descended man; and so he resembles Joseph, who went down to Egypt, and Job, who fell from a great height, and Huckleberry Finn, who went down the river. But the story is not ready to end; nothing has been said yet about the second King.

A great theme in fairy stories is that there are two Kings. Trouble happens with one's own father—the first King. Then one has to leave the first castle. After some time of suffering and isolation, a second King somehow appears in the picture, finds the hero (or heroine) while hunting, adopts him or her and sets a task. Then a complicated dance begins as the adventurer tries to establish a fruitful connection with the new King.

We remember that the boy in our story, having no craft—he shows some lack of father teaching in that detail—takes a job as kitchen helper in a castle which is not his father's castle. Here he experiences soot and ashes, even though he still retains his golden hair. After some time in the kitchen, the cook gives him an order to take food to the King. The story says it this way:

> Once when it happened that no one else was at hand, the cook ordered the boy to carry the food to the royal table, but because the boy did not want his golden hair to be seen, he kept his tarboosh on. Such a thing as that had never happened in the King's presence, and he said, "When you come to the royal table you must take your cap off." The boy answered: "Ah, Lord, I cannot; I have a sore place on my head." The King called the cook up, scolded him, and demanded how he could have taken such a boy as that into his service; and told him to fire the boy and get him out of the castle.

The gold hair helps us to survive in adolescence, but it is more an intrusion than a help, and the boy says it quite accurately: "I have a sore on my head." Such hair is a taste of heaven, but we don't know what to do with it when we meet the King—whether to let it show and brag about it, or hide it and be devious.

Everyone wants to be with "the King." We know how intensely young girls wanted to be in the presence of Elvis, the King, or more recently to be near "Prince." We hear of a woman who constantly breaks into David Letterman's house, and people who steal napkins from Prince Charles's rooms, or camp outside Michael Jackson's, or are willing to do anything to be invited to a White House party. Everyone wants to be in the presence of "the King." The Dalai Lama acts out "the King" for many people now, for some replacing even the pope.

The hunger for the father transmutes into the hunger for the King. But the story says that having golden hair doesn't give leave to remain in his chambers.

Perhaps each of us has taken some sort of kitchen job, got acquainted with ashes, even endured a katabasis, but that doesn't mean we can have a long stay with the King. The guards let us in and escort us out again. That is what the story says.

So several questions arise: Why do we have so much hunger for "the King"? And why, in our twenties and thirties, are the visits so short?

Each of us remembers from adolescence the teachers on whom we had a crush for a while, the brief visits with celebrities, with concert artists, the embarrassing conversations with famous writers to whom we go for advice. If the "King" accepts us we may find ourselves in an apprenticeship that we don't have the discipline to maintain. A woman who goes to the guru's chambers may discover to her horror that he wants to make love with her. Sometimes the concern of the "King" is genuine, and we say the wrong thing . . . we want praise and validation so badly that when we get confused the wrong thing pops out—and we retreat, hopelessly embarrassed.

Of course the King or Queen may not be physical: that is to say, in this world. Twelve-year-olds have inexplicable experiences of light for which they have no name, and they ordinarily know no mythology that can help them to place the experiences in a story. A fourteen-year-old understands all of mathematics in one flash, or knows exactly what the Indian saints are talking about; he or she travels to a part of the brain never visited before, has glimpses of a religious ecstasy. Such an event amounts to an ascension to the Seventh Heaven, followed abruptly by a fall back to earth.

As Romantics we long for that oceanic feeling we felt in the womb, when we were divine and fed by ambrosia. Addiction amounts to an attempt to escape limitations and stay in the King's room. Many of us go up the stairs even before the cook asks us to, and, through alcohol, sex, or cocaine, extend the visit beyond moments allotted for it. We could say that our entire culture is now obsessed with this one scene in "Iron John," namely, visiting the King. But whoever visits before being called, or stays too long, falls back into the ashes.

Singles' bars resemble the King's room. The sexual hunter inside both men and women, mingled for the moment with the lover, makes extravagant promises of ecstatic visits, long stays in

the heavenly chamber, and erotic delights. The spirit endures losses
during these needy unions.

Such hunting, Shakespeare says, is:

Enjoyed no sooner but despised straight,
Past reason hunted, and no sooner had
Past reason hated as a swallow'd bait
On purpose laid to make the taker mad;

Mad in pursuit and in possession so;
Had, having, and in quest to have, extreme;
A bliss in proof, and proved, a very woe,
Before, a joy proposed; behind, a dream.

All this world well knows, yet none knows well
To shun the heaven that leads men to this hell.

Singles' bars, then, are fantastic alchemical ovens where attempts to fuse crude metals go on day after day, night after night.

For whatever reason, visits to the King, when we are young,
do not last long. The alchemists would say that even though we
have done good ashes work, the soul is still contaminated with
infantile angers, unrealistic hopes, and rage at our parents, or at
ourselves. Another way to say that is that we know in the kitchen
what we have learned from the senses; we know wood and fire
and ashes, and that's it.

Our soul, when it is in the kitchen, resembles some sort of
crude or mixed rock. Spirit, being clarified and single, cannot make
a clear impression on this crude stuff until later.

The King, by contrast, who lives in his room high in the
castle among air and sunlight, suggests solar power and the holy
intellect. The King has arrived at unity; he is undistorted, unmin-
gled, as compared to the boy of ashes, or the sooty girl, and he
looks on matters differently. We should not be surprised if the
boy's visit in our story is short.

Edward Edinger, summarizing the conclusion of alchemists
on this point, says, "The lesser [wedding] is a union or fusion of

substances that are not yet thoroughly separated or discriminated. It is always followed by a death. . . . "

The alchemists talk of a longer wedding or a "great wedding" that happens later; and we will see it happen at the very end of our story also.

The Iron John story amounts to a dance, in which the young man gradually, and with many hesitations, succeeds in coming closer to the second King.

We know that in our life the story can end right there in the kitchen, all at once. If asked to bring the soup to the King, some say, "There's no one up there," or "Let him get his own soup." If a person confuses levels, he or she may say, "I serve myself soup, and I never serve anyone else, certainly not a King."

Those who ignore "the cook" may become stuck in the kitchen stage for years, happily or unhappily identified with the victim child, who knows only ashes. Some children feel a fear of crossing the threshold; it seems safer to remain stuck in ashes. Tough-talking writers such as William Burroughs or John Hawkes speak from their stuck places and insist that ashes are all there is.

If the visit to the King's room is so important—and so emotionally charged—we should look in more detail at what the ancient world meant by the word "King."

The King in His Three Realms

"King" and "Queen" have a long and honorable history in the invisible realm of myth and fairy stories, where the words do not imply human beings—let alone persons of gender—as well as a long history in the visible realm of monarchy where they do.

We'll distinguish among three kings: the upper Sacred King, the middle political king, and the third, or inner King.

THE SACRED KING

There is a King in the imaginative or invisible world. We don't know how he got there. Perhaps human beings, after having loved the political king for centuries, lifted him up into the invisible world, or perhaps it went the other way round. At any rate, there is a King in sacred space. From his mythological world he acts as a magnet and rearranges human molecules. He enters the human psyche like a whirlwind, or a tornado, and houses fly up in the air. Whenever the word *king* or *queen* is spoken, something in the body trembles a little.

"The King" and "the Queen" send energy down. They resemble the sun and the moon that pierce down through the earth's atmosphere. Even on cloudy days something of their radiant energy comes through.

These magnets or whirlwinds do things, are verbs: they affect our feelings and actions the way a magnet arranges tiny flakes of iron. The flakes move into a pattern. So a human being finds his or her feelings arranged in a pattern when in a room with a King. John Weir Perry calls the Sacred King "The Lord of the Four Quarters," and his book of that name lays out the mythology and rituals around this particular magnet.

The Lord of the Four Quarters sits with his Queen, who is Queen of the Four Quarters. Neither King nor Queen undermines the other's power. Both live in a mythological, eternal, and luminous realm, which we can call the "mythological layer," or the eternal realm.

That layer has often been felt as an overarching inner heaven. It is not empty, for the "magnets" or the "whirlwinds" or the "gods" live there. Dionysus is still alive there, Freya, Odin, and Thor, the Virgin Mary, Kali, Buddha, Zeus, and Allah, Athena and Artemis and Sophia. To think mythologically means to have the ability to imagine these "gods" and what they do, boisterously, vigorously, and well, while keeping the human layer and their layer well distinguished from each other.

I would estimate that people in the West lost their ability to think mythologically around the year 1000, and then the layer collapsed. Perhaps because Christianity would not allow any new stories, or new gods, or perhaps because after the Renaissance the exciting pursuit of science absorbed more and more imaginative energy, the layer was never reconstituted. European men and women gradually stopped feeding the abundant gods and goddesses with their imaginative energy. The inner heaven collapsed, and we see all around our feet its broken glass. The gods are lying all around our feet.

John Weir Perry says that the Sacred or Solar King is the principle of order and space. When the King is present, there is a sacred space free of chaos. The King does not create order; more simply, where he is, there is order. The Sacred King blesses; that is a second quality. Robert Moore, who has spoken wonderfully about the King, emphasizes a third quality: he encourages creativity as his realm.

The Queen's power is also great. Sometimes she is in the lead, sometimes he is. Because he and the Queen are in right space together, the fig tree blossoms, the apple trees bear fruit abundantly, ditches run milk and honey. The Celtic fairy tales, some of which begin with images of that sort, are not describing the state of things on earth, but the state of things in "Heaven," or the mythological layer.

The King in our story, high in his chamber, represents this Sacred and Eternal King. He lacks a Queen in our story; and we don't know if the storyteller lost the Queen, or if something is being said through the Queen's absence. He does have a daughter, though, and she, with her great power, will become the Queen later in the tale.

By his presence in the story, the king indicates that the landscape around Iron John is an ordered space. It is a *cosmos,* rather than a *chaos*.

THE EARTHLY KING

Kings as leaders of huge cities and empires, holding broad powers, are first noticed during the second millennium B.C., in the city-states of Mesopotamia. No one is sure if the Sun King in China preceded or followed the Mesopotamian king. The political king merges heavenly sun power and earthly authority. The Chinese elaborated this double kingship in fantastic details that still amount to models of mythological imagination. The Sun King and his Moon Queen, in any case, held societies together for about four thousand years. As principles of order, they began to fail in the eighteenth and nineteenth centuries in Europe. Under the title of Kaiser, Tsar, Emperor, Maharajah, Sultan, Bey—one after another, the kings fell, all through Europe and then throughout its colonies.

During the Middle Ages, kings would take tours of their earthly realms. Hundreds of people waited in English village lanes, for example, to see the king go by. They probably felt a blessing coming from the Sacred King as the physical one passed silently by.

The problem is that when the political king disappears from the lanes, even for good reason, we find it difficult to "see" or feel the eternal King. I am not saying that the king-killing was an error, nor that we should resurrect the king and send him out along the lanes again, but we need to notice that our visual imagination becomes confused when we can no longer see the physical king. Wiping out kings severely damages the mythological imagination. Each person has to repair that imagination on his or her own.

Our nation's rejection of the flesh-and-blood King George (1776) preceded the beheading of Louis XVI by a few years, and we celebrate that moment with Fourth of July fireworks. We repeat that rejection of the political king with less and less joy each July, perhaps because the brilliant and ascending explosion of victory, followed by the descending failure, casts its shadow down on our own fathers.

The surviving flesh-and-blood kings now live out their lives in the *National Enquirer,* along with Duke Ellington, Count Basie, and Prince.

Part of the popular confusion around fairy stories is that contemporary readers assume that "the King" in a fairy story is a political king. "I don't believe in that stuff," we say. "He looks like a bad king to me. Why doesn't he live in the kitchen?"

The political king is a part of a three-tiered world, and he derives his energy and authority from his ability to be transparent or receptive to the King above him. Few actual kings are that good, but the three-tiered world depends on his trying.

When the political kings lose respect, cannot do their work, lose their connection to the Sacred King, become dilettantes or gods, are killed, vanish from our sight, then things change. The imagination has more to do. It doesn't do it. Our fathers then become lessened in our mind's eye.

If the political kings now live in the *National Enquirer,* then our fathers are there, too. If the Sacred King lies like pieces of broken glass all around our feet, then our father is also a broken cup. Women know that about the Queen. If all queens live in the *National Enquirer,* then all women are there, trapped in a gossip sheet. If Sophia and Kali have fallen because of the collapse of the heavenly layers, and lie in the mud of the street, then all women lie in the mud of the street.

Women have taken on the task of lifting Sophia and Kali up again; it is not a job that we, as men, can do. Our job is to lift up Dionysus, Hermes, and the Zeus energy, even though we no longer see kings riding around in horse-drawn carriages. We need to see the Sacred King not "with but through the eyes" (as Blake put it), and to see our radiant inner King uncontaminated by the images of fallen Herods, or dead Stalins. As it is, our feet stumble each morning as we leave the house over bits of the Sun King lying on the sidewalk.

THE INNER KING

We have then inside us a third King, whom we can honor or not, and we'll call him the inner King.

The inner King is the one in us who knows what we want to do for the rest of our lives, or the rest of the month, or the rest of the day. He can make clear what we want without being contaminated in his choice by the opinions of others around us. The inner King is connected with our fire of purpose and passion.

When we were one or two years old, the inner King, we would guess, was alive and vigorous. We often knew then what we wanted, and we made that clear to ourselves and to others. Some families, of course, do not care what the children want.

For most of us, our King was killed early on. No King ever dies for good, but he falls over and dies. When the inner warriors are not strong enough to protect the King—and at two or three who could expect them to be?—he dies.

Another way to look at the King is to say that he stands for, depends on, gives substance to, our mood. A child has a mood—he or she wants to play, or stay in the room, or be loony. The grown-ups have bigger moods. The abusive, or depressed, or alcoholic, or workaholic, or crazy parent has an enormous mood, and it is the only mood that counts. The children and the other parent have to adapt to that big mood, serve it, cater to it, sacrifice their mood for that greater one. The King then gets sacrificed—he dies. By the time the child is twelve, he doesn't really know what his mood is anymore.

A man whose King is gone doesn't know if he has the right to decide even how to spend the day. When my King is weak, I ask my wife or children what is the right thing to do. I've had strange adventures in buying sweaters. For example, I can't decide which is better, the green sweater or the purple. My wife says, "The purple one is beautiful." The green sweater actually fades in my eyes, the color changes, becomes ugly. I can't believe that I ever found that sweater attractive.

Some people have a strong King when speaking or lecturing to an audience, a moderately strong King when exchanging views with five or six people, and a weak King when with one person.

Many men of the generation now forty-five or so projected their undeveloped inner King on Jack Kennedy, who spoke openly of Camelot, and on Martin Luther King, and on Bobby Kennedy. When forces in the United States opposed to any spiritual kingship killed the Kennedys and King in mid-career, it was a catastrophe for the men of that generation. Some men have told me in tears that they lost something then, and have never regained it; they have never gotten back on track.

Leaders, then, need to be strong enough so that the young men can let them carry their inner King for a while, and then to live long enough so that the young men can take it back, still undamaged, and let the King live inside them.

Young men coming into adulthood during the Reagan and Bush administrations have a different problem—the difficulty of finding anyone who can carry their King. Edwin Meese certainly could not do it, nor John Poindexter, nor any of the other men involved with the lies surrounding the Contras. Reagan, as actor, played the part, but could not be honest. The betrayal of the country during the savings and loan scandal by both Democratic and Republican senators makes the situation worse. If the younger men have no public man to whom they can give their King, how can they develop the King inside?

My generation gave their King to Roosevelt, Eisenhower, General Bradley, Senator Fulbright, and other men who carried it honorably. We knew nothing of the mythology around the King when we were twenty, but we did honor some men who, though they were not kings, did carry order, even blessing.

When the outward or flesh-and-blood king falls, his plunge downward entangles the frail Kings in the other two layers, increasing the speed of their descent. The fall of rotten kings accelerates the fall of the other two by sympathetic magic.

How then can the inner King be revived, when the mythology is gone, and there are no political leaders who can carry it, even for a few years?

The process of bringing the inner King back to life, when looked at inwardly, begins with attention to tiny desires—catching hints of what one really likes. William Stafford describes that as taking in our fingers the end of the golden thread. We notice the turns of thought, or language, that please us. One remembers at forty or fifty what sort of woman or man we really like. What were the delights we felt in childhood before we gave our life over to pleasing other people, or being nurses to them, or doing what they wanted done? Mythologically, catching hold of the end of the golden thread is described as picking up a single feather from the burning breast of the Firebird.

The diminishment of the father and the collapse of the outer King make the longing for the inner King intense, almost unbearable. I would say that, after the attention to tiny desires, the next step begins not with resolutions, but with a long grieving over the dead inner King, surrounded by his dead warriors.

The inner King, once recovered, requires feeding and honoring if he is to remain alive, and each man or woman has to figure out how to do that for him- or herself. Women too have a King as well as a Queen. The difference between them is a matter for another time.

Simply to be in touch with the Sacred King for twenty minutes was for Yeats worth all the years of labor that went before. Here is his poem:

> *My fiftieth year had come and gone.*
> *I sat, a solitary man,*
> *In a crowded London shop,*
> *An open book and empty cup*
> *On the marble table top.*
>
> *While on the shop and street I gazed*
> *My body for a moment blazed,*
> *And twenty minutes, more or less,*
> *It seemed, so great my happiness,*
> *That I was blessed, and could bless.*

THE DOUBLE STREAM INSIDE THE SACRED KING

The King in his upper room comes toward us with a shining face—he blesses, he encourages creativity, he establishes by presence alone an ordered universe. But there is, as Robert Moore has said so cogently and vividly, a second, darker side of the King who will curse young men, discourage creativity, establish—by his presence alone—disorder.

If these whirlwind or hurricane beings are a part of nature, then we can assure ourselves that day will be accompanied by night, and that plants will produce poisonous as well as healing substances.

The Sacred King sends his radiance down through the atmosphere, and the Poisoned King sends his radiance down as well. That means that in the political world there will be a Herod as well as an Arthur. We know that if Herod sees even a tiny bit of male creativity in his kingdom, he will move to kill all the young men to get rid of it. The Twisted King and the Whole King exist together in the eternal realm as some traditions hold the Devil to be the brother of Christ.

We can deduce then that every man on earth will experience a Destructive Brutal Warrior as well as a Constructive Warrior, and a Dark Trickster as well as a Playful Trickster. We learn from "Snow White" that young girls experience a Poisoning Queen as well as a Nourishing Queen; and we learn from Greek mythology that there is a Petrifying Athena, as well as an Enlivening Athena.

Two streams, then, flow down from the Sacred King. The Blessing King flows down directly into Churchill, and the Twisted King flows down directly into Stalin.

THE DOUBLE STREAM INSIDE THE FATHER

Michael Meade found a powerful African story which we've already retold here in part, and which begins with the father and son hunting together. The father catches a rat. After the son throws away the father's "rat" (which could be the father's occupation), the father gives the son a blow with the axe. The son, after lying unconscious for a while, wakes up and in the middle of the night slips into his father and mother's house, takes his clothing, and leaves.

After a "long walk in the dark" the boy comes to a village where everyone is asleep, except the chief, whose hut at the center of the village is brightly lit. The boy tells his story to the chief, and the chief says, "Can you keep a secret?"

"What secret?"

"I had a son, who was killed in a battle and never came home; I want you to be my son. Can you keep that secret?"

We are now looking at a mentor in this world, or a Sacred King in the other world. The boy agrees to become the chief's son, passes all sorts of tests, sits with him in his royal hut. Then one day the father appears in the village looking for his son. "I want my son back." So the father problem is still not settled.

We can say that for each of us this father question has to be dealt with. Sooner or later, we have to deal again with that side of the father who hit us with an ax.

In Kafka's *Metamorphosis* the son wakes one morning and finds he has somehow turned into a bug with a shell. We suspect the poisoned side of the Great Father is somewhere around. The insect son crawls under his own bed, and lives there, exercising occasionally by crawling around on the living room walls while the family is absent. The father returns unexpectedly one day, and, seeing the son-insect up on the wall, throws an apple that dents the shell and damages the son's soft interior body.

When the apple from the Garden of Eden hits the shell, we are out of psychological thinking and into mythological thinking. The father all at once carries something of a malignant Jehovah, and a shamer on some fantastic, enormous level.

Kafka is very good at describing how the father contains both Kings at once. In his story "The Judgment" the aged and apparently senile father changes size several times. While the son is carrying the father to his own room, having given that up to the father, the old man appears to be a small baby who plays with the son's watch chain. But once in the son's bed, the father leaps up and touches the ceiling with his fingers. He declares the son's best friend is actually his own confidant, and he condemns the son to death by drowning. His authority is so great that the son carries out the sentence immediately. As he slips over the bridge rail into the river he says, "Dear parents, I loved you all the same."

Each father inherits thousands of years of cunning and elaborate fatherhood. An apparently weak father can control the entire family from beneath with his silences. Should the father be an alcoholic, his alcoholism may be a massive operation, carried out with Napoleonic thoroughness, so that he rules his house by the most economical means. The Destructive Father does not give energy to those in his family but draws it out of them into some black hole he shelters in himself. He draws it out steadily, as the great tyrants we know of draw it from their citizens.

The King-father in the Grimm brothers' story called "The Six Swans" agrees, out of his cowardice when lost one day in the forest, to marry "the witch's daughter" as a way to get out. It was the father who let the forces of evil into that house. Our own father, through his cowardice or fears, may have arranged our disasters before we were born.

I have been in men's gatherings in which a man's attempt to deal with the ax-father comes out in shouts of rage that can go on for twenty minutes. Most men, if asked, remember very well the blow the father gave them and exactly where it fell.

One man says: "The ax hit on the left side of my head," another "on the back between my shoulders," another "straight down through the top of my head," another "right in the groin." Some men say, "He beat me when I was thirteen, and I'd kill him right now if he were in the room." We hear vivid stories of no guidance, no support, no affection, and in their place sarcasm, brutality, coldness. "You'll never be half the man I am." We hear abandonment, with a hint of murder thrown in from time to time.

The ability some men have to see the ax-side of their fathers I admire a great deal. Of course each one of them can get caught right there. James Hillman remarks: "If you are still being hurt by an event that happened to you at twelve, it is the thought that is hurting you now."

Other men—a surprising number of them—do not feel anger or blame. On the contrary, they feel a strong blood tie to their fathers, and to them the discipline was a minor thing. Some tell stories of generous, supporting fathers, who praised, loved, and protected them as best they could, and even initiated them as best they could in the absence of the old initiators. To the first group, this sounds like whitewashing of the father. It may not be.

Some men in the second group have been able to think of their fathers psychologically. If we adopt psychological thinking toward our father, we can bring out of ourselves forgiveness, complication, humor, symbolic subtlety, and compassion. The heart begins to melt. We understand how little love the father got, how little notice. We take his childhood traumas into account. Psychological thought, however, rarely *enlarges* a father. Rather than seeing what he did, good or evil, we see what he could not help but do. Psychological thinking may leave one's father the same size, perhaps smaller, simultaneously more acceptable and less original.

There is no right thing to do. There is no father who will be good all the way, either. We deduce that from the image of the two streams—one sacred, one poisoned—which flow down not only into physical kings on earth, but also down into our own fathers.

If we regard the father as insignificant, ridiculous, absurd, in the fashionably American way, we have diminished him so far that there is no longer a place for him in the story. If we insist he was an evil person, who shamed us all the time, we fall into victimhood and there is no longer a place for us in the story.

Mythology helps us to see the dark side of our own fathers vividly, unforgettably. Understanding that we and our father exist in some great story lifts us out of our private trance, and lets us feel that the suffering is not personal to us.

It is through the radiance of the Virgin Mary shining down into a woman that the Europeans see a woman's purity and sweetness. It is through the radiance of great witches, Baba Yaga, Kali, and Durga, that the Russians and the Hindus see a woman's violence, her strength, her openness to death, her longing to conquer death.

It is through the radiance of the Sacred King, the luminous Arthur, shining down into our own father, that we are able to see his bravery and his generosity; and we know that through the great Poisoned Fathers and Kings—Herod, Cronos, Stalin, the Thornbush Cock Giant—that we can see the father's devouring hunger, his fear of death, his insistence that everyone live in disorder.

THE LONGING TO LIVE WITH THE KING

Because of the tremendous hunger we each feel for the King, the Sacred or Blessing King, we want to start living with him right now. We want to leap over our father and move to his place. But it appears we cannot move there until we have dealt with the ax-father.

To the question, "Why can't we stay longer with the King?" we have to say: "Children visit the King, but adults make a place where the King can visit them."

We inquire then about the living space we have in our head for our own father. What sort of rooms have we made up for him? If we have the grudging, stingy respect for him suggested by Geoffrey Gorer and the sitcoms, the chances are the room will be in a run-down neighborhood, with sagging door, plastic curtains, a smelly refrigerator with rotten food in it. The demons of suspicion, we can be sure, have visited this place. They throw out the sofa one day without opening the windows. They put up paintings of Pinochet and Jesse Helms, and tie little black dogs to the radiator.

The son's first job then in a country like ours is to redo the room, clean it, widen it, refurnish it, honor the father's clear and helpful side. The men who love their fathers, simply and completely—and there are many of them—will find this work easy. They can put up paintings of George Washington. Some men, of course, know consciously only the positive side of their father, and don't have a clue to his dark side. I remember a young man about twenty-five who appeared at a small men's conference in Alaska. His father was a policeman who had been killed while on duty. In order to keep a positive father image for the children, his mother had lifted the father up on a pedestal; and so the father wasn't quite human. A few years later, some of his father's old policemen friends took one look at the young man and invited him over for a night of talk. Soon they began telling stories of how his father had cheated at cards, how good he was at it, and stories of his drinking, then stories of women. The old men gave that son a gift through stories.

Men with such an ideal father in their heads need to build an entire room for the father's twisted, secretive, destructive, vulgar, shadowy side, even if he was a hero to others. All of us in that situation need to add a room onto the apartment to house the Destructive King and his relatives.

By contrast, the son who always knew about his father's cruel and destructive side will find it easy to furnish one of these dark rooms. Perhaps a coffee table would be good, with Kafka's *Letter to My Father* bound in leather, some poison darts on the wall, walls papered with Jim Beam labels, and a bed whose headboard is elegantly carved with scenes from the life of Cronos, the son-eater.

In order to widen the Twisted Father's room, we need, like Kafka and Blake, to increase our capacity for horror, life-hatred, tyranny, jealousy, murderousness. Blake invented a god named Urizen who curses, condemns, and blasts "the fairest joys"; his tablets look like tombstones, and with his hands he writes out things you shall not do. Blake's fantasy amounts to an extra room added on to his father's apartment.

But that very same son needs to build a second room to house the generous and blessed side of his father. Again friends of the father may be helpful, because sometimes the father will hide his humor and generosity even from his wife and children. Many men have told me of help of that sort. "I found out that my father was a great dancer in his youth." "My father saved a man from prison, and never said a word about it to anyone." I appreciated it when old men said to me, "Your father was the only one who read books during the Depression." Some of us have to build this room against odds, recognizing that we have selective memory, that something in the culture wants us to be unfair to our father's masculine side, find self-serving reasons for his generous words, assume he is a monster, as some people say all men are. For some men, building the room means finding their father's grave and lying on it for a long time, howling.

If we haven't yet made two rooms, and furnished them, we can't expect our father, living or dead, to move in. Those men who have made both rooms inside their souls could begin to think of inviting a mentor in. He will also need two rooms.

I'm sure readers can continue for themselves the image I am proposing here. The King is a "man of the world," and he will never come to live in these cheap one-room apartments we have available. After the mentor has come, we might think of inviting the King to the refurbished rooms where the mentor has lived.

And God, whether male or female, also has, it is said, two

sides, and God will surely never come to live with a person who hasn't made space in the soul for the King, for the mentor, and for his own father's blessed and poisoned sides.

The Male As a Set-Apart Being

We know that each child begins in the womb as a female, and the fetus chosen to be male goes through hundreds of changes before he is born. John Layard reports that one old tradition holds that a stone, while still attached to the mountainside or the bedrock, is female. It becomes a male stone when it is moved away from its quarry place and set up by itself. The Easter Island stones, then, are male, and the Stonehenge rocks also.

We conclude, then, that every father is set apart. He stands alone, not only apart from his wife, but from his children. Sitting on the western cliff of the main Aran island, I wrote of my father:

> *Aren't you farther out*
> *from the mainland*
> *even than these granite cliffs?*
> *Perhaps I want you*
> *to be still farther from land*
> *than these Aran Islands,*
> *to be at the edge*
> *of all human feeling.*

Most of us want our father to be close, and at the same time, we want him to be "at the edge of all human feeling," where he already is.

Mythology is full of stories of the bad father, the son-swallower, the remote adventurer, the possessive and jealous giant. Good fathering of the kind each of us wants is rare in fairy tales or in mythology. There are no good fathers in the major stories of Greek mythology—a shocking fact; and very few in the Old Testament. Uranus, Cronos, and Zeus exhibit three styles of horrendous fatherhood. Abraham, a famous Old Testament father, was perfectly willing to sacrifice Isaac; and his grandson Jacob was good to Joseph, but apparently not to his other eleven sons, and he certainly didn't protect Joseph from his brothers' rage.

It is interesting that we find very few examples of close or chummy father-son relationships in mythological literature. King Arthur radiates generosity, but as uncle, as initiator and guide of young men, not as a father.

It is possible that we will never have the closeness we want from our fathers. "Male," John Layard says, "symbolizes that which is 'set apart.'"

I say this to speak to many young men who want from the father a repetition of the mother's affection, or a female nurturing they haven't gotten enough of. Whatever the father gives us, it will not be the same kind of closeness that our mother offered. And some men have to be satisfied with a relationship to their father that is not close. In many traditional cultures the men older than the father give and teach nurturing. The old man's power to nurture began with the foundation given by female nurturing, the mother's warmth, love, singing. Later the boy transfers to the earth as teacher; this is the time of the hunt, the cold, the wind, the weather. When the foundation of mother nurturing and earth companionship is in place, then the old men can move in and bring male nurturing and its vision.

Men seem set apart at birth; but we know a woman experiences set-apartness also, particularly when as an adult she begins to develop her masculine side.

The father's birth gift, then, is one thing, and the old men's gift another. The father gives with his sperm a black overcoat around the soul, invisible in our black nights. He gave, and gives, a sheathing, or envelope, or coating around the soul made of intensity, shrewdness, desire to penetrate, liveliness, impulse, daring. The father's birth gift cannot be quantified. His gift contributes to the love of knowledge, love of action, and ways to honor the world of things. It seems particularly important these days to name some of the father's gifts.

As we close this chapter on the King and the father, we recognize that we have hit something hard here. The sons and daughters in the United States still feel "too little father," and that is probably not going to get better. Fathers themselves have not changed so much; it is, rather, that they seem to us smaller, because we do not see behind them or through them the Blessed or Destructive King. The fathers seem opaque; the Sacred King seems farther away, and our eyesight is not too good.

When the mythological layer collapses, and the political kings fall, then the patriarchy, as a positive force, is over. The sun and moon energies can no longer get down to earth. Ancient Celtic mythology has an image for the end of the patriarchy, and it is this:

Eagles sit on the top branches of the sacred tree, with dead animals underneath their claws. Rotting bits of flesh fall down through the branches to the ground beneath, where the swine eat them.

We are the swine. When all the meat that comes down from above is rotten, then neither the sons nor daughters receive the true meat. Women have been and still are right in their complaints about the food they find on the earth, but men are not well fed either. Naturally everyone is dissatisfied, for neither men nor women are receiving the true meat.

That doesn't imply that we need to build up the patriarchy again, but that we need to understand that we are starving. The more difficult it is to visit the King, the more hungry everyone is. The perceived absence of the father is actually the absence of the King. Addiction does not have to do with Colombian drug lords, but with the absence of the King.

Men and women have been separated from the King before; this separation has happened many times in past centuries. It is interesting to go back to the story, then, and see what happens next.

CHAPTER FIVE

The Meeting with the God-Woman in the Garden

The Maternal Feminine and the Private Feminine

We have come a long way already in this story. The boy, after he left with the Wild Man, has been introduced well to soul. If you give a hair to the soul it will cover the hair with gold. If you make a road toward it, it will respond and cut down brush to make a road toward you. After this, the boy manages to get to the castle, drops into ashes, and, finally, visits briefly the King's chambers.

What is left? We can't stop the story here, because the feminine has not yet appeared. His mother, as the maternal form of the feminine, he has of course experienced, but that is all. And now he is about to meet the feminine in a nonmaternal form, in its powerful, blossoming, savvy, wild, instigating, erotic, playful form. She is the savvy woman on the earth plane. On the mythological plane she is "The Woman Who Loves Gold," as some fairy stories call her, or "The Woman with Golden Hair." The Russians call her "The Female Tsar," and the Celts sometimes call her "The Track of the Moon on the Water."

The Celts do a great deal of work in distinguishing two forms of the feminine energy, or "yin" energy, an earthly form and a starry, moonlike, or sunlike form. Some of their thought can be found in the extremely old story, preserved in *The Mabinogion*, of "Culhwch and Olwen."

The story says that Culhwch's mother went mad during pregnancy, and then in terror of the pigs gave birth to him in the pens where the sows were kept. One form of "yin" energy is the sow-mother, and we might recall that Demeter is also associated with pigs. The second form of the feminine, the more erotic and spiritual, the Celts associate with water and with the moon.

"Olwen" means "Path the Moon Takes on the Water." When one stands on shore looking at the shifting road, one cannot tell if one is looking at water or moon. The image catches the elusive, reflective, private, shape-changing, buoyant, silvery mood of the savvy feminine. The moon is attracted to the sun, and draws light from the sun, so to call her "The Silver Woman" or "The Woman Who Loves Gold" is not contradictory.

The Story: Meeting the King's Daughter

In ordinary, daily life, a man meets the maternal feminine at birth—before birth, in fact—and it is a solid meeting or not depending on the mother and her ability to bond. A man has many meetings with the feminine in grade school and teenage years. We meet the erotic feminine many times before we have actually taken the Ashes Road. Our story simply ignores these early meetings, for they, though sweet, are not "it."

The relatively unconscious man at twenty-four may have an affair with a relatively unconscious woman who is twenty-four and nothing happens. Even if she is a moon woman, nothing much happens if he and she have done no work. Usually both have less consciousness after the affair than they had before. John Cheever describes all this in his story, "The Chaste Clarissa."

Our story is going to talk of a meeting with the feminine woman that happens after the ashes, and the narrative implies that a fruitful meeting of that sort takes place only after the man has left the cellar and gone into "the garden."

Let's see how the story says it.

The King called the cook up, scolded him, and demanded how he could have taken such a boy as that into his service; and told him to fire the boy and get him out of the castle. The cook, however, had pity on the youngster and exchanged him for the gardener's boy.

Now the boy had to set out plants in the garden, and water them, chop with hoe and spade, and let wind and bad weather do what they wished.

Once in summer, when he was working in the garden by himself, it got so hot that he pulled his head covering off, so that the breeze would cool his head. When the sun touched his head, his hair glowed and blazed out so brightly that beams of sunlight went all the way into the bedroom of the King's daughter, and she leapt up to see what that could be. She spied the boy outside, and called to him, "Boy, bring me a batch of flowers!"

He quickly put his tarboosh back on, picked some wild flowers for her, and tied them in a bunch. As he started up the stairs with them, the gardener met him, and said, "What are you doing bringing the King's daughter such ordinary flowers? Get moving and pick another bouquet, the best we have and the most beautiful."

"No, no," the boy answered, "the wild flowers have stronger fragrance and they will please her more."

When the boy walked into her room, the King's daughter said, "Take your headthing off; it isn't proper for you to wear it in my presence."

He replied, "I don't dare do that. I have the mange, you know."

She however grabbed the tarboosh and yanked it off; his golden hair tumbled down around his shoulders, and it was magnificent to look at. He started out the door at a run, but she held him by the arm and gave him a handful of gold coins. He took them and left, but put no stock in them; in fact he brought the coins to the gardener and said, "I'm giving these to your children—they can use them to play with."

The next day the King's daughter again called the boy

to her and told him to bring her some more wild flowers. When he walked in with them, she reached for his little hat and would have torn it away, but he held on to it with both hands. Once more she gave him a handful of gold coins, but he refused to keep them and gave them to the gardener as playthings for his children.

The third day things went the same way: she couldn't manage to get his hat off, and he wouldn't accept the gold coins.

One day, perhaps in August, he takes off his turban or tarboosh. He reveals to the sky inadvertently and only for a moment the gold head of hair. The princess does not see the head itself. In a gorgeous display of the storyteller's wit, worthy of Shakespeare, sunlight bounces off the gold head, then up to the wall of the second-floor chamber.

The Swedes call these spots of light moving on a wall a "suncat." How beautiful it is for the sun to be allowed to take part in her first glimpse of the young man, for whom this meeting will be fateful. The Princess meets the man with gold hair, but the gold head also meets the sun. The golden hair has been inactive up to now, something to be kept hidden. Now it *does* something. The young man senses that he is being seen and replaces the cap, but it is too late. This moment was the *kairos,* as the Greeks called it, exactly the right moment for what was lying hidden in one's fate to be revealed.

We know we are in the presence of something elaborate here when the storyteller has the sunlight hit the gold hair, then bounce to the wall of the Princess's chamber, and from there sink into her eyes. Through the geometrical diagram the storyteller adopts a magnificent indirection, a way of introduction involving solar light. I can't praise this detail enough. It's clear that we are once again somewhere in the area of sacred intellect, only this time associated with woman.

Federico García Lorca says:

Woman who can kill two roosters in one second,
Woman who isn't afraid of light . . .

The mood of it all is the playfulness of light. If some alchemical themes showed up in the last section of the story when the boy carried his crude metals up the stairs for the "brief wedding," then we feel alchemical wittiness continue here.

We know from hundreds of texts that it is Mercury or Hermes who watches over the processes of alchemy. This garden scene, with the light shooting about like a ball of mercury that one tries in vain to grasp, is truly mercurial in its invention: witty, astonishing, playful, serious, delighting in leaps. Many a man can remember meeting a woman who turned out to be fateful for his life in some such playful way—a telephone number falls out of a wallet, or he goes to the wrong restaurant, or he and she stumble over the curb at the same moment, or they both choose the same book at the library, noticing it at the checkout desk, or the dogs' leashes get entangled, or they get assigned the same task at some benefit and fight over who should do it. All these experiences of coincidence, simultaneity, serendipity, synchronicity, light, suggest that something is about to happen that belongs to, or is part of, the "other world." We conclude then that this "woman" has some connection with the other world.

Let's set down the four things we know about this mysterious woman so far. First, she starts things; she requests flowers from the boy.

Second, she is the "King's daughter," so she is clearly related to Solar Fire, the Sacred King, or whatever words one wants to use to describe this being high in his sunlit chamber.

Third, she likes gold. She likes the boy's golden head a great deal. We notice that she offers gold coins in return for wild flowers.

Finally, she knows something. The King wasn't sure what was beneath the cap, but she knows.

Entering the Garden

All this began when the cook assigned the boy to garden work. The word *garden* in the mythological tradition suggests a walled garden. "Garden" suggests a place marked out, separated from farmyard, grain field, forest, or desert, in order that human beings can cultivate there precious plants or flowers. The gardener brings inside the walls rare roses, unusual grains, shoots from Persian pears, new varieties of apple trees, climbing vines. Natural plants develop by intent when inside the walled garden.

We know that the European walled garden of the Middle Ages drew many inspired traits from gardens that flourished in Persia, Arabia, and other Near Eastern countries. Among such traits were the geometrical design of the beds, the curiously shaped fountains at the center, and the strange association with alchemy. Alchemical texts of the Middle Ages show how the garden and the fountain looked. A stone fountain, for example, three or four feet high, built over a well, had sills or tunnels that carried water out to the four directions. The alchemists call such a fountain the *fons mercurialis,* that is, Mercury's Well, or the Well of Hermes.

The Greek god Hermes has a very ancient connection with walled gardens, in fact with all that is enclosed with or by intent. I find it charming that a can of peaches, for example, is said to this day to be "hermetically sealed." Hermes guides the forming of containers, the establishment of boundaried places, particularly those areas set aside for inward work. A nun's cloister, a meditation room, a deep well, a niche for a god, a relationship in which we intend to cultivate a holy tree, a closed tomb, the lover's room, the philosopher's study, the alchemist's vessel are all hermetic containers.

Universities were once walled gardens; and I have known people of fifty who today leave their business and enroll in medieval studies at the university. Some actually move into rooms at the college. For them such study is a walled garden.

Throughout Latin literature and later Italian, French, and Spanish literature, the image of the *hortus conclusus,* or walled garden, provided the theme and the setting for many poems. A good poem itself is a hortus conclusus—private, enigmatic, mysterious.

Critics in the twentieth century refer to Eugenio Montale's poetry and Stéphane Mallarmé's and Paul Celan's as hermetic. Gerard Manley Hopkins, in a poem I dearly love, describes the human desire for a walled garden, and as he goes on he makes the sounds of the poem into a walled garden. It is called "Heaven-Haven" and the subtitle says, "A Nun Takes the Veil."

> *I have desired to go*
> *Where springs not fail,*
> *To fields where flies no sharp and sided hail*
> *And a few lilies blow.*
>
> *And I have asked to be*
> *Where no storms come,*
> *Where the green swell is in the havens dumb,*
> *And out of the swing of the sea.*

Entering the garden we escape from the rain of blows offered by "the world" and find a temporary shelter. The Renaissance gardens in northern Europe retained the mood of the ordered courtyard of the classical Roman house.

"Where springs not fail" is a quality of the garden. If a man or woman has been sexually abused in childhood, or has lived in any form of a "dysfunctional family," he or she will need sooner or later a "heaven-haven." The story says that each of us needs it.

The walled garden is a shelter from the world, and a place to recover from broken trust. In "Allerleirauh" (Rough Animal Skins), the Grimm brothers' story, the garden takes the form of a hollow tree; in the tree the heroine, Allerleirauh, her body covered with a coat of rough furs, lives for a time.

The walled garden also is a place to develop introversion. Rilke says:

> *I am too alone in the world, and not alone enough*
> *to make every moment holy.*
> *I am too tiny in this world, and not tiny enough*
> *just to lie before you like a thing,*
> *shrewd and secretive.*
> *I want my own will, and I want simply to be with*
> *my will,*
> *as it goes toward action,*
> *and in the silent, sometimes hardly moving times*
> *when something is coming near,*

I want to be with those who know secret things
or else alone.

Translated by R.B.

We could say that the Greek goddess Demeter owns the surface of the earth, the wheat fields, barley fields, olive groves, vegetable plots, pastures. We remember that her daughter, Persephone, is playing one day on one of these flowery fields when Pluto, or Hades, takes her downward and inward. She goes to live with Pluto, whose name means "wealth," and so all of us go, when we go into the walled garden, to encounter the wealth of the psyche, which is especially rich in grief.

For men an unnamed god of duty holds down the surface of the earth; and all stock markets, all football fields, all corporation parking lots, all suburban tracts, all offices, all firing ranges, belong to him. There a man makes a stand, makes a farm, makes an impression, makes an empire, but sooner or later, if he is lucky, the time comes to go inward, and live in "the garden." The Wild Man here is like Persephone. It is in the garden that a man finds the wealth of the psyche.

We could say that in the walled garden, as in the alchemical vessel, new metals get formed as the old ones melt. The lead of depression melts and becomes grief. The drive for success, an insistent tin, joins with Aphrodite's copper, and makes bronze, which is good to make both shields and images of the gods. The enclosed garden then suggests cultivation as opposed to rawness, boundaries as opposed to unbounded sociability, soul concerns as opposed to outer obsessions, passion as opposed to raw sexuality, growth of soul desire as opposed to obsession with a generalized greed for things.

This little poem of Lorca's gives a hint of that mysterious growth of soul desire that the garden encourages:

The rose
was not searching for the sunrise:
almost eternal on its branch,
it was searching for something else.

> *The rose*
> *was not searching for darkness or science:*
> *borderline of flesh and dream,*
> *it was searching for something else.*
>
> *The rose*
> *was not searching for the rose.*
> *Motionless in the sky*
> *it was searching for something else.*
>> *Translated by R.B.*

This new work in the garden means a coming out of basement space into wind and weather. Seeds sprout, seasons change, leaves fall, bulbs send up new stalks in the garden. Theodore Roethke says:

> *I study the lives on a leaf: the little*
> *Sleepers, numb nudgers in cold dimensions,*
> *Beetles in caves, newts, stone-deaf fishes,*
> *Lice tethered to long limp subterranean weeds,*
> *Squirmers in bogs,*
> *And bacterial creepers*
> *Wriggling through wounds*
> *Like elvers in ponds,*
> *Their wan mouths kissing the warm sutures,*
> *Cleaning and caressing,*
> *Creeping and healing.*

Manure alters itself into leaves, roses, and apples; our disasters we understand to be not our own fault, and it may not be proper to blame ourselves for all of them, or any of them. While in the garden we are still doing work "in the darkness," but the darkness resembles black earth now. The Persian poet Rumi in one passage mentions joyfully how poems and images rise in him almost effortlessly. Then he says:

> *But the real work is being done outside*
> *By someone digging in the ground.*
>> *Translated by Coleman Barks*

In the garden the soul and nature marry. When we love cultivation more than excitement we are ready to start a garden. In the garden we cultivate yearning and longing—those strangely un-American feelings—and notice tiny desires. Paying attention to tiny, hardly noticeable feelings is the garden way. That's the way lovers behave.

The enclosed garden is a right place for lovers. Trysting lovers in medieval literature—Tristram and Isolde, for example—have their dangerous meetings there. In the garden one might meet a young girl, a wise old man, or the King walking "in the cool of the day." It is astonishing how often the image of gardens appears in love poetry; particularly among the Arabs. Al-Muntafil said:

> There is a mole on Ahmad's cheek that draws all
>   those who are not now in love;
> it is a rose-garden, whose gardener is an
>   Abyssinian.
>> Version by R.B.

The poem beautifully calls up the "dark man" who somehow belongs in the garden. The most important events in the lives of the great lovers take place in the Garden Not Open to Everyone, and by extension we can say that the most significant events in our soul lives take place in this same garden.

The enclosed garden encourages true desire for the infinite more than the greed for objects; and we know that all true desire is dangerous. Ibn Hazm says:

> The meeting that has to be secret reaches
> an intensity that the open meeting cannot reach.
> It is a delight that is mixed with danger,
> like walking on a road over shifting sand-hills.
>> Version by R.B.

When two people are contained inside the intimacies of a love affair, especially one that has to be secret, they may feel solids in them turning to liquids, and liquids changing to air. The heat of Eros is a delight mixed with danger.

Initiation, then, asks every young man at a certain point to become a lover: that is, to develop the lover in him from seed to flower. We know from Shakespeare's *Romeo and Juliet,* and other Renaissance accounts, that it was not at all unusual for a young man at that time to take two or three years off, and spend it learning to be a lover. We spend those years in graduate school instead. He would learn how to play a musical instrument because the resonance of the strings affect the heart; he would learn poems "by heart," practice setting them to his own music, and then sing them to introverted women sitting behind iron window bars. It was garden work, with longing in it.

Robert Moore offers the phrase "appreciative consciousness" as a way of describing the lover's nature. If one appreciates the harmonies of the strings, sunlight on a leaf, the grace of the wind, the folds of a curtain, then one can enter the garden of love at unexpected moments. Moreover, after a man or woman has fallen in love, the leaf looks better, turns of phrase have more grace, shoulders are more beautiful. I noticed that we even love small towns:

> *When we are in love,*
> *We love the grass, and the barns, and the*
> *   lightpoles,*
> *And the small main streets abandoned all night.*
> *   —R.B.*

Lovers are full of praise:

> *It was among ferns I learned about eternity.*
> *Below your belly there is a curly place.*
> *Through you I learned to love the ferns on that*
> *   bank,*
> *And the curve that the deer's hoof leaves in sand.*
> *   —R.B.*

Moreover, when a man falls in love with a woman, or with a man, he is in the garden. Rumi says:

Come to the Garden in spring.
There is wine, and sweethearts in the pomegranate
   blossoms.
If you do not come, these do not matter.
If you do come, these do not matter.

   Translated by Coleman Barks

Garden work may begin unexpectedly. An illness that confines the sufferer to a room for weeks may be his enclosed garden. An accident may bring it on. Thoreau, on the other hand, chose to live for some months in a cabin he built himself, and he and his cabin and Walden Pond were his garden. He knew very well that he had become a lover, and said, "A match has been found for me at last; I have fallen in love with a shrub oak."

Some men entering the garden begin by getting up at 5 A.M. and keeping an hour for themselves each morning before work. A father, in order to do that, may have to resist his own insistence that his life belongs to his work, his children, and his marriage.

Making a garden, and living in it, means attention to boundaries, and sometimes we need the boundaries to prevent caretaking from coming in and occupying all our time.

I am too tiny in this world, and not tiny enough
Just to lie before you like a thing . . .

Addiction to perfection, as Marian Woodman reminds us, amounts to having no garden. The anxiety to be perfect withers the vegetation. Shame keeps us from cultivating a garden. Men and women deeply caught in shame will, when they tend their garden, pull out both weeds and flowers because so many of their own feelings seem defective or soiled.

What do we love so much that we want to protect it from strangers? That is a good question for garden makers.

No matter how deeply I go down into myself
my God is dark, and like a webbing made
of a hundred roots, that drink in silence.

   —Rainer Maria Rilke
   Translated by R.B.

The Woman with Golden Hair and Delicious Confusion

The young woman in our story has managed to bring into her own room this boy with the gold hair under his cap. What would it be like for an ordinary boy to meet the Woman Who Loves Gold?

I remember a man telling me of a summer he spent at fifteen working as a busboy in a Catskills resort. He and the other boys were doing all right until one day a tall, blond, beautiful, self-contained, high-cheekboned sixteen-year-old girl walked into the dining room. It was all over in a moment. The fifteen-year-old boy sank under the waves, bubbles came up, he was lost.

It is interesting that neither he nor his equally moved friends ever talked to her. Instead they spent hours after work discussing who spoke to her today, what she wore at breakfast, whom she walked up with, who sat at her table. Her face and its beauty, which seemed inaccessible, or invulnerable, made them all feel like hicks, inarticulate clods of earth, hopelessly matter-ridden louts. She was above matter.

For three weeks the obsession went on; they woke up every morning feverish. Then the summer ended; she left, that was it. There was only one event in the summer, that one.

The sixteen-year-old girl was not the Woman with Golden Hair, but the boys didn't know that. They saw what they saw: they saw the Track of the Moon on the Water and were deliciously confused.

The girl, on her side, is equally confused. She may in reality be lacking in self-esteem, be insecure, shamed, even victimized, but on the outside, in the radiance from her face, she is queenly, self-possessed, golden, and invulnerable. The Gold Woman in the other world sends her radiance down through the atmosphere, and the radiance appears on the girl's face. Her beauty is a good enough hook for the boys' otherworldly longing; perhaps she even fits some template in their genetic memory. They take one look and summer is complete.

If the boys had been eighteen, one of them might have spoken to her, and courted her. He might even have made love to her; and in the course of all that he would have realized that she wasn't "she." What a disappointment! "How could I have been so wrong?" he says to himself. When she asks him why he has lost interest, he may even tell her of his disappointment.

We are looking at the source of a lot of desperation in certain men here, and a lot of suffering in certain women. A man may repeat the courting and disappointment over and over. One man about thirty-five told me that confusion about the layers had ruined his life. His life had gone like this: he sees a woman across the room, knows immediately that it is "She." He drops the relationship he has, pursues her, feels wild excitement, passion, beating heart, obsession. After a few months, everything collapses; she becomes an ordinary woman. He is confused and puzzled. Then he sees once more a radiant face across the room, and the old certainty comes again. Her face seems to give out a whisper: "All those who love the Woman with Golden Hair come to me." She doesn't seem to realize she is sending out that whisper. Of course the whisper gives her great power because men offer to rearrange their lives for her. But it isn't real power, and when men leave her, she feels insignificant and small, abandoned, powerless. A generation ago millions of American men gave their longing for the Gold-haired Woman to Marilyn Monroe. She offered to take it and she died from it.

The glory of the Sacred King drifts down to a public figure, a leader, and to a father who can receive it. The glory of the Woman with Golden Hair drifts down from its eternal luminous space onto a public figure such as Marilyn Monroe or Meryl Streep and then to a sixteen-year-old girl in a Catskills resort. Underneath the invulnerable face is an ordinary human girl, highly vulnerable, being pulled up and down by these impersonal ruthless forces.

During the twelfth and thirteenth centuries all this was understood. The troubadour poets, instructed by the religious intelligence of the Muslims, wrote poems to the Golden Woman. They kept the planes clear by describing her as "the wife of the Lord of the Castle." By this device the poet also provided plausible reasons why he needed to keep the mood of secrecy, and containment. The wives of the lords were savvy women and knew that soul desire was being served here. Some women of the time became troubadour poets themselves. When a woman troubadour, such as the Countess of Dia, who was a very great poet, praises a man, she looks through him to a luminous figure standing behind him, just as the men poets do when they praise a woman.

If an ancient Greek saw a man who had Zeus energy, he would never say, "That man is Zeus." His mythology distinguished the layers. Now that mythology has collapsed, contemporary men again and again confuse a living woman with the Woman Who Has Golden Hair. A living woman with stomach, small intestine, and a disturbed childhood is not the woman of light. A person who discreetly farts in an elevator is not a divine being, and a man needs to know this.

What does it mean when a man falls in love with a radiant face across the room? It may mean that he has some soul work to do. His soul is the issue. Instead of pursuing the woman and trying to get her alone, away from her husband, he needs to go alone himself, perhaps to a mountain cabin, for three months, write poetry, canoe down a river, and dream. That would save some women a lot of trouble.

I am not saying that falling in love is an illusion each time, and that romantic love is always to be treated with suspicion and discounted. The whole matter is delicate. It is possible that Robert Johnson, often so accurate and marvelous in his writings, suspects romantic love too much. Another mistake that Jungians make is to adopt that hideous word *anima,* and to regard every good-looking woman you meet as your *anima.*

When a man says to a woman, "You are my anima," she should quickly scream and run out of the room. The word *anima* has neither the greatness of the Woman with Golden Hair nor the greatness of an ordinary woman, who wants to be loved as a woman.

When a woman whom a man has never met appears in his

dream, it may mean that the Woman with Golden Hair is approaching. This poem is called "A Dream of an Afternoon with a Woman I Did Not Know."

> *I woke up, and went out. Not yet dawn.*
> *A rooster claimed he was the sickle moon.*
> *The windmill was a ladder that ended at a gray*
> *cloud.*
> *A feed grinder was growling at a nearby farm.*
>
> *Frost has made clouds of the weeds overnight.*
> *In my dream we stopped for coffee, we sat alone*
> *near a fireplace, near delicate cups.*
> *I loved that afternoon, and the rest of my life.*
>
> —R.B.

John Fowles remarked that his novel *The French Lieutenant's Woman* sprang from a single image he saw for ten seconds in a dream. A woman appeared, her face partially concealed by a scarf, standing at the end of a dock in a storm.

Meryl Streep enacted this scene magnificently in the movie. Later scenes make clear that the Mysterious Hidden Woman, as I have called her elsewhere, loves privacy, overhanging trees, long skirts, the shadowy places underneath bridges, rooms with low lighting. One intense sexual storm in a hay barn means more to her than three years of tepid lovemaking; she wants passion and purpose in a man, and she carries a weighty desire in her, a passion somewhere between erotic feeling and religious intensity.

Dante, who knew the troubadour poets of Provence down to his toes, wrote a number of poems about the naïve girl in the Catskills resort; or, more accurately, he wrote about a woman who was herself conscious of what she carried, so she was not naïve, but savvy.

> *The woman I worship carries ecstatic love in her*
> *eyes.*
> *Whatever she looks at grows less worldly.*
> *When she goes by, each man turns to look at her*
> *And if she notices him his chest trembles.*

So that, dropping his eyes, he grows pale,
And his chest feels hollow at each of his weaknesses,
Self-absorption and self-mothering leave ahead of
*   her,*
All you women, help me to say this rightly.

When a man hears that voice, sweetness and
*   thoughts*
Of ways to serve others come in his chest;
I say then much praise to the first man who
*   glimpsed her.*

And when she smiles for even a short time, there is
*   a feeling*
Of someone present I cannot speak of, nor keep in
*   remembrance,*
This is all some sort of miracle, fresh, amazing.
*   Translated by R.B.*

The Irish beauty Maud Gonne came to visit the Yeats house one day when W. B. Yeats was eighteen. That was it for him. He wrote many poems for her, became a public speaker for her, loved her and proposed to her for thirty years, until he gave up and decided to marry an ordinary woman. Even after he had made this decision, he had a hard time keeping her out of his head. While his friends were looking around to find a wife for him, he wrote this poem:

One had a lovely face,
And two or three had charm,
But charm and face were in vain
Because the mountain grass
Cannot but keep the form
Where the mountain hare has lain.
*   —"Memory," from Collected Poems*

Mountain hares are wild; he points out Maud Gonne's connection to all wildness. We remember that the boy in our story remarks about the God-Woman: "Wild flowers would please her more."

Just as the political king and our personal fathers receive a radiance that drifts or pours down from the Sacred King, so Maud Gonne and every living woman receive that radiance pouring down from the Holy Feminine or the Gold Woman.

We know that the phrase "the feminine" is not interchangeable with the phrase "a woman." Women participate in the feminine as the water in a jar participates in the light when light passes through it. Kabir says: "Take a jar full of water, and put it down on the water—Now it has water inside and water outside." So femaleness is as abundant as ocean or sunlight, endless, beyond jars, yet is caught here and there, enveloped here and there— sometimes in women's bodies, sometimes in men's bodies. But each body contains only a taste of the ocean, a fragrance from the sea. Blake would say, "The naked woman's body is a portion of eternity too great for the eye of man."

In our story this jar of ocean water appears as the King's daughter. Why could we not complete the initiation of a young man without her? We all have ideas on that, and I'll offer one.

Every man and every woman on this planet is on the road from the Law to the Legends. Surely every person reading this book is. The Legends stand for the moist, the swampish, the wild, the untamed. The Legends are watery, when compared with the dryness of the Law. It takes twenty years to understand the Laws, and then a whole lifetime to get from there to the Legends.

The Law stands for the commandments we need in order to stay alive, the rule that says which side of the road we drive on, the law of gravity. We need to learn the axiom that we cannot take water into our lungs and keep breathing; the dictate that keeps us from murdering each other over a slight rebuke; the canon against self-slaughter; the postulates that encourage prudence, politeness, and appropriateness; the precepts that help us control our madness. Some men stay with the rules. Yeats, talking of such men who become scholars, says:

All shuffle there; all cough in ink;
All wear the carpet with their shoes;
All think what other people think;
All know the man their neighbor knows.
Lord, what would they think
Did their Catullus walk that way?

We are each on the way from the Law to the Legends, from dogma to the Midrash, from the overly obedient man to wildness. The boy in our story is clearly walking in that direction. Evidence for that is his conversation with the Wild Man about his golden ball and his later departure with him. The closer a person comes to the Legends, then the closer he or she comes to depth, moistness, spontaneity, and shagginess. Some Celtic tales describe "a bird with a human head" who tells a young hero about a shaggy horse, which then carries the young man to the shore of the ocean, and down into it, where the youth throws loaves of bread to the dragons at the right moment. So we move from Saint George toward the dragon.

How does this motion begin? The writer and analyst John Layard says that when a man is ready to make a decisive move toward "The Legends," a feminine figure whose face "looks both ways" may appear in his dreams. It is as if she has two faces: one looks toward the world of rule and laws, and the other toward the world of dragonish desire, moistness, wildness, adult manhood. This dream figure is not a flesh-and-blood woman, but a luminous eternal figure. She is the Woman with Golden Hair.

We assume that something similar happens to a woman who is ready for a decisive move. At a certain moment a male figure whose face looks both ways will appear in her dreams. But I am only guessing. Women know more about that than a man does.

In any case, "The Woman Who Looks Two Ways" has appeared in our tale now. The Russians in their fairy stories call her "The Tsar Who Is Also a Woman"; she can be called "The Woman Attracted by Gold," or whatever name you would like to make up yourself. If she could be named once and for all, then, as the Tao

Te Ching says, she would not be the real luminous being, so let's not worry about her name.

The world of the Law and the world of the Legends are two distinct parts of the universe, and perhaps after the Woman Who Sees Both Ways appears the man is able to see these two worlds with more precision because she can see them. His story moves faster.

In her ability to get the plot of life moving, the Woman with Golden Hair resembles the Hindu feminine, the Shakti, more than the Western feminine, whom custom imagines as receptive and passive. Shakti, whom we see in many Indian paintings, is erect, instigating, up-leaping, fiery, outrageous. In some paintings Shiva lies nearby on the ground, or even under her feet, apparently asleep; he is by contrast receptive, cool, laid back, deeply inside himself.

The relation of this instigating woman to Mary Magdalene bears looking at. Her impulse to cause trouble, throw the spark into dry wood, pull energy out of the stagnant psyche, stir the sea with a single hair, deserves some study and some notice.

Antonio Machado, drawing his knowledge from the old Arab and Persian culture, remarks that sooner or later the preoccupied or walking man or the intent man sits down at the side of the road.

> Close to the road we sit down one day.
> Our whole life now amounts to time, and our sole
>   concern
> the attitudes of despair that we adopt
> while we wait. But She will not fail to arrive.
>   Translated by R.B.

Hermes and the God-Woman

Saturn is the god of ashes, and he is the lethargic, depressed, cinder-biting god whom the young man worships when it is the right time in his life for ashes. Saturn is dense, condensed, heavy, driven; he becomes discipline in lucky men, and sour bitterness in unlucky men. He is the god of correct failure.

Hermes is the god of the interior nervous system. His presence amounts to heavenly wit. When we are in Hermes' field, messages pass with fantastic speed between the brain and the fingertips, between the heart and the tear ducts, between the genitals and the eyes, between the part of us that suffers and the part of us that laughs. Hermes is Mercury, and we know that mercury cannot be held in the hand—it rolls everywhere, separates into tiny drops, joins again, falls on the floor, rolls under the table, moves with amazing quickness. It is correctly called quicksilver.

This mercurial energy is called, among other things, Odin in northern Europe, Mercury in Italy, Hermes in Greece. Its day of the week is Wednesday (Odin's Day) and *mercredi* in France.

Sometimes when friends are talking in a closed room, the heat of the conversation begins to increase: witty things are said; contributions flow from all sides; leaps of imagination appear; the genuinely spiritual follows an instant after the genuinely obscene. Hermes has arrived. At some beautiful moment of the conversation a silence falls that feels mysterious; everyone hesitates to break it. In Spain until the fifteenth century that silence was called "Hermes' silence." So López-Pedraza says in his fine book on Hermes.

The old tradition maintains that true learning does not take place unless Hermes is present. That is depressing, because university English departments, and sociology departments, and religion departments usually get rid of teachers with Hermes energy first. The whole Ph.D. system was created by Germanic Hermes-killers. Hermes is magical, detail-loving, obscene, dancelike, goofy, and not on a career track.

Hermes slips in true information in that split second between the moment your tongue starts a word and the moment it finishes. You plan to say, "This is my mother," and you say, "This is my wife." I did that. My mother looked very pleased. You plan to say "farther," and it comes out "father," because Hermes moves faster than our thought. What people call a Freudian slip is really a Hermes precision. Hermes punctures pomposity, piety, sureness, self-satisfaction.

Hermes has been active in the garden, by choosing the instant for the boy to take off his headcloth, by sending the ray up into the Princess's room at the right second, in the choosing of wild flowers rather than tame, and in the giving away later of the gold coins. All this sun work is his. The planet Mercury is the nearest of all planets to the sun, and so he is the sun's closest relative.

Alchemists knew that mercury has the ability to liquefy gold and silver. We sense how stuck and stiff the masculine can become, and the feminine can become just as stuck. Mercury softens them in some way so that each can flow. In the presence of Hermes, a flow between masculine and feminine in our story has begun to happen.

The young man, Iron John's student, receives a multiple blessing: one from Aphrodite, which is another name for the Woman Who Loves Gold, and one from Hermes. Hermes and Aphrodite get along well together. Several surviving Greek sculptures show Aphrodite running her fingers through Hermes' hair. We know that not every god and goddess make a good union: Hera and Zeus are an example of that. But Hermes and Aphrodite together are so good that they became the model for the hermaphrodite. It is a soul union—of the Hermes in a man with the Aphrodite in a woman, or the other way around.

The Woman Who Loves Gold pulls off the boy's tarboosh, knowing perfectly well, as the King did not, what lies beneath. She gives the boy gold coins in return for the wild flowers, and each time he remarks, "I'll give them to the gardener's children to play with."

That implies that whatever one receives in the garden is to be given away. And the head covering needs to remain on. A woman may be too eager for a young man to show his gold. In general the public wants artists to show their gold immediately. But the Iron John story implies throughout that an artist should be cautious in showing his or her paintings during the twenties, or in publishing a book too early.

If, like Keats, you are going to die at twenty-five, then everything has different timing. But for those of us who have agreed to live longer, it is important to put the head covering on, and to say about the coins: "I'll give them to the gardener's children to play with."

We have already spoken of Hermes' part in hermetically sealing off certain interior space, keeping out what needs to be kept out, and holding in what wants to be held in. Men who can prevent themselves from giving everything away to work and to the world find themselves able at last to enter the walled space, inside which certain magical events take place.

Hermes with his wells and his walls arranges the garden:

> *And I have asked to be*
> *Where no storms come,*
> *Where the green swell is in the havens dumb,*
> *And out of the swing of the sea.*

Iron John wants the young man to experience the garden. Once the garden—which may take ten years to develop—has been experienced, then we could say that the young man has begun to honor his own soul, has learned to become a lover, and has learned to dance.

CHAPTER SIX

To Bring the Interior Warriors Back to Life

Michael Meade reminds us of the old Celtic motto: "Never give a sword to a man who can't dance." Our story says the next step for the boy is warriorhood; warriorhood follows the garden.

The initiator offers the sword only after the young man's heart has been touched by the lover's privacy and the lover's dance. We notice that the Marines take the boy without that provision; they offer a sword to a man whether he can dance or not.

The Marines develop the outer warrior; we'll begin with the inner warrior.

The Warriors Inside

The warriors inside American men have become weak in recent years, and their weakness contributes to a lack of boundaries, a condition which earlier in this book we spoke of as naïveté. A grown man six feet tall will allow another person to cross his boundaries, enter his psychic house, verbally abuse him, carry away his treasures, and slam the door behind; the invaded man will stand there with an ingratiating, confused smile on his face.

When a boy grows up in a "dysfunctional" family (perhaps there is no other kind of family), his interior warriors will be killed off early. Warriors, mythologically, lift their swords to defend the king. The King in a child stands for and stands up for the child's mood. But when we are children our mood gets easily overrun and swept over in the messed-up family by the more powerful, more dominant, more terrifying mood of the parent. We can say that when the warriors inside cannot protect our mood from being disintegrated, or defend our body from invasion, the warriors collapse, go into trance, or die.

The inner warriors I speak of do not cross the boundary aggressively; they exist to defend the boundary. The Fianna, that famous band of warriors who defended Ireland's borders, would be a model. The Fianna stayed out all spring and summer watching the boundaries, and during the winter came in.

But a typical child has no such protection. If a grown-up moves to hit a child, or stuff food into the child's mouth, there is no defense—it happens. If the grown-up decides to shout, and penetrate the child's auditory boundaries by sheer violence, it happens. Most parents invade the child's territory whenever they wish, and the child, trying to maintain his mood by crying, is simply carried away, mood included.

Each child lives deep inside his or her own psychic house, or soul castle, and the child deserves the right of sovereignty inside that house. Whenever a parent ignores the child's sovereignty, and invades, the child feels not only anger, but shame. The child concludes that if it has no sovereignty, it must be worthless. Shame is the name we give to the sense that we are unworthy and inadequate as human beings. Gershen Kauffman describes that feeling brilliantly in this book, *Shame,* and Merle Fossum and Marilyn Mason in their book, *Facing Shame,* extend Kauffman's work into the area of family shame systems and how they work.

When our parents do not respect our territory at all, their disrespect seems overwhelming proof of our inadequacy. A slap across the face pierces deeply, for the face is the actual boundary of our soul, and we have been penetrated. If a grown-up decides to cross our sexual boundaries and touch us, there is nothing that we as children can do about it. Our warriors die. The child, so full of expectation of blessing whenever he or she is around an adult, stiffens with shock, and falls into the timeless fossilized confusion of shame. What is worse, one sexual invasion, or one beating, usually leads to another, and the warriors, if revived, die again.

When a boy grows up in an alcoholic family, his warriors get swept into the river by a vast wave of water, and they struggle there, carried downriver. The child, boy or girl, unprotected, gets isolated, and has more in common with snow geese than with people.

> *The snow geese, treading blowing Dakotah snows,*
> *Over the fence stairs of the small farms come,*
> *Slipping through cries flung up into the night,*
> *And setting, ah, between them, shifting wings,*
> *Light down at last in bare and snowy fields.*
>
> *The drunken father pulls the boy inside.*
> *The boy breaks free, turns, leaves the house.*
> *He spends that night out eating with the geese.*
> *Where, alert and balancing on wide feet,*
> *Crossing rows, they walk through the broken stalks.*
>   —R.B.

It is no wonder that such a child, when a teenager, looks for single rooms, maternal women, gurus, systems, withdrawals, "non-attachment." When he is older, thirty or thirty-five, he will still feel unprotected, and be unable to defend himself from other people enraged at their own unprotection.

Every adult or older sibling who wants to enter the child's psychic room does so, because it is as if there is no doorknob at all on the inside of the door. The door moves freely in, opening us to improper intimacies that the mother may insist on, to improper belittling the father may insist on, to sexual fondling any older child or baby-sitter may insist on, to incest, physical or psychic. The door moves freely, we could say, because the doorknob is on the outside.

I think it's likely that the early death of a man's warriors keeps the boy in him from growing up. It's possible that it also prevents the female in the boy from developing. We know that Dickens, for example, endured a horrendous childhood, and we also notice that his female characters tend to be sentimental and girlish. It's possible that these girlish beings are projections of his stunted interior woman, whom his warriors could not protect from the violence all around him.

The inner boy in a messed-up family may keep on being shamed, invaded, disappointed, and paralyzed for years and years. "I am a victim," he says, over and over; and he is. But that very identification with victimhood keeps the soul house open and available for still more invasions. Most American men today do not have enough awakened or living warriors inside to defend their soul houses. And most people, men or women, do not know what genuine outward or inward warriors would look like, or feel like.

The Outer, or Disciplined, Warrior

The mythologist and cultural historian Georges Dumézil has given a great gift with his discovery and massive documentation of the idea that the fertile earth of Indo-European civilizations is composed of three separate soil layers: the King, the Warrior, and the Farmer. These three threads make up the tapestry. There are three sorts of ceremonies, three ways of living life, three world views with gods and goddesses for each way.

Roman culture had Jupiter in the king area, Mars in the warrior area, and Quirinus in the agricultural area. The ancient Greek culture had Zeus and Hera in the king and queen area, Ares in the warrior area, and Dionysus and Ariadne in the farmer and wine-grower area. Northern Europe had Odin in the king area; the warriors had Thor, and farmers had Frey and Freya.

The agricultural vision sees "fecundity, abundance in men and goods, nourishment, health, peace, sensual gratification." The habitual identification of gods and goddesses with fertility themes during the nineteenth century now appears to be an obsession with this nourishment level.

The royal vision, from the King and Queen's eyes, sees sovereignty, political parenthood, royalty, the sacred and how to administer it. We have discussed that vision in Chapter 4.

Dumézil has established that the warrior vision makes up the middle level. The warrior's eyes see combat and the use of force in combat. If Dumézil is right, one-third of the visions the Indo-European race has ever had in the near or far past amount to visions from the head of the warrior. We could say that a third of each person's brain is a warrior brain; a third of the instincts carried by our DNA relate to warrior behavior; a third of our thoughts—whether we like it or not—are warrior thoughts. That is a sobering idea.

Robert Moore, the psychologist and theologian, has thought cogently and intensely about the warrior, and we'll sum up a few of his ideas. He emphasizes that for men the warrior is "hardwired." It is not software. He may say to men: "You have plenty of warrior in you—don't worry about it—more than you'll need. The question is whether you will honor it: whether you will have it consciously or unconsciously."

The warrior's area of expertise and experience is the battlefield. The war that takes place there can be physical war, psychological war, or spiritual war. Inside that reverberating and ritual space, armies, tribes, divinities, even ideas, arrange themselves in adversarial fashion. Flags go up, voices deepen, brains sharpen, urgency tightens muscles. Old philosophers in the warrior mode imagine opposites: straight and crooked, long and short, sour and sweet. Extroverted men in the warrior mode, like General Patton, imagine battle, steel on steel, the holiness of the battlefield—as holy to them as the black-seeded field is to the farmer—they imagine the rushing in of adrenaline, personal combat, the delight of danger, even the joy of noble death.

Moore emphasizes that the quality of a true warrior is that he is in service to a purpose greater than himself: that is, to a transcendent cause. Mythologically, he is in service to a True King. If the King he serves is corrupt, as in Ollie North's case, or if there is no King at all, and he is serving greed, or power, then he is no longer a warrior, but a soldier.

The Aztecs, when they took over the Toltec culture in Mexico about A.D. 1200, lifted the warrior caste above the kingly caste. This was an organizational move novel to the Toltec world, and this single change doomed the entire Aztec culture. The Japanese, whose society has honored the warrior for centuries, tell a story about a pond that had lost its King; uncertain what to do, the pond's inhabitants finally elect a heron (who is associated in Japan with the warrior) to be King. The heron eats up everyone in the pond.

When a warrior is in service, however, to a True King—that is, to a transcendent cause—he does well, and his body becomes a hardworking servant, which he requires to endure cold, heat, pain, wounds, scarring, hunger, lack of sleep, hardship of all kinds. The body usually responds well. The person in touch with warrior energy can work long hours, ignore fatigue, do what is necessary, finish the Ph.D. and all the footnotes, endure obnoxious department heads, live sparsely like Ralph Nader, write as T. S. Eliot did under a single dangling light bulb for years, clean up shit and filth endlessly like Saint Francis or Mother Teresa, endure contempt, disdain, and exile as Sakharov did. A clawed hand takes the comfort-loving baby away, and an adult warrior inhabits the body.

How can any complicated culture live without strong warrior energy? The outward warriors inside some women are today strong, sometimes stronger than those in men. Forces in contemporary society recently have encouraged women to be warriors, while discouraging warriorhood in boys and men.

Michael Meade emphasizes strategy as an essential quality of the true warrior. Strategy includes cunning, worldliness, intelligence. A hero in some old story who is attempting to find the Woman with the Golden Hair, or to capture the Three Black Stallions who live under the ocean, may discover a giant or a witch, or both, blocking his road. The soldier part of him says, "Attack the giant or the witch head on. Kill them!" The warrior has to be called on to devise a strategy. The strategy here is that the boy will enter the giant's forest beating a small drum, and when the giant asks him why he does that, the boy says he is showing the way for the ten thousand small men who are following. He explains that the men are small, but each carries a tiny hammer, and these will be able to knock out the giant's brains when he lies down to sleep. A giant loves sleep, and small things terrify him, so he usually makes a deal. The warrior's vision includes such witty strategy.

The Eternal, or Sacred, Warrior

Neil Forsythe includes an imposing range of mythological material about the Eternal Warrior in his book *The Old Enemy: Satan and the Combat Myth*. The physical warrior, whether Roland or Joan of Arc or Patton, loves the battlefield. The field the Holy Warrior loves is the field of good and evil, where the Forces of Darkness battle with the Forces of Light. Ancient literature, such as the *Ramayana,* carries many more descriptions of these impalpable, invisible battles than of the battlefields in which human beings live and die.

In the Marduk epic, the name of Marduk's enemy, Tiamat, suggests in the Babylonian language the chaotic forces of the sea. Mythologically, chaos and evil are related. The chaos of Tiamat has a female tone, and the chaos of Humbaba, the Babylonian giant, has a male tone.

Christian texts call all chaotic forces Satan, thereby giving them a male tone; and so the holy battle for Christians pits against each other the two brothers, Christ and Satan.

Milton, embodying in his life many of the qualities of the outward warrior, lost his eyesight battling in words the landed gentry who wanted to return to power after the execution of Charles I. He imagined eternal warriorhood when he composed *Paradise Lost*. He loved the battlefield of good and evil as much as Patton loved the battle of tanks in North Africa.

The ancient Persians created the most elaborate of these divine battlefields where Ahura Mazda (whose last name still adorns some light bulbs) battles as the Warrior of Light, and the Destructive Spirit, Ahriman, battles as the Warrior of Darkness. Judaism imagines Yahweh to be the Warrior of Light, and Satan to be the Warrior of Darkness.

The author of Job implies that inside Yahweh there is a dark side. When Yahweh wipes out Job's health and family, Job glimpses the "monstrous and fearful side of God," as Neil Forsythe phrases it. The Eternal Battle then can be a war between God and His Enemy, or a war between the two halves of God. As human beings, we feel these wars inside ourselves.

Antonio Machado said:

Every man has two
battles which he fights:
he fights with god in his dreams,
and he fights the sea when awake.
 Translated by R.B.

A Sacred King and Queen live in the Luminous Realm, near Dionysus and Jesus, but the Holy Warrior also lives there, "hardwired" into the universe. His battle against chaos, against the sea, against greedy giants, against the Great Mother, against the Great Titan Father, against dwarfs, devils, and all God's enemies, will never end. Judaism adopted as God a Jehovah Warrior God rather than a King God; and we have all inherited from Judeo-Christianity those tightened muscles, and armor-covered chests, of the Warrior Who Fights Forever.

The Sacred Warrior has a blessed side and a poisoned side. It is no surprise, then, if earthly warriors have a sacred and a twisted side also. One man is a self-sacrificing warrior fighting for a cause beyond himself; another man is a madman soldier, raping, pillaging, killing mindlessly, dropping napalm over entire villages.

The Holy Warrior invades us from eternal space as a hurricane energy and a whirlwind force. The warrior power, nourished on electric or magnetic energy, moves behind the veil of flesh, and alters moods and impulses, shines through the screen of skin and bones, makes the body do what the power wants.

Each whirlwind force, whether Wild Man, Warrior, or King, can be imagined as a large claw that reaches through the wall and takes the human baby out. The invading claw is dangerous. But because of the claw the human being lives for moments in the other world. The old Viking warrior, for example, who went berserk—bear-shirted—made a journey to the other world, from which he eventually returned. North European folklore includes story after story about that experience. A practiced warrior falls asleep in his chair one day inside his house. At that very moment a huge bear appears on the battlefield, attacks and fights the enemy. Should the bear be wounded on his right paw, the man, when he wakes up exhausted and confused, will find a wound in his right hand.

The physical warrior, when well trained, can go through a door, and in the next room will meet the dark-minded, hot warrior. Literature describes Celtic and Viking warriors who went "too far" into that world, following the clawed hand; and men and women cooled them down and reintroduced them with great care to the human community again. We let our warriors go berserk, and then simply discharge them out into the streets.

We can say, then, that knowledge of what warriorhood is, and how to deal with its dark side and how to admire its positive side, has been lost. Simultaneously, the warrior himself, or our image of him, has suffered a collapse in all three worlds.

Milton, as Blake remarked, really wanted Satan to win. To the old mythologists, Milton's longing is a massive betrayal. We, and Milton, romanticize chaos. Perhaps we, as industrial people, secretly want chaos to come in and loosen up our rigidly stratified lives. India goes on exulting in Krishna's victories over giants and demons, and worshippers in Bali act out each day in the temples fantastically vivid scenes from the battle between evil principles and good principles and the victory of the good in the *Ramayana*. But we are not quite sure that we want Krishna to win, and we prefer Woody Allen to the *Ramayana*. We plan to meet God's enemies with a little humor and a fine for noncompliance. A lack of imagination makes us unable to see what chaos is; and the recent history of Iran makes clear that a humorless fundamentalism will not replace the missing imagination. Holy warriorhood in the Muslim world has been reduced to a war between Iran and Iraq, just as our heated imaginative delight in the wars of the imagination during Arthur's time have become concretized into the "Cold War."

When the Holy Warrior falls, he entangles the warriors in the other two places in his fall. The chivalric tradition, which sprang up in the European eleventh and twelfth centuries, tried, by drawing on Arabic and Persian sources, to sustain the warrior ideal in cultivated life by modifying it toward elegance, compassion, sacrifice, and partnership-thought. As late as the eighteenth century in Italy, the language of the warrior included images of the lover.

The aikido student and master Terry Dobson, who has taught so many of us the goodness possible inside the warrior, found this passage spoken in 1465 by the French knight, Jean de Brueil:

> Battle is a joyous thing. We love each other so much in battle. If we see that our cause is just and our kinsmen fight boldly, tears come to our eyes. A sweet joy rises in our hearts, in the feeling of our honest loyalty to each other; and seeing our friend so bravely exposing his body to danger in order to fulfill the commandment of our Creator, we resolve to go forward and die or live with him on account of love. This brings such delight that anyone who has not felt it cannot say how wonderful it is. Do you think someone who feels this is afraid of death? Not in the least! He is so strengthened, so delighted, that he does not know where he is. Truly, he fears nothing in the world!

Here we see the lover and the warrior mingling. But that mingling is now mostly gone. The physical warrior disintegrated into the soldier when mechanized warfare came on.

Some people believe that the conscious warrior and his ideals ended during the American Civil War's last battles, which amounted to slaughter. General Grant saw it and chose to remain drunk. At Ypres in 1915, one hundred thousand young men died in one day, all of whom died without seeing the machine gunners who killed them.

Anything left of the warrior vanished with the mass bombings of Dresden, the bombs on Nagasaki and Hiroshima, and the B-52 bombings of rice fields in Vietnam.

Contemporary war, with its mechanical and heartless destruction, has made the heat of aggression seem disgraceful. Ares is not
present on the contemporary battlefield. The Vietnam veterans
suffered soul damage in that they went into battle imagining they
served a warrior god, and came back out of it godless. "Women
hate war," it has often been said, "but love the warrior." That is
no longer true. Most women in the West see no reason to distinguish the warrior from the soldier or the soldier from the murderer.
It was a madness associated with the warrior that—during the last
war—destroyed the very fabric of culture which it was once the
job of the warrior to preserve. Women in other countries may see
that differently. A Russian woman from Kiev, whose generation
of women have lived for many years without men their own age,
said to me, "All the young men who were left after the battle for
Kiev went to Moscow to defend it. Not one came back." She went
on, "I know that women in the United States are angry with the
men because they are too aggressive, and so on. We don't feel that
way. If the Russian men had not had great aggression in them,
the Germans would be in Moscow right now. The matter of
aggression looks different if you have been invaded."

We can all add further details to the account I've given of the
decline from warrior to soldier to murderer, but it is important to
notice the result. The disciplined warrior, made irrelevant by mechanized war, disdained and abandoned by the high-tech culture, is
fading in American men. The fading of the warrior contributes to
the collapse of civilized society. A man who cannot defend his own
space cannot defend women and children. The poisoned warriors
called drug lords prey primarily for recruits on kingless, warriorless
boys.

And it all moves so swiftly. The massive butcheries of 1915
finish off the disciplined or outward warrior, and then within thirty
years, the warriors inside Western men begin to weaken. The
double weakening makes us realize how connected the outer world
and the inner world are, how serious the events of history are.

Our story goes back to a time when the warrior was still
honored. We'll see now how the storyteller introduces the warrior.

The Story: The Battle Scene

Not long after, the country was swept up in war. The King gathered his forces and was not positive that he could succeed against the enemy, who was powerful and retained a large army. The gardener's boy said: "I am quite grown now, and I will go to war, if you'll just give me a horse." The other men laughed and declared: "When we've gone, you go look in the stable—we'll certainly leave a horse behind for you."

When they had all gone, the boy went into the barn and led a horse out; it was lame in one leg, and walked hippity, hoppity. He climbed on it and rode to the dark forest.

When he came to its edge, he called three times: "Iron John," so loud that it echoed through the trees.

In a moment the Wild Man arrived and said, "What is it you want?"

"I want a strong war-horse because I intend to go to the war."

"You will receive that, and more than you have asked for as well."

The Wild Man turned then and went back into the woods, and not long afterwards, a stableboy came out of the trees leading a war-horse that blew air through its nostrils and was not easy to hold in. Running along after the horse came a large band of warriors, entirely clothed in iron, with their swords shining in the sun. The boy turned his three-legged nag over to the stableboy, mounted the new horse and rode out at the head of the soldiers. By the time he neared the battlefield, a large part of the King's men had already been killed, and not much more was needed to bring them to total defeat.

The boy and his iron band rode there at full speed, galloped on the enemy like a hurricane, and struck down every one that opposed them. The enemy turned to flee, but the boy kept after them and pursued them to the last man. Then, however, instead of returning to the King, the boy took his band a roundabout way back to the forest, and called Iron John out.

"What do you want?" the Wild Man asked.

"You can take your horse and your men back, and give me again the three-legged nag."

So it all happened as he requested, and he rode the hoppity hop back home.

When the King returned to his castle, his daughter went to him and congratulated him on his victory.

"It wasn't me," he said, "who managed that, but a strange knight and his warrior band who arrived to help."

The daughter asked who this strange knight was, but the King didn't know, and added: "He galloped off in pursuit of the enemy, and that's the last I saw of him." The girl applied to the gardener and inquired about his boy, but he laughed and said, "He is just now arrived home on his three-legged nag. The farm help made fun of him, shouting: 'Guess who's here? Moopygoop.' Then they said, 'You've been under a lilac bush, eh? How was it?' He said back to them, 'I fought very well; if I hadn't been there, who knows what would have happened?' They all fell over themselves laughing."

The passage begins with the statement that the Kingdom has been invaded. If the characters in a fairy story all make up one psyche—namely, ours—we would have to conclude that it is our own psyche that has been invaded.

The battle, I would think, appears at this moment in the story not because an enemy has just occupied the psyche one or two days ago, but because the gardener's boy realizes at last that the invasion has taken place. And it is now intensifying.

Observers have noticed for centuries that when the effort for change heats up the psyche, the heat itself attracts demons, or sleeping complexes, or bitter enemies of the spirit—trouble of some sort.

People who have joined a meditation group will tell you, for hours, stories about this phenomenon: they begin to meditate; everything goes better than ever for them for two or three weeks, and then suddenly, the landlady kicks them out of their apartment; a filling falls out of a tooth; the laundry loses their clothes; someone breaks into their car, and so on.

Those stories point to renewed or intensified invasion. But who is invading?

During all the time we were busy going to college, or setting up a career, or longing for purity, a mysterious force was invading the Kingdom. How often men and women in their twenties feel suddenly in danger. A secret voice says, "You must make a change now. If you don't, it will be too late."

When I was about thirty, I described the invader as a python:

> *The ape, alone in his bamboo cage, smells*
> *The python, and cries, but no one hears him call.*
> *The grave moves forward from its ambush,*
> *Curling slowly, with sideways motion,*
> *Passing under bushes and through leaf tunnels,*
>
> *Leaving dogs and sheep murdered where it slept.*
> *Some shining thing inside us, that has*
> *Served us well, shakes its bamboo bars.*
> *It may be gone before we wake.*

There is an invaded country and there is an invader, there is a spiritually hopeful part of us and a dangerously hostile part. There is a dovelike part of the soul, and a toothed part of the soul. César Vallejo says:

> *And what if after so many wings of birds,*
> *The stopped bird doesn't survive!*
> *It would be better, really,*

> *If it were all swallowed up right now, and let's end*
> *it!*
>
> Translated by R.B. and Douglas Lawder

The invasion is more than a distraction or an annoyance. The story says that the King is losing the battle. Apparently the center of the psyche cannot protect its own territory. An enemy has been activated, and the soul is no longer partnered, supported, harmonious, nor *in harmonium*, as Wallace Stevens would say.

Remembering the battlefield where the eternal warrior fights, we might assume that the enemy invading the soul is evil itself, but it doesn't feel that way. The invader might be chaos, but the enemy also feels as if it were a part of our own soul. "The lion and the honeycomb, what has the scripture said?" Bees make honey inside the dead body of the hostile lion.

If the King is actually losing the battle, it is time for the warrior in us to learn how to fight. We notice that the warrior pursues the battle to the end, with no halfway measures in mind— no pulling back.

The wolf who swallowed the six kids has to be killed; nothing is said about a halfway measure such as therapy for the wolf. All this is inner work with inner wolves but the attitude needs to be decisive. If there is no decisive move, the wolf will simply go on eating your "kids."

We feel ourselves in a religious situation here, perhaps in a religious ritual. That which is "killed" transforms. We know that when a man, for example, joined the Mithraic religion in Roman times, a priest stabbed a bull in his presence, and the novice said, "Just as the God kills the bull, I kill my own passions."

We also know that in the Mithraic cave room, where the religious ceremonies were held, a painting of the bull execution rotated on hinges, and on its reverse side it showed wine—for the bull's blood has been transformed into wine—and wheat, which grows out of the dead bull. Similarly in Egypt, wheat was shown each spring sprouting from the layer of earth that had been carefully placed around and on top of Osiris' dead body.

It's possible that the battle scene we are discussing happens in a ritual space, and we expect that some sort of wheat or corn or honey will come from these "bodies."

But first of all we can regard the battle scene as the boy's initiation into warrior intensities. It tells the boy that it is right for him to be in contact with the enemy. Being passive, or hiring an expert to fight your enemy, won't do. I like it very much that the enemy in our story is never named.

Gaining a Four-legged Horse

A remarkable detail that leaps up out of this scene and demands some interpretation is the three-legged horse that the boy finds in the stable. This three-legged horse doesn't feel like good news when we see it standing there, and it obviously feels worse when one rides it. We might look at what a horse could be in such a story as this, and what the difference might be between three legs and four.

"Four" is complete in that it stands for the four-gated city, the four directions, the four rivers of Paradise, the four seasons, the four letters of the Holy Name, the four horses of the sun carriage, and the four strings of the sistrum. The old rhyme goes:

One for sorrow,
Two for mirth,
Three for wedding,
Four for birth.

Three, on the other hand, falls a little short. A three-gated city is not as impressive as a four-gated city, and a planet with only three directions would seem odd to us. Dawn, noon, and sunset add up to three parts of a good day, but night is left out. Fall, winter, and summer would not be acceptable to farmers, for they need spring. So we have to think that something important is gone.

As for the horse, its associations range over heaven and earth. The horse has reminded human beings of ocean waves, of the dead, of thunder, of sexual energy, particularly sexual energy of men, of the Great Mother, for Lady Godiva rode on a horse, of glory and kingship, and of divine energies, such as the four horses of the Apocalypse.

The horse, when contrasted with its rider, reminds men and women of the animal side of human beings, and of the body. The rider stands for the intelligence or intellect or mind, and the horse stands for the animal desires and instincts and energies that have their home there.

I am going to consider the fourth leg as a shamed leg. I assume that the boy's animal body has been crippled by shame; his hobbledehoy walks so because it has a shamed leg.

We have already spoken of shame and its power. Shame can come in from many sources: from parents who deliberately shame us in order to make us more controllable, from addicted parents who shame us as a side effect of their own addiction, or from peers who shame us to get rid of some of their shame. Asking a parent for a response and not receiving it is cause enough for shame; we can ingest a shame-bound parent, and receive shame by inheritance; every invasion, whether sexual abuse or physical abuse, produces in five minutes shame that lasts for thirty years. Simply making up a false personality to please our parents can generate shame for a lifetime. The shaming we receive from irritable schoolteachers, manic Catholic priests, or our own internalized perfectionist increases the store of shame that gets poured into our hollow leg, and each drop of shame increases our commitment to isolation. We attend secret meetings of apology, submission, resentment, and collaboration.

When we were very tiny, our horse had all four legs, and it joyfully lived in whatever sensualities it could gallop to. By the time a child in our culture is twelve, one of the legs at least will be crippled by shame, whether it lives in a "dysfunctional" household or not.

None of us knows at twelve how to heal our horse of shame. The story suggests that a boy's horse needs to be brought to an older man, or to a mentor, or, lifting the scene to the imaginative level, it needs to be brought to the Wild Man. We take the nag out of the barn, where "the older boys" have left it for us; we ride to the edge of the forest; and then we ask the Wild Man for a better horse. We know we have to return it, but just to experience what it would be like to ride on a horse without a crippled leg, even for a few minutes, is worth it all.

In one Swedish version the four-legged horse arrives straight out of the earth. In our version he appears from the forest with fifty or so armed men running alongside him, "their spears shining in the sun." These intent men will be helpful now. Their iron is important.

Iron John, by lending us the horse, does not do away with our early shaming; that cannot be done away with. But we can work to prevent further shaming. And we can learn what connection we still have to that earlier, four-legged horse. That is what the Wild Man means when he says: "I will give you what you ask, and more."

Warriorhood in Teaching, in Literature, and in Science

In Tibetan monasteries of the twelfth and thirteenth centuries young Buddhist novices would line up along a corridor, facing each other. The Buddhist teacher walking between would shout questions at them: "What was Buddha's face before he was born?" The young men hear high-spirited shouts from each other and from the master, shouting replies. Adrenaline floods into the brain, the strings of the musical instrument of thought are tightened, the brain becomes a falcon diving and climbing into air, climbing away from the wrist, on the hunt for food.

Father Ong, a priest and the author of *Orality and Literacy,* wrote an article recently about the fate of that combative method of teaching in the West. The famous debates about angels in the Middle Ages belonged to this combative teaching which we ridicule these days, though Henri Corbin has shown that those debates amounted to a battle between Aristotle and Avicenna. Fundamental soul matters—for example, the existence of what Corbin calls "the imaginal world"—were at stake. Avicenna affirmed that it was a third realm between spirit and body; Aristotle denied it.

Father Ong notes that combative debates survive in some European universities but have almost ceased in American universities. Men who have no family tradition of lively argument may feel themselves overwhelmed in such debates. Moreover, some men and women found that they did not enjoy this way of learning: the competitive mood, the aggression, the fierceness of phrase, did not please them, and some pity for the loser affected the joy of the combat.

But the disappearance of fierce debates is a loss. When the playful verbal combats disappear, then warriorhood becomes reduced or restricted to wrestling, football, the martial arts, guerrilla warfare, blood-and-guts movies.

Both science and literature advance by means of ritual battles between generations. Eliot invents a new move in the poetic monologue, and drives Robert Browning from the field. So-called "New Criticism" does ritual battle with "historical criticism" during this time. Later, the leftist criticism of the thirties attacks the New Criticism, and so on. If each generation embodies some impulse of warriorhood, literature propels itself forward and escapes stagnation. Language bones breaks, but the flow continues.

José Ortega y Gasset describes in detail such combat among the astronomical thinkers, beginning a hundred years or so before Galileo. Science adopted generational struggle during the Renaissance as a means of progress, and still uses it.

Blake fought a mental fight against Newton:

I will not cease from Mental Fight,
Nor shall my Sword sleep in my hand
Till we have built Jerusalem
In England's green & pleasant land.

The warrior ideals have a place in business as well. Since the time of the shoguns, the Japanese have studied the self-sacrificial acts the warrior ideal requires, and that study seems to have strengthened the responsibility or duty they accept toward the employees of their companies. In the United States, the company owners during the nineteenth century had so little sense of duty that the unions had to step in to protect the workers. These days the chief executives in America move from company to company lightly, vote themselves bonuses just before bankruptcy, sell out the retirement fund, and so on. These men are certainly not building Jerusalem.

It is odd how few strong swords the taxpayers bring forward against these outrages, or against the savings and loan greediness, or against the presidential campaigners' refusal to debate the issues.

I mentioned in an earlier chapter the man who was literally unable to extend his arm if his hand was closed around a sword, even a wooden one. The collapse of the warrior means that the sword is thrown away. I have met many good men since who say that if someone gave them a sword, they would break it or stick it into the earth and walk away.

The Pelasgian Creation Myth

We know that more than one American man today needs a sword to cut his adult soul away from his mother-bound soul. Australian aboriginal initiators use that sword precisely to cut that psychic umbilical cord. The sword has the edge that cuts clinging away from love, cuts boyish bravado away from manly firmness, and cuts passive-aggression away from fierceness. The Tibetans refer to such a sharp interior sword as "the Vajra sword." Without it, they say, no spiritual life is possible, and no adult life.

We also may need a sword to cut us apart from our own self-pity. Victimhood may have been inattentively joined to us when we were children, in a joining we could not prevent, achieved in a trance by a molester, a brutalizing brother or sister, a violent father or violent mother. The victim's soul becomes bound in a Siamese-twin fashion to self-pity, resentment, depression, low self-esteem, passivity, and rage. Who is going to cut those emotions away from the soul?

The Greeks admired a Pelasgian creation myth, which was different from and older than the Olympian creation myth. The myth says that once upon a time there was an egg floating on the ocean. Then a sword began to move toward the egg, and the sword cut the egg in two. It turned out that Eros was inside the egg.

If the egg had remained as it was, there would have been no Eros in the world. No sword, no Eros, the myth says. The parent's love for the child, the man's love for a woman, the woman's love for a man, the bee's love for the hive, the worshipper's love for God—none of that comes into being without the sword.

Such a history of creation is a history of discriminations. Once matter appeared, the Great Cutter arrived and divided matter into heavy stuff and light stuff. The light rose and the heavy sank. Then the Divine Cutter appeared once more, and divided the light stuff so that one part became Fire and one part Air. Then the Divine Cutter divided the heavy matter so that one part became Earth and one part became Water. Then the Divine Cutter, or *Logos,* divided earth so that one part became mainland, and one part island. The sword once more divided water into salt water and fresh water. The sword kept on dividing and dividing. These cuttings resulted at last in the finely articulated, singing, beautifully detailed, shining world of minute particulars that the landscape painters love. Why should we be afraid of cuttings? We can feel how different this story is from "And God created Heaven and Earth."

Pythagoras, who loved this story of creation, said that if we looked closely, we could also see the tracks the Divine Cutter left as he or she advanced into the invisible realm. The Cutter leaves behind as its tracks pairs of opposites that exist everywhere; we might mention right and left, straight and crooked, the male and the female, the limited and the unlimited, the moving and the resting, and so on. We'll glance at those opposites later in this chapter.

Jung referred to the value of distinctiveness in his odd piece called "Seven Sermons to the Dead." We note that a hawk always remains a hawk, even when the hawk is living among owls; an owl remains an owl, even when living among porcupines. But human beings are suggestible and can lose distinction. When they merge into "the masses," as in Fascism, they fall into indistinctiveness. The Gnostics imagined a place called the Pleroma, which is an enormous abundance, but also an enormous indistinction. It is desirable, then, for men and women to aim for distinction consciously. It is dangerous if they do not do so.

A great deal of debate goes on these days over how much distinctiveness the genders should aim for. The implication of the Pelasgian myth is that the "prodigious complexity" we all love depends both in nature and in culture on a love of distinctiveness.

Warriorhood in Marriage and Relationship

Conscious fighting is a great help in relationships between men and women. Jung said, "American marriages are the saddest in the whole world, because the man does all his fighting at the office."

When a man and a woman are standing toe-to-toe arguing, what is it that the man wants? Often he does not know. He wants the conflict to end because he is afraid, because he doesn't know how to fight, because he "doesn't believe in fighting," because he never saw his mother and father fight in a fruitful way, because his boundaries are so poorly maintained that every sword thrust penetrates to the very center of his chest, which is tender and fearful. When shouts of rage come out of the man, it means that his warriors have not been able to protect his chest; the lances have already entered, and it is too late.

Michael Meade has suggested that both marital partners begin by identifying the weapons that have come down through their family lines. Perhaps the woman has inherited the short dagger, used unexpectedly, and the spiked mace, which she swings down late in the argument onto the foot soldier's head. The husband may have inherited a broad sword, which he swings when frightened in large indiscriminate circles; it says "never" and "always." "You always talk like your mother." He might add the slender witticism spear to that.

Some people also use the "doorway lance." When the argument is over, and the woman, let's say, is about to go to work, the man says: "By the way," and the lance pins her to the doorframe.

Man and wife might say which weapons he or she plans to use in the particular fight coming up. During such preliminary conversations the man's warrior and woman's warrior are welcomed in the house and honored. A good fight gets things clear, and I think women long to fight and be with men who know how to fight well.

When both use their weapons unconsciously or without naming them, both man and woman stumble into the battle, and when it is over the two interior children can be badly wounded.

The adult warrior inside both men and women, when trained, can receive a blow without sulking or collapsing, knows how to fight for limited goals, keeps the rules of combat in mind, and in general is able to keep the fighting clean and to establish limits.

Marie-Louise von Franz once told a story about a woman friend. "This woman had gone through several marriages. Each marriage would go well until an argument came. Then she would throw a fit, and say damaging things. The terrible quarrels would continue, and finally the man would leave. One day we heard she had found a new husband, and we said, 'Oh-oh, here it goes again.' But something else happened. A few weeks after the honeymoon, the same old quarrel arrived and she brought out her poison and said terrible things. The husband turned pale, but to her surprise, said nothing, and left the room. She found him upstairs packing his bags. 'What are you doing?' she said. 'I know,' he said, 'that I am supposed to act like a man now and shout and hit you, but I am not that sort of man. I will not allow anyone to talk to me in the way you have, and I am leaving.' She was astounded. She asked him not to leave, and he didn't. The marriage is still going on."

This story is not perfect. If a woman has a fair argument, it is not right for the man to leave; he should stay and fight. But von Franz's use of the word *fit* implies that her friend had a habit of going over the line into possession. Her fits belonged metaphorically to Kali's realm, rather than to the human realm. Men cross that line often as well. The inner warrior can tell a person when the partner is on this side of the human line, and when on the other side.

Marian Woodman remarks in *The Ravaged Bridegroom,* "Anger comes from the personal level, rage from an archetypal core. . . . The rage in both sexes comes out of centuries of abuse.

If it is taken into relationships, it destroys. Attacking each other in a state of possession has nothing to do with liberation." The interior warrior in both men and women can help them to fight on the human plane. If men and women have only soldiers or shamed children inside, they will have to settle for damaging battles constantly.

Iron vs. Copper

We notice that the soldiers in our story, when they arrive running alongside Iron John's horse, are "clothed in iron." Iron belongs to Mars and Ares. Iron was believed to be related to blood, because of the red hiding inside iron. The ancients distinguished between two sorts of iron: magnetic iron, which is associated with the sky-gods and has "fallen from the heavens," and ordinary iron, which is associated with earthly dark gods, such as Set, who pursues and kills the solar god, Osiris.

In astrology, iron governs the planet Mars. Iron is often considered lucky, especially when found on the road. Horseshoes can be used as protection against evil; and nails are set into cradles to protect infants, or into beds to protect women in childbirth; scissors may be hidden in the bed also.

Blake associated iron with intellect and with spiritual warfare. We notice in fairy tales that the energy of the benevolent Father-Spirit appears at times in the form of small men dressed in iron. When the boy in our story brings iron to the battlefield with him, he brings a great array of lucky and helpful powers: horseshoes, magnetic iron, blood, the planet Mars, the sky-gods, the Father-Spirit, intellectual fight.

So far in this chapter we have linked warriorhood to self-sacrifice and service to the King, to intellectual combat, to clean fighting in marriage, and to the sharpness of the Vajra sword. The Vajra sword should move in such a way as to cut apart what has been inappropriately joined. When the sword has done its work and the Logos-Knife has cut well, we will find ourselves less needy and more ready to enter the pairs of opposites. We recall some of the pairs of opposites that Pythagoras named: light and dark, limited and unlimited, male and female, the resting and the moving, and so on.

What if we feel too young to inhabit the dangerous space between male and female? What if we don't like the fierce tension between straight and crooked and don't feel up to so many opposites? The child in a messed-up family may feel a ghastly tension between the addicted parent and the clean parent, between the cold of the angry father and the heat of the loving mother, or between the cold of the furious mother and the heat of the sorrowing father.

In such a situation it's relatively easy to give up iron work and take up copper work. A child can easily become a professional bridge. The child can become a conductor made of that good conducting metal, copper.

A man's copper work probably begins early by placing one hand on his father's wrathful chest and the other hand on the earth; or perhaps he places one hand on his mother's anguished heart and the other on the earth, or one hand on an adult's isolated head and the other on the earth.

The boy who becomes a conductor values himself for the complicated current that runs through his body, for his ability to conduct wrath to the ground by a quiet reply, for the self-sacrificing stretching out of his arms to touch each pole.

Many of us know this sensation of conduction from early childhood: the mother and father talk to each other through the child. The shame of the alcoholic father, for example, goes through our body heading east, and the anxiety of the dependent mother goes through our body heading west. Fury and contempt pass each other, meeting somewhere in the son's or daughter's chest.

If the child is a boy, the intense isolation of the father can run through him with little resistance . . . copper is such a good conductor that the boy doesn't heat up. The intensity of female suffering can flow through him without heating him up very much either. I'm not sure how it is with girl children—I suspect they heat up a little more.

The son loses his distinctiveness as a man by learning to be a conductor; the daughter who accepts this task becomes, similarly, a bridge, not a woman. When either son or daughter reaches adulthood, they will notice many opportunities for similar bridging.

This way of treating opposites has become extremely popular in the last forty years. When a man or woman becomes a conductor, the act of conducting gives us the sense that we are not shamefully narrow and limited, but that we have something for everyone. Of course, in order for a person to maintain the illusion of being both limited and unlimited, both child and bridge, both flesh and copper, that person has to ignore many perceptions that slip into him or her at odd hours.

If a man has become copper as a boy, he will likely continue working with that metal when grown up. He may place one hand on the crown of his furious wife's head and the other hand on the earth. He may become a public apologist, conducting to earth—through his own body—centuries of justified female fury.

As fathers lose touch with the warrior, fewer fathers give any modeling beyond the copper bridge when faced with female anger. "My father never stood up to my mother, and I'm still angry about that." Hundreds of men have spoken that sentence at gatherings. Sometimes all that would have been necessary would have been for the father to stand up for his boundaries, or for the limits of verbal abuse, and simply say firmly, "Enough!" If the father cannot set limits to the mother's raging, nor the mother to the father's "loss of temper," the children turn into copper wires.

The more the man agrees to be copper, the more he becomes neither alive nor dead, but a third thing, an amorphous, demasculinized, half-alive psychic conductor. I believe that a woman sometimes finds herself channeling the rage of dozens of dead women who could not speak their rage while alive. Conducting that rage is dangerous.

Conducting large amounts of charm and niceness is also dangerous. Ingesting excessive amounts of copper is an occupational hazard for ministers, therapists, and priests, resembling the hazards of ingesting lead that some factory workers endure. Contemporary ministers channel spiritual comfort, coddling, and soothing, but at the expense of risk-taking and solitariness. Many a male minister gives up his longing for solitude, and for the harshness and zaniness of male companionship; and when they bury such as a minister, he's really made mostly of copper.

Men and women, then, often become conductors not from bravery or openness to change, but from a longing for comfort, for peace in the house, for padded swords, for protective coloration, a longing to be the quail hiding in fall reeds.

Becoming a conductor for male and female currents is not the same thing as achieving androgyny. The Hermaphrodite is an image from alchemy and becomes possible, as we mentioned earlier, on an inner plane after years of distinctiveness: that is, years of cutting, opposites, and discrimination. A false androgyny is achieved early on through conduction, but usually neither Hermes nor Aphrodite is present.

This is a difficult subject, and it is difficult to qualify statements in the right way. None of us has received very good advice on copper work. Women in the early days of the feminist movement demanded that men should do more conduction of anger for them. Women have long been tired of being copper for men's domination fantasies; I suppose the early feminists did not notice how much conduction men were already doing.

Sustaining the Tension Between Opposites

Through the image of a human being becoming a copper wire, I am trying to bring up into words a sensation that most of us have experienced in our childhood homes. We lose our childhood and a lot of our playfulness by becoming copper wires. What happens to us as we get older?

We become suspicious of all forms of merging. Romantic love involves a great deal of merging; and it isn't that we need to reject it but to examine it. It is right to examine all mergings: mergings of molester and victim, of tyrant and citizen, of company and employee, of church and worshipper, of decade and style, of group mind and personal mind, of husband and wife.

Chekhov composed in his story "The Darling" a masterpiece on this last form of merging. We meet a woman who, when married to a theater producer, complains that audiences respect only musical comedies. After her husband dies, she marries a lumber merchant, and learns to talk intensely of "two-by-fours," "underflooring," "oak joists," and so on. When that husband dies, she falls in love with a veterinary surgeon and talks passionately of hoof-and-mouth disease, natal fever, hog cholera, et cetera. Having no children, she becomes attached to the veterinarian's small son, and soon speaks feelingly of how unfair principals are, how difficult life in the playground is, et cetera. The story ends with the boy in his sleep shouting: "I've given it to you! Get away! Shut up!"

We could easily write a parallel story in which a man adapts in a feeling way to wife after wife. To merge so well is beautiful, and yet. . . . Some truth-telling child inside each of us, men or women, must learn, when faced with excessive merging, to say as the little boy did, "Get away! Shut up!" Some merging is right, some is not.

It is our intuition that can tell us when the merging is appropriate or inappropriate; then it is the warrior inside who can teach us how to hold boundaries. In the non-copper mode, the boundaries are kept but the relationship remains vital.

Frost said, "Something there is that doesn't love a wall." But we know that a boundary is not a wall. In marriage, there can be boundaries, and valid points of view on each side of the boundary. They don't have to merge into one view.

When Robert and Elinor Frost's infant son died, and Robert buried the boy himself, he found that his wife hated the way he dug the grave, and she hated the way he spoke of it:

> *"And it's come to this,*
> *A man can't speak of his own child that's dead."*
>
> *"You can't because you don't know how to speak.*
> *If you had any feelings, you that dug*
> *With your own hand—how could you?—his little*
> *grave;*
> *I saw you from that very window there,*
> *Making the gravel leap and leap in air,*

Leap up, like that, like that, and land so lightly
And roll back down the mound beside the hole.
I thought, Who is that man? I didn't know
   you. . . ."

"My words are nearly always an offense.
I don't know how to speak of anything
So as to please you. But I might be taught,
I should suppose. I can't say I see how.
A man must partly give up being a man
With women-folk. . . ."

He said twice over before he knew himself:
"Can't a man speak of his own child he's lost?"

"Not you! Oh, where's my hat? Oh, I don't need it!
I must get out of here. I must get air.
I don't know rightly whether any man can."

"Amy! Don't go to someone else this time.
Listen to me. I won't come down the stairs."

    —from "Home Burial"

I love Robert Frost because he is able to sustain the tension between opposites, here between man and woman, with neither attitude understood as wrong, but as different.

When a person becomes old enough to sense the opposites and realize that he or she has to take an attitude toward them, two possibilities spring to mind—first, bridging them with Aphrodite's metal, copper, which we've already spoken of, and second, living in the opposites, while not coming down hard on one side or the other.

Living in the Opposites

We can talk, then, of living between the opposites. To live between means that we not only recognize opposites, but rejoice that they exist. Pythagoras, as we mentioned above, left behind a careful list of opposites that he vouched for. Male and female make up one pair, the light and the dark another, the one and the many another, the odd and even another. To live between we stretch out our arms and push the opposites as far apart as we can, and then live in the resonating space between them.

Living in the opposites does not mean identifying with one side and then belittling the other. The aim is not that a man, for example, should choose the male role and then regard the female as the enemy.

The Catholic church, obsessed with the opposites of pagan attitudes and Christian attitudes, identified with one side during the Inquisition, and the result was disastrous. In any religion it is tempting for ascetic men to identify with the male pole. Then, disguised as spiritual warriors, they can remain angry at women all through life. More and more women in recent decades have begun identifying with the female pole, and maintain that everything bad is male, and everything good is female.

Rejoicing in the opposites means pushing the opposites apart with our imaginations so as to create space, and then enjoying the fantastic music coming from each side. One gets a sense of the power of that by sitting between a sitar and a tabla when both are giving off music.

One can feel the resonance between opposites in flamenco dancing. Defender and attacker watch each other, attractor and refuser, woman and man, red and red. Each is a pole with its separate magnetic charge, each is a nation defending its borders, each is a warrior enjoying the heat of extravagant passion, a distinguished passion which is fierce, eaglelike, mysterious.

Admiring Paris' Choice

We remember that Ares in Greek mythology had a sister; her name was Eris (Discord), and she was the one who caused trouble for Paris by lending him a golden apple, and telling him to give it to the goddess he liked the best. That is trouble. Paris saw Hera and her Rooted Earth Energy, Aphrodite and her Erotic Joy, and Athena and her Ecstatic Spiritual Knowledge. Eris says: "Choose!"

Most of us pretend not to hear that word. Paris' task is to choose one goddess, and that means two will be left angry with him. When a person chooses the one thing most precious, it is a serious act. Choosing ends well, but not for the rejected divinities.

"I want it all." "Go for it" is the current cliché expressing some horrible greediness, naïveté, and love of the unlimited. Some naïve men and women do not want to choose, but want events to choose. Richard Wilbur wrote a marvelous poem on that longing:

> *I read how Quixote in his random ride*
> *Came to a crossing once, and lest he lose*
> *The purity of chance, would not decide*
>
> *Whither to fare, but wished his horse to choose.*
> *For glory lay wherever he might turn.*
> *His head was light with pride, his horse's shoes*
> *Were heavy, and he headed for the barn.*

Choosing a goddess is very different from identifying with one side of a pair of opposites. The question here is what you really love. Eris says choose what you want and then pay for it. A man chooses his life's desire, and the warrior in him agrees to the unpleasant labors that will follow. It is not different for a woman.

The warrior gives a man or woman permission to live in suffering. Yeats in old age said:

> *All men live in suffering*
> *I know as few can know,*
> *Whether they take the upper road,*
> *Or stay content on the low,*
> *Rower bent in his row-boat*
> *Or weaver bent at his loom. . . .*

Suffering here means the difficult tasks accepted for the sake of your desire, but also the painful awareness of other roads not taken.

The passion in our nature urges a human being to choose "the one precious thing," and urges him to pay for it through poverty, conflict, deprivation, labor, and the endurance of anger from rejected divinities. It is the warrior that enables the human being to decide to become a musician only, or a poet only, or a doctor only, or a hermit only, or a painter only. It is the lover in a man or woman who loves the one precious thing, and tells him what it is; but it is the warrior in Rembrandt or Mirabai who agrees to endure the suffering the choice entails.

The yeshiva student may find that the goddess of sexuality attacks him. Sakharov chose, and he received hostility from the Establishment, rejection by his own children, and exile to Gorky.

Alchemists of the Middle Ages made a lot out of the scene in which Paris chooses among the goddesses. A sixteenth-century woodcut, which Edward Edinger reprints in his *Anatomy of the Psyche,* shows, near Paris and the goddesses, a king lying on the ground, sound asleep. At the instant Paris indicates his choice with his wand, the king wakes up.

If we choose "the one precious thing"—the object of our desire—then, according to the alchemists, the inner King in us that has been asleep for so many years wakes up. During all the conductor years in which we buried our iron, and made ourselves into copper bridges, the King had no choice but to sleep. As long as nothing is clear, as long as we have not chosen whether to be conductor or human, the King—and the Queen—sleeps on.

Paris' choice marks out one goddess, or life-road, from another. There is something fierce in it.

We could say that New Age people in general are addicted to harmony. The alchemical woodcut says that a child will not become an adult until it breaks the addiction to harmony, chooses the one precious thing, and enters into a joyful participation in the tensions of the world.

When the battle in our story is over, the boy is now naïve in one less way, in that he knows what a sword is. Of course, like everything else in the story, the battle happens over and over. We find our three-legged horse; we ride to the forest; we ask the Wild Man for a whole horse; without anger we join the tensions of the world. Each time we use the warrior well, we are not so much fighting battles as awakening the King.

Moving from Copper to Iron

This process of reviving the inner warriors goes on for years, and it is associated with the change from copper to iron. Each of us needs to imagine how to bring the interior warriors back to life, and it is not physical work so much as imaginative work.

The Fianna loved Ireland, and were willing to defend her borders. What do we love well enough to want it defended?

Protecting boundaries and the King means, in the metaphor we mentioned above, getting the doorknob on the inside of the door. Growing older does not make this happen on its own. A man at thirty-five or forty-five, as soon as he hears a hand fumbling with the doorknob outside, may fall into a trance, and let it all happen again. It is the warrior's job to break the trance. Gradually, a man or woman learns to recognize the marks of the trance, and the sort of woman or man who throws us into the trance. Metaphorically, the task is to move the doorknob to the inside of the door. The more honor we give the inner warriors, the more likely it is that they will warn us when someone is rattling it.

Each time we ask our warriors' intuition to smell out shamers, we gain shrewdness. We may lose some "boyish naïveté" of course, some "optimism about human nature," but we are no longer a wounded six-year-old. The wounded child may still need to be nurtured and defended, but the child no longer possesses us.

The warrior's task is to warn us when the person talking to us intends to pass on some of his or her shame. For example, when we have finished a talk or a lecture, someone might say, "I liked your talk, except for one thing. Would you like to know what it was?" Now is the time. The person may have goodwill or not. If the warrior says not, a possible answer is, "I don't think I'll be shamed by you today, if that's all right with you." There's no need to hit the person with a stick. Sometimes simply speaking the word "shame" is enough to keep the boundary. The person looks shocked, and says that he had no such intention in mind . . . oh, certainly not.

Protecting the inner house implies replacing some of the copper with iron. "Maid Maleen," a story the Grimm brothers collected, advises Maleen and her maidservant, both unprotected, to eat nettles, which are in fact a source of iron. Eating nettles suggests accepting the thorns as well as the rose, living in scarcity, doing the unpleasant, and avoiding talk of how things might be better. Talking about reality is a good way to bring in iron.

A practical way of preventing oneself from being a copper bridge is to become conscious of conduction the moment it is happening. Conduction is unconscious, and naming it helps move it to communication. "I don't think I'll be a conductor for you any longer."

Warriorship inside, then, amounts to a soul alertness that helps protect a human being from being turned into copper wire, and protects us from shamers, unconscious swordsmen, hostile people, and greedy interior beings.

The Odyssey says there are suitors inside who want to marry the soul. These toothy suitors have plans for your life. If a person never lifts a sword, he or she may get high marks for gentleness, but may end up as a slave to the suitors, or the target of an arranged wedding. We could say about a person who refuses to lift a sword:

His head was light with pride, his horse's shoes
Were heavy, and he headed for the barn.

That can happen to a culture also. If a culture does not deal with the warrior energy—take it in consciously, discipline it, honor it—it will turn up outside in the form of street gangs, wife beating, drug violence, brutality to children, and aimless murder.

One major task of contemporary men is to reimagine, now that the images of eternal warrior and outward warrior no longer provide the model, the value of the warrior in relationships, in literary studies, in thought, in emotion.

And we might imagine what follows after warrior intensities. Doesn't the energy that loves to fight need to learn to play all over again? How does that happen?

CHAPTER SEVEN

Riding the Red, the White, and the Black Horses

We know that our society produces a plentiful supply of boys, but seems to produce fewer and fewer men. Some contemporary cultures—the New Guinea tribes would be examples—force the boys to be men through various cunning, heated, imaginative, reckless austerities and teachings that may happen too quickly to produce a solid man. We come in at the opposite end of that spectrum, in that we have no ideas at all on how to produce men, and we let it all happen unconsciously while we look away to Wall Street and hope for the best.

Michael Ventura, in a magnificent essay called "The Age of Endarkenment" (published recently in the *Whole Earth Review*), speaks of adolescent wildness and its challenge to our lack of ideas. Their music, their fashions, their words, their codes, he says, announce that the initiatory moment has come. Those extravagances are a request for a response. Ventura remarks:

Tribal people everywhere greeted the onset of puberty, especially in males, with elaborate and excruciating initiations—*a practice that plainly wouldn't have been necessary unless their young were as extreme as ours.* . . . The tribal adults didn't run from this moment in their children as we do; they celebrated it. They would assault their adolescents with, quite literally, holy terror; rituals that had been kept secret from the young until that moment . . .

rituals that focused upon the young all the light and darkness of their tribe's collective psyche, all its sense of mystery, all its questions and all the stories told to both harbor and answer those questions. . . . The crucial word here is "focus." The adults had something to teach: stories, skills, magic, dances, visions, rituals. In fact, if these things were not learned well and completely, the tribe could not survive. . . . Tribal cultures satisfied the craving while supplying the need, and we call that "initiation." This practice was so effective that usually by the age of fifteen a tribal youth was able to take his or her place as a fully responsible adult.

Ventura notices that for about forty years, the young in our culture have generated forms—music, fashions, behaviors—"that prolong the initiatory moment . . . as though hoping to be somehow initiated by chance somewhere along the way." It doesn't happen: Mick Jagger gets middle-aged and still the adults offer no response to the opening.

The prolongation of the initiatory moment—and the lack of response to it from adults—has everything to do, Ventura says, with the massive drug market in the United States.

Each of us has to know a great deal more about initiation than we do before we can meet this initiatory demand. But it wouldn't hurt to think.

An Overview of Classic Initiation

There are many sorts of initiation, many models, many sequences of rituals and teachings. All sequences of initiatory stages are linear, and initiation itself resembles a sphere. With that warning, we could look at a linear view of male initiation laid out in five stages. First, bonding with the mother and separation from the mother. (We do the first moderately well, and the second not well at all, particularly in the suburbs and the ghetto.) Second, bonding with the father and separation from the father. (We often postpone the father bonding until we are fifty or so, and then separation still has to be done.) Third, the arrival of the male mother, or the mentor, who helps a man rebuild the bridge to his own greatness or essence. King Arthur is an example of such a male mother. (This step happens haphazardly if at all.) Fourth, apprenticeship to a hurricane energy such as the Wild Man, or the Warrior, or Dionysus, or Apollo. When he has done well, the young man receives a drink from the waters of the god. (Such a drink is one thing the adolescents are asking for.) And finally, fifth, the marriage with the Holy Woman or the Queen.

The events of our story fit roughly into this model of classic initiation. Iron John represents the adult mentor who reconnects the boy to his greatness and to his "Gold Head." Iron John as Wild Man is also himself the divine energy from whose waters the boy is allowed to drink.

Having abandoned initiation, our society has difficulty in leading boys toward manhood. Mythologically, we can say that the Great Father in his primitive form blocks the young men on their path, and the Great Mother in her primitive form blocks the young men also. These blockages we have to add to our explanation of why we have so many boys and so few men. The main reason I think is our own ignorance of initiation, and our dismissal of its value.

The personal father who draws down through himself primarily the blessing, the orderly, and creative side of the Sacred King will be able to help his son pass through the initiatory stages joyfully. But we know that the Twisted or Poisoned side of the Sacred King will also be drawn down through the father. The Poisoned King will "lay his curse on the fairest joys" as Blake said, and by that means damage the son's generativity, self-esteem, and sexuality, so that he will be effectively blocked from the garden. Some fathers commit incest with their sons, some psychic incest. We have described this Twisted side of the Great Father at length in Chapter Four.

We need to look at the two sides of the Great Mother as well. From her positive side acceptance, nourishing, praise, and courage flow down to the son. But the Great Mother also has a Twisted or Poisoned side, for she too is an immense hurricane energy that puts her clawed hand through the wall. Sometimes that clawed hand takes the human part of the mother out, and leaves only the mechanical part that repeats psychic patterns well known to her grandmothers, great-grandmothers, and great-great-grandmothers. Our story sums up the possessive side of the Great Mother in a single idea: "It is necessary to steal the key from under the mother's pillow."

Marian Woodman asks us to distinguish between the conscious mother, who is aware of the power she exercises over son or daughter, and the unconscious mother, who keeps running Great Mother programs in her brain over and over, hardly distinguishing between partnership and domination.

The Twisted side of the Great Mother doesn't want the boy to grow up because if he does he will pass out of her realm. She doesn't curse him as the Twisted side of the Sacred King does, but she holds him.

The Celtic story called "Culwch and Olwen," which we touched on earlier, calls attention to a young man named Mabon, who is imprisoned under the water. Salmon can hear his weeping night and day. Culwch's companions tell Arthur that Culwch cannot complete his tasks until Mabon is rescued from his underwater prison, and that can't be done until Eidoel is brought down from his solitary tower, and that can't be done until the Great Salmon, the oldest living creature, has been found, and so on, and so on. The boy imprisoned under the water is the young male caught in the habitual possessiveness of the Great Mother. The personal mother does not do this jailing, but rather it is done by the Great Mother, to whom one's personal mother is receptive or transparent. We must repeat that it isn't the personal mother who imprisons the son—she wants him to be free. It is the possessive or primitive side of the Great Mother that keeps him locked up.

How the imprisoning takes place is described in other stories. One such story is the Russian tale called "The Maiden Tsar," in which a merchant's son, whose name is Ivan, loses his mother by death when very young. His father remarries, so that Ivan now has a stepmother. "Stepmother" is a code word in fairy tales for the Poisoned side of the Great Mother. A disturbing fact is told: the stepmother has fallen in love with Ivan. We could say that the Great Mother has fallen in love inappropriately with the uninitiated boy.

The father goes on a trip, and the tutor he has hired to teach Ivan takes the boy fishing on the bay. A number of boats appear far away, come closer, and on the largest boat there is a powerful golden-haired woman who greets Ivan as if she knows him. To his delight, she promises to return the next afternoon. She is called "The-Maiden-Who-Is-Also-a-Tsar." We recognize her as the Golden-Haired Woman. That night the stepmother gets the tutor drunk and finds out all that has happened. She gives the tutor a pin, and tells him to slip it into Ivan's collar as soon as the ships arrive in sight the next day, and that will put him to sleep. The tutor does exactly that; Ivan grows tired, lies down, and does not wake.

This act of the Great Mother, in collusion with the tutor, is more subtle than the father's curse, and it leaves no mark: as soon as the ships are gone, the tutor pulls the pin out; Ivan wakes up. But the boy's growth, or initiatory process, stops just before he is able to bring the wild flowers to the Holy Woman; it is stopped dead by the stepmother. During the moments crucial for his next step of consciousness, he was asleep.

I like it that the tutor, nominally male, and the stepmother, nominally female, do this bad-news work together. The story suggests by the word "tutor" that the educational system, which puts boys and girls to sleep for years, right up through graduate school, is in collusion with the dark side of the Great Mother. Essays on deconstruction theory are written by people with pins in their necks. Each of us knows enough about collectivized education to take this idea much farther. The colleges call themselves Alma Mater. And the negative matter in materialism puts whole nations to sleep.

Marian Woodman has referred to this pin as a "false phallus," inserted near the head. She associates it with certain kinds of intellectual conversations proceeding from her rationalist mind that the unconscious mother indulges in with her teenage son. Sometimes the intellectual ideas the mother brings to the son late at night are a blessing, sometimes not. Such a boy could end up years later isolated in a high mental tower.

But if the union takes place on a feeling level, he could end up imprisoned under the water where the salmon hear him weep night and day.

Our culture has paid attention in recent years, and rightly so, to men's physical incest with their daughters, which is hideous and revolting in its range and damage. And we have paid some attention to psychic incest as well between father and daughter. We are aware of a disturbing rise in the number of sons who report sexual abuse by mothers, as well as by fathers, uncles, and older brothers; but the culture still does not take very seriously the damage caused by psychic incest between mother and son.

Mari Sandoz in *These Were the Sioux* mentions that the young Sioux boy never—after the age of seven or so—looked his mother in the eyes. All requests were passed through his sister. "Would you ask Mother to repair these sandals?" "Dumbo wants his sandals fixed," and so on. When the task was finished, the mother did not hand the sandals to the son, saying, "Here are your sandals," but again, the object went around a circuitous route. Much sexual energy can be exchanged when the mother looks the son directly in the eyes and says, "Here is your new T-shirt, all washed."

Such precautions between mother and son seem absurd to us, unheard of, ridiculous, inhuman. And yet the Sioux men, once grown, were famous for their lack of fear when with women, their uninhibited conversations in the tepees, their ease in sexual talk with their wives. We recognize that the Sioux women were more aware of the possibilities of psychic incest between mother and son than we are.

I've mentioned that American mothers sometimes confide details of their private lives to their small sons, details that might better go to adults their own age. Frank disclosure is often better than silence, but it becomes harmful if the son feels he has to do something about it. The boy in many a kitchen gets drawn to his mother's side, and he says in some form those terrible words: "Mama, when I'm grown up, I'm going to have a big house for you, and you'll never have to work again."

Twenty to thirty percent of boys now live in houses with no adult male present; and most speak these words, silently or openly. But psychic incest is by no means restricted to single-parent homes. The emphasis placed in recent decades on the inadequacy of men, and on the evil of the patriarchal system, encourages mothers to discount grown men. Contemporary women have also become aware of their own rich interior lives. One could say that the European novel, a lovely phenomenon of the last two centuries, has taught more than one contemporary woman what a rich reservoir of impulses and longings she has in her soul that can be satisfied or remain unsatisfied. Few women say now, "The boundaries of my life are my husband's," or even think it. A twentieth-century woman feels complicated sensibilities in herself that no ordinary or mortal man can meet.

I am suggesting then that two contemporary trends have come together. One is the increasing emphasis in the American culture on the adult man's inadequacy, even his absurdity, and the second is the woman's increased awareness of her own interior emotional richness.

When these two trends come together, hope for change and fulfillment falls on young sons. The mother looks to the son for emotional satisfaction, and her fantasies in that regard may have deepened in recent years. It's not uncommon for grown men to turn to young women for sexual companionship; a grown woman may turn to her eight-year-old son for soul companionship. Her fantasies could include dreams that he will redeem the crudities of other men, that he will develop a mind open to women's values, and that she will have a soul companion in him. Perhaps in her fantasies he will live out some heroic scenario that she could not. Above all, she hopes he may learn to be kind to women, kinder than his father was, and will be able to satisfy his own woman sexually. In short, she will hope that he will become a better lover to "his woman" than his father was or is. Who could "his woman" be?

Hundreds of times one man or another has said to me that now, at forty or forty-five, he realizes that his task throughout his life has been to be a substitute husband, lover, and soul companion for his mother. He envisions himself as a white knight for womankind. If I ask such a man, "How do you feel about men?" he is likely to say, "I have never been able to trust them."

If we understand the second stage of initiation to be bonding with the father (and separation from the father), such a man is nowhere near that step. He does not trust men; and we guess that he would never trust the Wild Man enough to go off on his shoulders.

The boy who is called on by his mother too early feels helpless when he realizes that he is too small to do what is asked of him. His emotional energy is too fragmented to support his mother's needs, and his male confidence is far too unsteady for him to replace his father.

It isn't unusual for such a boy to feel himself a failure in relation to his father, with whom he has virtually no relationship. Then, when he doesn't save his mother, he feels a failure in relation to her as well. He begins life with a double failure.

One needs to be able to say these truths without laying a lot of blame on the mother, for Freud has already singled her out, wrongly, for the main responsibility. The whole initiatory tradition, of which Freud knew very little, lays the primary responsibility on men, particularly on the older men and the ritual elders. They are to call the boys away. When they don't do that, the possessive side of the Great Mother will start its imprisonment, even though the personal mother doesn't want the negative holding to take place. The mother often doesn't even see these things happen; but the boy sees them.

Out of shame over his inadequacy, and in some fear of being pulled over onto the mother's side before he has stabilized himself as a man, the boy finds in himself an inexplicable anger, a rage that prevents the mother's dream of a delicate man from becoming real. This anger may exhibit itself when the teenage son talks ugly to his mother in the kitchen. This is his private form of heavy-metal lyrics, bewildering to her. The inexplicable anger may turn up later in hundreds of other ways: isolation, workaholism, or the deeds of a thoughtless Don Juan or James Bond who rip off women sexually, and then demean them, or in the case of Bond, shoot them if they get in the way.

Placing high expectations on the small son, longing that he replace a defective father, which stops the male initiatory process at the earliest stage, is called "the stepmother falling in love with Ivan."

The lack of mythology, too, particularly the loss of Greek mythology in the culture at large, and the relegation of fairy tales to children, contributes to the inability of mothers to see what is happening. It's as if many women are shrewd about the dark or negative side of the Sacred King but naïve about the negative side of the Great Mother.

Recently an audience of very alert women, when asked for adjectives that touch on the Great Mother, offered a wonderful abundance of words: nourishing, moist, accepting, earthy, passionate, non-judgmental, gentle, supportive, loving. But no one said "unconscious." Women get little help in distinguishing between the positive side of the Great Mother and the negative side. We need people to remind men again and again how difficult it is to become a conscious father, and people to remind women how difficult it is to be a conscious mother. There is a part of a man or woman that is hidden even to himself or herself.

We know that there are many exceptions to what I've said, and all sorts of mothers and fathers. Some fathers are good to both sons and daughters; some mothers do not ask the sons or daughters to save them, or become their substitute marriage partners.

But when a son *is* called on too early, the one thing that boy did wrong is that he didn't save his mother. He didn't make her happier, or take away her pain. He failed to replace his (inadequate) father, and so the father is in shame, but the son is in guilt, because he should have been able to do it.

A traditional way of differentiating guilt from shame is this: Shame, it is said, is the sense that you are an utterly inadequate person on this planet, and probably nothing can be done about it. Guilt is the sense that you have done one thing wrong, and you can atone for it. Some sons called on too early will feel both shame and guilt.

We remember that Orestes, while being pursued by the Furious Invisible Women after he murdered his mother, bit off a finger and threw it at them; when they saw that, some of the black Furious Invisible Women turned white, and left him alone.

A traditional strategy, then, when one feels too much guilt is to bite off one part of your body, and throw it behind you. A man in guilt may decide to fail during the first half of his life. That's his punishment for not having saved his mother. Some men go into a profession they hate, having bitten off their joy, and only at fifty return to what they love. A man may marry "the wrong woman" in the midst of his guilt; another may become impotent. Still another may become a compulsive seducer, and so continue to feel guilt over never satisfying any woman's real emotional needs. Some men who fail to rescue their mothers become therapists, and attempt to rescue a woman over and over. They bite off the finger of their emotions, and listen to other people's emotions the rest of their lives. If the horse in our story had done that, he would have bitten off one of his own legs.

When a man finds himself unable to get the key from under his mother's pillow, perhaps he has loved his mother too much, or worried about her too long. When a man finds himself unable to descend into the ashes, or enter the garden, perhaps he has loved his father too much, or worried about him too long.

Not all men, then, move through the stages of initiation with the speed that Iron John's student does, who achieved a clean break with both mother and father early on. And what of the men who are really unlucky, the man who does not love his mother or his father, the man severely beaten or abused or forcefully abandoned? These are the suffering men whose pain is deeper than any of us can imagine.

Such a man becomes a cold-hearted survivalist, living in the Idaho of the mind with his dogs and an AK-47.

This survivalist man is fighting in some small Pacific island years after the war is over. His masculine beauty does not come out, and the rigid boundaries, the angry boy inside, the dead King, the robotlike interior soldiers, throw his family and his wife into despair. He is in despair himself. His mother did not protect him from his father, as he sees it, and his father did not protect him from his mother. In that state, the two hemispheres of his brain do not commune well with each other. He does not know what his feelings are; they do not come up into words. He can fall into wife-beating or violence at a traffic light in fifteen seconds, and that will only put him farther into despair.

How can a man get out of this mode, which leads to battering other nations and other people obsessively and destructively all his life? How can men, loved or unloved, get out of their monotonously aggressive mode? That is a question our whole nation has to ask in the wake of the cold war's collapse.

Our story says that such a man needs a male mother, in this world or in the eternal world, to whom he can bring his three-legged horse, and from whom he can receive a horse with all four legs.

The Story: Festival of Golden Apples

It's time to return to our story now. The young man we are watching, much luckier than most of us, has passed through the ashes and the garden and the battle. He rode to the battlefield on a whole horse lent to him by the Wild Man. He has returned his war-horse to the forest, and ridden home on his hobbledehoy to the jeers of the stable boys. But he knows what he has accomplished.

Why not end the story here? The young man, during the battle, has entered the realm of conflict joyfully, as if it were his proper territory. True warriors are precious, so much so that when a man has developed an inner and outer warrior, one is tempted to say, "This is enough." Living in the marvelous opposites of the midbrain, its dreamlike furies, its secret defenses of passion, its heightened adrenaline-inspired blood flow, a man can give spirit to the world, protect the community, and be in passion himself.

Men receive the warrior gift, that high ecstasy of service, from impersonal warrior mansions high in the genetic heavens; but there are things that life requires of us besides warriorhood. The ability to fight as well as to dance, which is evidence of wholehearted intent to be in the world, is not so savory when the man can only imagine another person or another country as an enemy, and cannot imagine any way of relating but to fight. Men as brilliant as Savonarola, Saint Ignatius of Loyola who founded the Jesuit Order, Karl Marx, General Patton, Nietzsche, and Ibsen have all gotten stuck in the warrior mode.

The warrior mode, moreover, has a poisoned or negative side. The warrior's twisted or poisoned side amounts to brutality, pillage, insistence on unconditional surrender, mindless killing, wife-beating, rape, betrayal of all the King's human values.

Men invigorated by warrior energy need the ability to modulate out of the warrior mode. We know that we can't end the story here because the release from aggression or the passage through has not yet appeared.

Returning to the story, we remember that the last section ended with the victory over the King's enemies. We guess that the King's daughter has become curious about the identity of that mysterious knight who saved the kingdom. We remember that she suspects that the gardener's boy is someone unusual. It occurs to her that the only way to find out if the gardener's boy is the mysterious knight is to invite all the knights in the neighborhood to come to the court for a festival, and so to show themselves.

> The King said to his daughter: "I'll arrange a great festival that will last three days, and you will be the one who throws out the golden apple. Perhaps the mysterious knight will appear."

After the announcement of the festival had been made,

the young man rode to the forest's edge and called for Iron John.

"What do you need?" he asked.

"I want to catch the golden apple the King's daughter is going to throw."

"There's no problem: you virtually have it in your hands right now," Iron John replied. "I'll provide you more: red armor for the occasion, and a powerful chestnut horse."

The young man galloped to the field at the proper time, rode in among the other knights, and no one recognized him. The King's daughter stepped forward, and she threw a golden apple into the group of men; and he was the man who caught it. However, having caught it, he galloped off and was gone.

When the second day arrived, Iron John had him fitted out with white armor, and provided for him a white horse. This time also the apple fell into his hands; once more he did not pause for even an instant, but galloped off.

That made the King angry, and the King said, "This behavior is not allowed; he is supposed to ride over to me and report his name."

"If he catches the apple the third time, and gallops off again," he told his men, "chase him. What's more, if he refuses to return, give him a blow; use your sword."

For the third day of the festival, Iron John gave the young man black armor and a black horse. That afternoon the young man caught the apple also. But this time, when he rode away with it, the King's men galloped after him, and one got close enough to give him a leg wound with the end of his sword. The young man escaped; but his horse made such a powerful leap to do so that the young man's helmet fell off, and everyone could see that he had golden hair. The King's men rode home and told the King everything that had happened.

Three themes or details in this passage seem to demand attention here: the meaning of the golden apples, the curious nature of this festival, and the sequence of three colors insisted on for the horses.

The Golden Apples

The golden apples in this story, as in many other stories, hint that the events are happening in some special space or time, that they are connected with ritual.

Paris had a golden apple to bestow, and we recall that he was asked to choose among Hera, Athene, and Aphrodite. The apple associates with immortality, and we know that some young men, when about to be sacrificed in the Greek ritual of Adonis, were given a golden apple as a passport to paradise. The word *paradise* means walled space in ancient Persian, and the Celts imagined paradise to be an apple orchard in the West where death is. This correlates with all sorts of details in old European life. For example, it is the apple that is bobbed for at Halloween, when the dead return to this world. Ritual banquets used to begin with the egg of the East, and end with the apple of the West. One more delicious detail about the apple is this: if one slices an apple transversely, one will see in the dark pips the sacred pentangle with its five points. That is the secret sign for the Holy Woman or Sophia. The apple is the earth; and the pentangle is its secret configuration. So Sophia is, in such thought, the soul of the earth.

We have a hint here that the King's daughter, the Woman Who Loves Gold, has chosen the boy to be a Sacred King.

It is natural that our story would now pass into ritual space. We notice that the knights do not fight during this festival: the fighting took place in the last section. The festival the King calls for does not involve javelins knocking men out of saddles, armor being pierced, sword blows that invade the intestines or take an arm off at the shoulder. Some change is being asked for in the expression of warrior energy. We could say that here the young man learns to modulate out of aggression through display, form, and ritual. The young men display their beauty as they pass in procession, and "luck" determines who gets the apple.

Threshold Space

Victor Turner, the anthropologist, has recovered in recent decades the almost forgotten concept of ritual space. Human beings enter and leave ritual space over a ceremonial threshold, or "limen." Such ritual space can also be called liminal space. Before one enters it, one undergoes some ritual preparation, and the physical spot also requires some preparation to set it apart. Inside that ceremonial place, both time and space become changed, different from what they are in a profane place.

Change or transformation can happen only when a man or woman is in ritual space. Entering, one first needs to step over a threshold, by some sort of ceremony; and second, the space itself needs to be "heated." A man or woman remains inside this heated space (as in Sufi ritual dance) for a relatively brief time, and then returns to ordinary consciousness, to one's own sloppiness or dullness.

The Catholic church remembered ritual space in the Latin mass, but for Protestants it fell into oblivion. With exceptions, Protestantism has spread its ignorance of ritual space everywhere in the world. Living in an age that has lost the concept, we can easily make two mistakes: we provide no ritual space at all in our lives, and so remain "cool"; or we stay in it too long. Some fundamentalists insist on remaining for forty years in ritual space without an exit—no sloppy humanness allowed. If a person enters no ritual space he or she remains soft clay; if one stays too long, the human being ends up as a cracked pot, overbaked and blackened.

Dionysus, it is said, founded Greek theater. We know that Dionysian initiation work took place in exquisitely maintained ritual space. Greek tragic theater amounts to a transfer of this elaborate ritual space to a public event.

Ritual space has several more characteristics. When we are in it, our desire energy does not rush forward toward its climax, whether that be orgasm or battle; but delight replaces fury, and a turn of phrase or a turn of a symbol replaces the turn of the sword.

We add that men and women in ritual space can become introduced to the unknown man or the unknown woman inside themselves. The King and his daughter instituted the festival be-cause—and this is a beautiful detail—they wanted to know who "the mysterious knight" was.

Lovemaking in India and Tibet sometimes goes on within ritual space. Religious teachers help a man and a woman to set up such a heated space in which the pair joins sexually, but in which neither man nor woman goes on to orgasm. The lovemaking may last two or three or four hours. Ceremonies, some very elaborate, prepare the space. The man prepares with knowledge and needs imaginative energy because his task is to visualize several goddesses in detail as he looks in the woman's eyes, and the woman prepares with knowledge and uses her imaginative energy to visualize sev-eral gods in detail as she looks into his eyes. The two persons ride on their instincts as on a horse; that horse holds them in ritual space, even if their instincts before that moment have enjoyed a lifetime of plunging on toward their goals.

Enjoying ritual space, then, is an intimate and imaginative act, and enjoying such space resembles being enclosed in a bowl or in a basket. Morris Berman has pointed out that museums characteristically present hard things, such as axes and spears, as evidence of early culture. But culture very likely begins with baskets made of reeds that are "soft" and hold emptiness.

Each person's interior emptiness, one could say, has its own shape. In ordinary life, we try to satisfy our longings, and fill the emptiness, but in ritual space, both men and women learn to experience the emptiness or the longing and not to fill it.

Such a man can be in the presence of innocence without moving to have sexual intercourse with it, enjoy his fierceness without acting it out physically, know his mother's neediness with-out moving to satisfy it. A warrior can enjoy the beauty of his sacred warriorhood without engaging in battle.

In the festival, each knight joins the other knights in a parade or display where there is no violence. Having moved into ritual space, he slows down his speed, gives grace to his movements, offers a bow to the King and Queen, pushes through no boundaries, offers no hostility, is there to be *seen*. We could say this graceful display moves the Princess to throw the apple—at precisely the right moment.

Biologists once thought that herons and geese created their puzzling ritual dances for fertility or survival reasons, that they were, in the word we use about ourselves, practical. But biologists in recent years, after extensive observation of herons, deer, geese, peacocks, and so on, have concluded that some ritual dances have no particular value for survival—they amount to *display*. Display embodies beauty and expressiveness often united with a zany grace. Human beings tend to display at the front end; we emphasize the beauty in the face, and the face becomes emotionally expressive. Deer, however, display at both ends: white-tailed deer show beauty in the facial area and in the anal area with their gorgeous tails. Heron dances, peacock strutting, stag processions can all be considered as artistic or superfluous displays.

Longing is expressed, beauty, high spirits. The energies that are caught there, held in a formal moment, activate something in other birds or animals watching. So the displays are activating dances. The events are meant to be seen.

Our culture allows certain displays, related to macho strutting, or cruising down the main street in large cars, that happen when the young man (or woman) is in the pre-warrior or warrior stage. Gangs exhibit a great deal of that sort of display. That is a part of adolescent fire, but it is not what I am talking of here.

Ritual space carries the young man out of machismo, out of battle, out of dominator fantasies. Blake called the highest stage of consciousness "constant creativity" or "The Shining City of Art." The golden apple lets one into the paradise of form. The knights in the festival participate in display as an expression of the love of form and beauty. It is closer to art than strutting. They are being led by ritual space away from war and toward community.

When an old Celtic warrior, such as Cuchulain, returned from battle, the whole community would take part in the ritual. Sometimes a group of women, his mother among them, would bare their breasts at him to awaken compassion, and the men would place him, still in the madness of the heated midbrain, into three tubs of water, one after the other, to cool him down. The first tub of water would vanish on contact, the second would boil away, and so on. We asked the Vietnam men to become soldiers. But there have been no ceremonies emphasizing compassion, no acknowledgment of heat, no honoring of a requested madness.

The Vietnam veterans would be in better shape today if we had arranged a festival in every small town in the country, in which the veterans had ridden by, and a young woman had thrown them golden apples. That parade would have honored their return to domestic life, and included them in ceremonies of the golden apples, thousands of years old.

The Vietnam era commanders had no ritual to help the veterans when they arrived home. The army flew them to New York and dumped them in the street. We all know what happened. More Vietnam men have now committed suicide since the war than died during it. The black wall in Washington is an attempt to remedy the failure; it is also a testimony to the army's lack of imagination, and to our reckless forgetting of all that men in the past knew about this supremely important change from warrior to non-warrior.

Many adolescent boys now are experiencing battle intensities in the cities. We meet these overheated young men with jail sentences or with averted eyes. They receive nothing, and more adolescents commit suicide every year. Soon we will need a black wall to evoke our ritual failures with adolescents.

We remember that the boy, during the enemy invasion, rode his three-legged horse to the forest edge, and exchanged it temporarily for the war-horse Iron John gave him. Though the story doesn't repeat the image, we assume that during the later festival, he each day rode his hobbledehoy to the forest as well. That has to be, because strange horses stabled in the horse barn would have been noticed.

If the three-legged horse, metaphorically, is his own body with one shamed leg, the young man exchanges his body three more times for a whole horse and experiences what it is like to ride to a display without shame. The heron and the peacock and the deer express in their vivid and outrageous display what the absence of shame is like. "The pride of the peacock is the glory of God," Blake says.

The contemporary man in the Kmart or the church basement or the lawyer's office has no Iron John from whom he can receive a four-legged horse. We know the young man has to return the borrowed horse, and yet the experience of inhabiting a body with no shame would teach him what pride is.

We guess that during the pause between the battle and this festival, the boy's interior warriors have become strong enough so that now he doesn't have to hide in corners and haystacks, but can appear at a public function. He is able to parade with other men, and call, so to speak, for the apple to be thrown.

A dear friend told me a story like that. This man's father fled the family in shame when his son was five, and the son felt for years shamed himself through this abandonment. In his twenties the son went to Japan and spent ten years studying the martial arts with a strong mentor. It was only after learning that art that he was able to return to his own family and take his rightful place there. To be without a supportive father is for a man an alternative phrase for "to be in shame." His support, as the boy's in our story, came from a substitute father—in his story, the martial mentor; in our story, Iron John. Only when a man's interior warriors are strong enough can he go into the joy of display.

With this strength he can also enter into the delight of form. Shapeless clothing, verse that is sloppy, chaotic furnishings: all are linked in secret ways to shame. The universe is not ashamed, and it delights in form. The sun rising over the ocean and setting in the ocean, the moon's lonely shinings and hidings, the leaves unfolding and falling are its displays.

Poetry is a form of display. The poet bird repeats vowels and consonants in order to widen his tail. Meter and counted syllables make up a peacock tail. The poem is a dance done for some being in the other world.

How sweet to weigh the line with all these vowels:
Body, Thomas, the codfish's psalm. The gaiety
Of form lies in the labor of its playfulness.
The sound counted, recounted, nourishes someone.

The delight in form, then, moves one away from the old duality of hero and enemy, right and wrong, male adversary and female adversary. When a man or a woman enters ritual space, each takes actions meant *to be seen,* and the joy of display helps pull energy away that would otherwise be invested in conflict. The knights who parade before the King's stands, patiently waiting to receive a "golden apple," are lovely emblems of the new stage in which the infinitive *to win* fades and is replaced by the infinitive *to be seen.*

Our festival, then, has taken place in ritual space. That space, heated by the Holy Feminine and the King, becomes hot enough to allow change. Warriorhood that has not been repressed or skipped over can modulate into beauty, delight, display, and art.

Riding the Red, the White, and the Black Horses

The story says that Iron John gave the young man a different colored horse, saddle, and armor on each of three successive days, and we sense that some information is being offered in that detail. All we can do is to investigate the three colors and their associations, and see what happens.

We recall that the Queen in "Snow White" was sewing one day near an ebony window frame as the snow fell outside; and when she pricked her finger, three drops of blood fell on the snow. She said, "I want a child as white as snow, as red as blood, and as black as this window frame." The fairy-tale hero or heroine, whether in Russian, German, or Finnish tales, who chances to see a drop of red blood fall from a black raven into the white snow, sinks immediately into a yogic trance. That suggests the vast power red, black, and white have or have had over human consciousness up through the Middle Ages.

We'll look briefly at both the African and European associations around red, white, and black. Victor Turner has gathered in his *Ritual Process* and *A Forest of Symbols* a great deal of information about the three colors in Africa. For the Ndembu tribe in Zambia, with which Turner lived for years, much in their religious system depends on distinctions suggested by these colors.

Red for the Ndembu is the blood of birth, menstrual blood, and blood shed by a weapon. The Ashanti add more associations to that: red for them stands also for red earth, and so earth cults; also for war and witchcraft and the sacrifice of men and beasts. European associations hover close to the African ones. Margaret Walker in her *Women's Encyclopedia of Myths and Secrets* names red as the "blood-red thread of life." Europeans also add anger to it: "He saw red." Red suggests bull-like rages. "Never wave a red cloth at a bull."

White for the Ndembu and Ashanti peoples calls up semen, saliva, water, milk, lakes, rivers, "blessing by flowing water," the sea, and priesthood. Turner says of the Ndembu: "Whiteness represents the seamless web of connection that ideally ought to include both the living and the dead. It is right relationship between people, merely as human beings, and its fruits are health, strength and all good things. 'White' laughter, for example, which is visibly manifested in the flashing of teeth, represents fellowship and good company" (*The Ritual Process*). Because of the association of white with semen, white suggests the masculine principle as red suggests the female principle. The opposition is not a simple one, however, because a white pullet means life and fertility, as against the red cock, which equals death and witchcraft. Turner says: "There is no fixed correlation between the colors and the sexes. Color symbolism is not consistently sex-linked, although red and white may be situationally specified to represent the opposition of the sexes."

For Europeans white retains the connection to blessing and to milk, and it does suggest some qualities of good fellowship and strength. It also calls up the purity of children and brides, and by extension persons with high moral purposes, such as the white knight, who fights for purity, the Virgin, and good.

Black is charcoal, river mud, and black fruits among the Ndembu, and it stands for badness and evil, the blackened corpse, suffering, having diseases, lack of purity, and for night and darkness. Turner adds that black also refers "to the concept of mystical or ritual death and to the related concept of the death of passion and hostility . . . for the Ndembu, 'to die' often means to reach the end of a particular stage of development 'through death to maturity.' " For Europeans, too, black means death and mourning. They add depression: "He is in a black mood." Also black suggests the left-hand path: "She is a black witch," or "He is a black magician." European and Egyptian alchemists' associations around black are very close to the Africans': black stands for crude matter, the "*prima materia*," lead, and Osiris' body when in the underworld.

The Great Mother Sequence

European fairy tales, when we examine them, insist on these three colors just as the Ndembu do, and in Europe, these three colors appear in a certain order. The best-known order or sequence of these colors is that mentioned in "Snow White": white, red, black. We can call this order the Great Mother sequence. White, red, black names the three phases of the moon: first the white of the Virgin as the New Moon; then the red of Motherhood as the Full Moon; and finally the black of the Crone as the Old Moon.

Barbara Walker, in her book on the Crone, goes over these three stages and their colors in great detail. We could say that each of us experiences innocence first, then love and battle, then death, destruction, and knowledge. The old Viking myths report that when a human being dies, three cocks crow—first the white cock, then the red cock, then the black cock. So we all travel that road and it is a broad one. It is the Great Mother road—white, red, black.

The Alchemists' Sequence

The alchemists, Egyptian or European, have the same three colors, but begin with black. First is the black of the *prima materia,* the black of lead, the black of matter utterly untouched by spirit or consciousness. They want the black to deepen. "The black beast" must come forward, the old texts say, before our growth starts. "Beauty and the Beast" says that as well.

In the second stage the black beast whitens, as the horizon before dawn slowly whitens. White here stands for a purification that is going on; imagination, spirit, and humor are developing. "But in this state of 'whiteness' one does not *live* in the true sense of the word; it is a sort of abstract, ideal state. In order to make it come alive it must have 'blood,' it must have what the alchemists call the *rubedo,* the 'redness' of life" (Jung).

The alchemists' third stage is the red of the rising sun. Now sulfur appears, flaring up, passion.

This is the path of men and women who want increased personality, more spirit, occult knowledge, who want spiritual lead to turn into spiritual gold. It begins maybe at forty-five, not at birth. We walk the lead–gold path at the same time we walk the life–death road.

The Masculine Sequence

Our story remembers the third road. If the Great Mother sequence lays out the feminine mysteries of life and death, and the alchemists' sequence lays out a neutral sequence, true for both men and women, then we could say that Iron John's sequence lays out the masculine mysteries of wounding and growth. This road begins with red. It goes red, white, black.

If the young woman begins with the white of innocence or the white dress of confirmation, the boy begins with red. Red is the color of Mars. The old men initiators among the Gisu and Masai in Africa lead the young "moran" men immediately into the red: the young men are encouraged to flare up, fight, see red, get into trouble; and in emotions they are encouraged to express pride, to be arrogant, antisocial, quarrelsome, and be friends with anger. The girls encourage them to fight. An elder guides each young man, so that the fights don't result in fatal wounds. The young man may stay in the red stage for ten or fifteen years. During that time, the girls make love with them but will never marry such a man, because he is still unfinished; he has no respect, the elders say, he is too red.

When a young man is red, he shows his anger, he shouts at people, he flares up like a match with a sulfur tip, he flushes red with anger, he fights for what is his, stops being passive, walks on the balls of his feet, is a red hawk, is fierce. Of course no one trusts a red man very far.

A great Russian fairy story called "Prince Ivan and the Fire-bird" provides a vivid scene for the start of the red. A young warrior rides along and suddenly sees on the forest floor a feather "that has fallen from the burning breast of the great Firebird." Metaphorically, it is a red feather.

His horse advises him not to pick it up, for if he does, it will bring trouble. The young man picks it up anyway. Since the feather has fallen from the breast of the Firebird, we know it is connected to the heart—it is burning, fiery. It calls to the man as a vocation calls or as initiation calls.

The Middle Ages paid a lot of attention to Iron John's sequence, and we can see this movement from the Red Knight to the White Knight to the Black Knight clearly in the adventures of Parsifal. When Parsifal leaves his mother's house, where there were no adult men, he is a clumsy, naïve fool. Almost immediately he kills the Red Knight and takes his armor—he himself becomes the Red Knight. How many misunderstandings he causes; how much rudeness and arrogance he has; how much antisocial behavior he indulges in during his Red Armor time! But without the red, no white.

We try these days to move young men by compulsory education directly from childhood into the White Knight.

And we could say that sometimes a mother wants her son to

be white when he is already in red. (Conversely, a man in midlife may want his wife to be white—and respectable—when she has already moved into red.)

We know that the Wild Man in our story gives the young man a red horse on the first day. The second day he gives a white horse. What shall we say about white?

A white knight is gleaming and shining. We usually make fun of that, but a white knight is also engaged. He fights for the good, and he is no longer randomly antisocial. Ralph Nader is a white knight; he engages the corporate world.

We remember that Saint George was riding a white horse and wearing white armor when he engaged the dragon. Looked at positively, we could say that going into white means that a man can have a relationship with the dragon. That doesn't imply killing the dragon. We know that the Christian crusaders, who found the Saint George and the dragon myth in Palestine, distorted it on returning home. In some old versions the dragon transforms into a woman, or gives treasure; he transforms himself. The dragon in the old myths is not evil. He's a dark water-energy, a little regressed maybe, but his hunger is old and understandable.

A typical Celtic hero gets into a relationship with a dragon by throwing loaves of bread into his mouth. Of course he has to throw accurately, so we could say that some precision and skill enters with white.

The danger with the white knight stage in our culture is that he is often insufferable because he has not lived through the red. White knights in our culture support the cold war and project bad redness out onto the American Indians, or red communists, or wild women, or black men. If a man hasn't lived through the red stage, he is a stuck white knight who will characteristically set up a false war with some concretized dragon, such as Poverty or Drugs. The Bush-Dukakis debate was the sad debate of two stuck white knights. Such debates will be remarkably boring.

We could say that the moment the young Russian rider picked up the feather from the Firebird, he was already on his way, as the horse knew, to the black.

On the third day Iron John gives the young man in our story

a black horse, with black saddle, black bridle, black armor. He is riding his black horse when he makes his decisive descent into woundedness, and is wounded "by the King's men."

We can see increasing darkness at the edges of Rembrandt's paintings as he gets older. If you place in order Lincoln's photographs during his last four years, you can see him go into the black. People who are in the black usually give up blame. A mother once got into the White House and woke Lincoln up at five in the morning, saying that her son had been sent by train to Washington a few days before, had had no sleep, had been assigned to guard duty on arriving, had fallen asleep, and now was going to be shot at eight that morning. If Lincoln had been in the red, he might have shouted for the guards, "Who let this woman in here? Get her out of here!" If he were in the white he might have said, "Madam, we all have to obey rules. Your son didn't obey the rules, and I feel as bad about it as you do, but I can't intervene." He didn't say either of those things. He said, "Well, I guess shooting him wouldn't help him much," and he signed a piece of paper. We notice that humor comes in with the black.

If we take nothing else away from the Iron John story, we could usefully take this idea that the young male moves from red intensity to white engagement to black humanity. Each man is given three horses that we ride at various times of our lives; we fall off and get back on.

I don't think we should consider one horse better than another; all we could say is that none should be skipped. We need three skills, for each horse has its own sort of gait; each horse shies at different things, responds to a rider differently.

Teachers and parents often tell us to skip the red horse. Some men did not live through the red in adolescence. Such a man then will have to go back to red later, learn to flare up, and be obnoxious when he is forty.

Ministers often find themselves forcibly confined to white because they skipped red, and their congregations won't let them go back to it. But then they can't go forward into black. Politicians have to look white, while actually being God-knows-what color. Anwar Sadat undoubtedly got to the black while in prison; more politicians probably should be put in prison. It would probably be good for poets as well.

When a person moves into the black, that process amounts to bringing all of the shadow material, which has been for years projected out there on the faces of bad men and women, communists, witches, and tyrants, back inside. That process could be called retrieving and eating the shadow.

Robert Frost ate a lot of his shadow, which is certainly a part of his greatness. He talks of the shadow in his marriage. A husband and wife are driving through the woods in a buggy pulled by a single horse. Suddenly a man steps out of the trees and stabs the horse to the heart. The couple, Frost says, were "The most unquestioning pair that ever accepted fate."

We assumed that the man himself
Or someone he had to obey
Wanted us to get down
And walk the rest of the way.

A man then who goes into the black has to "walk the rest of the way." It takes a long time to move into the black. How many years pass before a man finds the dark parts of himself that he threw away? When he does find those parts, and retrieves them, other people will begin to trust him.

When he is able to ride on the black horse, then the horse itself will carry him to the place where the King's men wound him. At that instant his golden hair falls down over his shoulders so that everyone will know who he is . . . but that's another part of the story.

CHAPTER EIGHT

The Wound by the King's Men

Something is left over from the story of the festival with the golden apples, and that is the wound to his leg the young man has just received.

> That afternoon the young man caught the apple also. But this time, when he rode away with it, the King's men galloped after him, and one got close enough to give him a leg wound with the end of his sword. The young man escaped; but his horse made such a powerful leap to do so that the young man's helmet fell off, and everyone could see that he had golden hair. The King's men rode home and told the King everything that had happened.

> We all feel something mysterious and weighty around this leg wound. It represents something we half remember.

A Wound to the Genitals

With Freud fresh in our minds, we would probably assume first that there is a sexual wound lurking in all of this. It's always possible that leg is a euphemism for genitals. We know that the Fisher King, the most famous of all the Arthurian wounded men, had received some sort of genital wound. Parsifal, in Chretien de Troyes' version, asks his female cousin about that, and she says:

"Good sir, he is a King, I assure you, but he was wounded and maimed in a battle so that he cannot move himself. For a javelin wounded him through the two thighs. He is still in such pain that he cannot mount a horse, but when he wishes to divert himself, he has himself placed in a boat and goes fishing with a hook; therefore, he is called the 'Fisher King.' "

Some commentators report that he has a piece of iron lodged in the testicles. Iron is usually associated in fairy stories with the imprisonment of men—as glass is with the imprisonment of women. The Fisher King's sexuality is then somehow in prison, or iron has wounded it. But no one is sure what "wounded sexuality" means. It's possible that by the eleventh century Rome's hostile attitude toward sexuality had finally reached the Celtic countryside. The Fisher King could no longer "mount a horse"—the old vulgar sexuality had been dismissed, put away.

Because our story is probably pre-Christian by several centuries, I doubt if the Fisher King's constant pain applies to this story. The story doesn't suggest anxiety about sexual functions. I think the explanation of the wound lies elsewhere; that is to say, it is a leg wound more than a "thigh" wound.

A Wound That Lames

There is nothing like a wound in the head, or in the shoulder, or in the chest to concentrate your attention on head, shoulder, or chest. The new wound acts to concentrate the young man's attention on his thigh. As our story has proceeded, the young man has become more and more in touch with underworld treasures—its ashes, its armed men, its horses—and now the young man is sent, so to speak, to the lower half of his own body.

There is a vivid wound in the Grimm brothers story called "The Water of Life." A young man goes through an elaborate set of trials in trying to bring back "the water of life" to save his sick father. A princess tells him where the fountain is, and that he must draw the water before the clock strikes twelve. He succeeds in getting the water. "Just as he was passing through the iron gate, the clock struck twelve, and the gate slammed with such force that it took off a piece of his heel." A leg wound again close to the end of the story—and we would guess that it will slow him down.

A wounded leg affects locomotion. It's as if the boy's first wound, to his finger, sped him up, and this one slows him down, way down. The old tradition says that feeling is associated with slowness. Perhaps this wound deepens his feeling.

Jacob, once the fast and slippery one, so clever in his head that he could trick Esau, later is called on to wrestle with God, and during that mismatch he suffers a dislocation of the upper leg, after which he walks with a limp. An old tradition says that Jesus walked with a limp, a legend Robert Graves mentions in *King Jesus*.

We could speak of grounding here, in the sense that a copper wire goes straight down into the earth itself. Does a wounded leg give one a better connection to earth? Oedipus' pinned-together ankles would seem to have provided a poor connection for him in infancy. But later he gets grounded. After he blinds himself, he walks slowly, being led through the Holy Grove by his daughters. The connection with earth is so good that on his death the ground opens and he disappears into it.

We remember that Hephaestus also had a limp. People in early times thought blacksmiths were dangerously magical and precious because they dared to melt metal, and some tribes it seems deliberately lamed their blacksmiths in order to keep them from wandering off to some other tribe. Such a blacksmith gets "grounded," as we "ground" a child if he stays out too late.

Some old traditions say that no man is adult until he has become opened to the soul and spirit world, and they say that such an opening is done by a wound in the right place, at the right time, in the right company. A wound allows the spirit or soul to enter. James Hillman, referring to Hans Castorp in *The Magic Mountain,* and the spot of tuberculosis on Castorp's lung, says, "Through the little hole of his wound, the immense realm of the spirit enters."

People too healthy, too determined to jog, too muscular, may use their health to prevent the soul from entering. They leave no door. Through the perfection of victory they achieve health, but the soul enters through the hole of defeat.

The Persian poet, Rumi, sums all this up beautifully in his poem about the lame goat.

> *You've seen a herd of goats*
> *Going down to the water.*
>
> *The lame and dreamy goat*
> *brings up the rear.*
>
> *There are worried faces about that one,*
> *but ah, now they're laughing, because look,*
>
> *as they return,*
> *that goat is the leader!*
>
> *There are many different kinds of knowing.*
> *The lame goat's kind is a branch*
> *that traces back to the roots of Presence.*
>
> *Learn from the lame goat,*
> *and lead the herd Home.*
>
> —from *Mathnawi*, III, 114–1127
> *Translated by Coleman Barks*

The Boar Wound That Kills Adonis

The detail of the wounded leg leads us in an entirely different direction if we remember the ritual woundings of Adonis and Attis. Sir James Frazer sets out in *The Golden Bough*, particularly in the volume called *Adonis, Attis, Osiris*, the results of his enormous research on this matter. We know that in the Cybele, Inanna, Venus, and Isis cultures of the Mediterranean and Mesopotamian areas, the Boy-Who-Would-Be-Wounded was imagined to be the Great Mother's lover and, at the same time, her son.

The boy's double role is easier to grasp if we understand that at that time all vegetation—flowers, grass, wheat, grapes, lettuce—was imagined to be male. Since we say "Earth Mother," we, if we think of it at all, assume that vegetation is female. For them it was male.

The earth lives through the year; the leaves fall. The earth lives forever; the "vegetable world" dies. The Great Mother, like the earth, lives on and on, year after year, but the green vegetation dies in summer heat and again in winter cold. In order for the human world and the natural world to move in harmony, the religious establishment in those cultures arranged for a boy to be sacrificed on June 21 and again on December 21. The boy, a sort of magic boy, grew up and was cut down. In sympathy, people would grow flowers in shallow pots with little soil, called "Gardens of Adonis." Such gardens were pots of short-lived flowers, such as lettuce and fennel, which grow quickly, and as Ad de Vries remarks in his *Dictionary of Symbols and Imagery* are tended "for eight days, and then allowed to wither, in order to be thrown into the sea with the image of Adonis . . . the gardens were often on the roofs." "The Gardens of Adonis last but a day" was a line in an old tune.

> *Time, like an ever-rolling stream*
> *Bears all its sons away.*

The young man, chosen ritually and sacrificed ritually, received in some areas the name Adonis, in other areas Attis, in parts of Greece Hyacinthus, in Mesopotamia Tammuz. He was an uninitiated boy; he had no resource of energy comparable to the Great Mother, and he died while she lived.

Robert Graves has a great deal to say about this ritual, but I don't believe, as he sometimes seems to, that this was a great conspiracy of Great Mother priestesses to humiliate and sacrifice men. Men and women both, in their religious longing that "what is below shall be like what is above," prepared and carried out the ritual. I do not see it as part of a war between men and women.

We have forgotten these events. The sacrifices have dropped into oblivion, but historians of the time, buoyed by thousands of references in ancient literature, make clear that the death wound was given by a boar. The boar, with his curved moon-tusk, gave Adonis a wound in the genital area, and that wound was fatal.

In very ancient Greek times, the temple probably arranged a fatal boar hunt. The boar arrives straight out of nature, and carries in his face, tusks, powerful legs and neck, and unpredictable motions, the terror of impetuous forces in nature such as floods, firefalls, waterfalls, wind-weather. His tusk has a beautiful curve, like a breaking wave, or the new moon, or the harvester's scythe.

Tales of young men wounded by boars are thousands of years old. We know those tales go back to the layer of European culture around the wild pig and the domesticated pig. The pig was the earliest domesticated animal, and the pig culture was succeeded by a layer of sheep culture and for some a layer of cattle culture. Myths were often rewritten as the symbolic animal changed.

John Layard, who spent years living among the Stone Age culture of Malekula, found to his surprise that Malekulan culture was still absorbed fully in the pig and boar culture that Europe had passed through centuries before. The Malekulan people expressed all their symbolic and religious ideas through the life and habits of swine and, one could say, experienced all their transcendence through the boar. The boar acts then in Greece as a holy animal.

This is how Ovid describes the attack on Adonis:

> But the young hunter
> Scorned all such warnings, and one day, it
> happened,
> His hounds, hard on the trail, roused a wild boar,
> And as he rushed from the wood, Adonis struck him
> A glancing blow, and the boar turned, and shaking
> The spear from the side, came charging at the
> hunter,
> Who feared, and ran, and fell, and the tusk
> entered
> Deep in the groin, and the youth lay there dying
> On the yellow sand.

> —from *Metamorphoses*, Book 10
> *Translated by Rolfe Humphries*

Scholars believe that in later Greek times, a priestess or priest, dressed in a boar mask and carrying the harvester's scythe, gave the ritual wound to the boy's belly or genitals, and he bled to death. It appears also that the young man received a golden apple before the ritual, so that he could be admitted to the paradise in the West.

This sacrifice is shocking only to those who have not read the extensive literature. Margaret Walker, who is sober and reliable, says about Adonis in her *Encyclopedia of Women's Myths and Secrets*:

> Adonis: Greek version of Semitic Adonai, "The Lord," a castrated and sacrificed savior-god whose love-death united him with Aphrodite, or Asherah, or Mari. In Jerusalem, his name was Tammuz. . . .
>
> Another form of the same god was Anchises, castrated: "gored in the groin" by Aphrodite's boar-masked priest. His severed phallus became his "son," the ithyphallic god Priapus, identified with Eros in Greece. . . . Castrating the god was likened to reaping the grain, which Adonis personified.

We recall that "Abraham" stopped the sacrifice of "Isaac," which we presume had been going on for centuries. During Abraham's time Palestine was living in the sheep culture, so a ram was substituted instead.

This whole area lies much in shadow, and very few people talk about it. We do know that at some time, different in each of the cultures studied, the boar wound stops being fatal.

The Boar Wound That No Longer Kills

Bruno Bettelheim made a detailed study of aboriginal initiation rituals and summed up some of his findings in *Symbolic Wounds*. According to Bettelheim, the aborigines say that the Great Mother instituted certain rituals belonging to male initiation. Only later, apparently, did the men take them over.

When the old men do take over a ritual, they hold to the

basic ceremony, but the mood of it changes. If the old form, in their view, weakened men, the new form may strengthen them. Keeping that model in mind, it's possible to imagine that the old men initiators in Greece took over the boar ritual and altered it so that the sacrifice of the young men stopped.

The Odyssey in fact announces that such a time has come. Odysseus' adventure with a boar when he was a boy, which Homer reports, would be important then. Odysseus, the story says, was hunting boar "with his grandfather," which suggests that the entire ritual was now under the care of the old men. Homer tells the story in the nineteenth book of The Odyssey, and Robert Fitzgerald phrases it this way:

> Patter of hounds' feet, men's feet, woke the boar
> as they came up—and from his woody ambush
> with razor back bristling and raging eyes
> he trotted and stood at bay. Odysseus,
> being on top of him, had the first shot,
> lunging to stick him; but the boar
> had already charged under the long spear.
> He hooked aslant with one white tusk and ripped
> out
> flesh above the knee, but missed the bone.
> Odysseus' second thrust went home by luck,
> his bright spear passing through the shoulder joint;
> and the beast fell moaning as life passed away.

We could say that we have two kinds of men by this time: those men whom the boar kills, and those men whom the boar only scars. There are men who do not survive an encounter with the negative side of the Great Mother, and there are men who do. When the fight takes place under the care of the old men—the grandfathers—the boar attack only leaves a scar. The man himself remains alive, and, when old, is cunning like Odysseus and full of knowledge.

The boar ritual began as a killing of an uninitiated boy, and it changed into a ceremony that marked a late and decisive stage in the initiated man's ordeal. This alteration reminds us of a development that Osiris went through in Egyptian religion, which contributed to the stability of Egypt. Osiris, once imagined as the son of Isis, became her "brother" and "husband."

Odysseus, as James Hillman has pointed out, is not a one-sided hero, like so many Greek heroes who flare up and die out as shallow flowers. Odysseus surprises us with his strength in the male line: he gives honor to his own father and a great deal of warmth to his son. Mythologically, Odysseus unites in himself the adventuresome young man, the "puer," and the steady old man, the "senex."

It is interesting that when the Romans translated *The Odyssey,* they gave Odysseus the name *Ulixes,* which some believe to be a union of *oulas,* wound, and *ischea,* thigh. Ulysses' name, then, becomes, literally, thigh wound. He receives the wound and lives. The Romans must have felt this detail in Odysseus' life to be very important.

Later in *The Odyssey,* in the twenty-fourth book, there is a marvelous scene in which Odysseus returns secretly to Ithaca, and stays in the swine herder's hut (pigs again). His old nurse washes the traveler, and when she sees the wound in the thigh, suddenly realizes who he is. The new sort of man can be recognized through the scar on his thigh.

Something beyond the ordinary then is happening when the King's men wound the young man in the leg. We can make a distinction now between the boar wound that takes the boy to paradise and the boar wound that leaves him with a scar on his thigh. If we have that scar, our "old nurse" can recognize us. Others can see who we are, but our own eyesight apparently is also clearer.

It is likely that in "Iron John" we are dealing with an initiatory wound, perhaps a wound given physically by old men initiators at some time in the past. We can speculate that the mentors gave a young man a thigh wound at some late stage of initiation. Odysseus, as we mentioned, has the scar of such a wound, and we know that he was the initiated man; for example, he is "the thirteenth" in his band as they visit Circe.

What is a scar? The native Americans have a magnificent

tradition about scars, which Lame Deer alludes to briefly in his autobiography. I have heard the tradition said this way: "When you die, you meet the Old Hag, and she eats your scars. If you have no scars, she will eat your eyeballs, and you will be blind in the next world." That story moves awfully fast but it certainly defends the value of scars.

If one has no scars, one becomes blind in the next world, but perhaps the man without scars is blind also in the imaginative world. Odysseus gives evidence that his scar helps him to see, for as he travels from one mysterious island to the next, the men with him get crushed by rocks, or eaten by the Cyclops, or turned into pigs (pigs again!) by Circe; he sees something they don't, and he lives through these dangers, though just barely.

It seems to me, then, that the wound the young man receives from the King's men is not specifically a sexual wound; and the wound goes farther than a simple laming, which it also is. It hints at an initiatory ritual administered by old men which we have forgotten. Apparently the leg wound, when accomplished ritually, or done in threshold space, strengthened young men. We will look at what sort of strength that may have been.

The Wound As Male Womb

Dionysus, we recall, was born from Zeus' thigh. Because Dionysus' destiny was to be "A Man with Two Mothers," Zeus' thunderbolt ended his stay in Semele's womb. One story says that Hermes saved the unborn boy, and sewed him up inside Zeus' thigh. The story has much magical thinking in it, but we notice the opening in Zeus' thigh. Another story says that Zeus himself made the opening in his own thigh in order to provide a womb for Dionysus.

This sort of thinking is thousands and thousands of years old. André Leroi-Gourhan, who spent years studying the enigmatic Dordogne cave paintings, concluded that the famous scene of the wounded mammoth, the shaman in trance, and the bird-headed wand, amounts to a study of "the wound." We know from Siberian sources that the shaman must needs be a wounded man, and a spear gave Christ a wound in his side before his death.

Leroi-Gourhan speculates that the Dordogne painters are using a visual language whose visual "words" are multiple. For example, a spear when drawn is also a phallus, so that a pictured wound is also a vulva. To receive a spear, then, is, in Dordogne art, to have a vulva, or to receive a womb.

Shakespeare with his staggering genius understood the parallel well. His first long poem was "Venus and Adonis," and it tackles head-on this old Mediterranean story of male sacrifice. Shakespeare presents Venus as an older hot-blooded woman, and Adonis as a young, hot, and unpracticed boy. At her urging, they make love, but those readers who recognize classical mythology know that a boar hunt is coming. The boar attacks Adonis and somehow turns his thigh into a woman's thigh. This is how Shakespeare says it:

> *'Tis true, 'tis true; thus was Adonis slain;*
> *He ran upon the boar with his sharp spear,*
> *Who did not whet his teeth at him again,*
> *But by a kiss thought to persuade him there;*
>   *And nuzzling in his flank, the loving swine*
>   *Sheath'd, unaware, the tusk in his soft groin.*

Shakespeare calls attention to a strange thing: it is as if the boar is to the young man as a man is to a woman. The boar in fact opens a sexual passage; he creates a sheath; the young man receives a female opening:

> *Sheath'd, unaware, the tusk in his soft groin.*

The passage is stunning to me: secret knowledge is hinted at here. The union of sheath and wound appears by the lightest possible touches, accomplished by Shakespeare's amazing genius in being able to turn an image just to the side.

The "loving" boar, then, resembles Zeus' own knife, or Hermes' knife; it opens a wound in Adonis' thigh that resembles the womb created in Zeus' thigh. And we recall the association of Dionysus with this very wound.

The Wound As a Man's Commitment to the God of Grief.

Dionysus, we note, is the Greek god most connected with wounds and woundedness. The Titans, the myth says, gave Dionysus a mirror when he was an infant, and then while he was distracted tore him apart and ate him. As we mentioned earlier, he was reconstituted from the heart, which the Titans overlooked. Some of the other Greek gods, Apollo and Zeus, for example, stand for wholeness, radiance, and sun-like integrity; but Dionysus stands for the ecstasy that can come from tearing and being torn. The ecstatic wine comes only if the cluster of grapes is torn apart, trampled, enclosed.

Dionysus is the clump of grapes that hands tore apart in the Greek villages and threw into the wine vat. When the men and women were tramping on those grapes, it is known that they would sing: "O Dionysus, I did not know, I did not know." When cattle culture came to Greece, the village people ritually killed a bull in the spring, and as they ate the raw flesh, spoke the name "Dionysus" over and over. Ethical philosopy wants Apollo, morality, and perfection. The pagans want tearing and ecstasy.

W. B. Yeats, writing late in his life, imagines an argument between a Catholic bishop who wants sinlessness and a gypsy wild woman named Crazy Jane. Yeats has her say to the bishop:

"A woman can be proud and stiff
When on love intent:
But love has pitched his mansion in
The place of excrement;
For nothing can be sole or whole
That has not been rent."

That expresses beautifully the pagan and Dionysian praise of tearing and being torn; and the tiny explosion that happens in the head during the last four lines is a testimony to Yeats' greatness, but also to the power of this old pagan idea.

I think we have said as much as we can now about the leg wound. We conclude that some young men in the past, presumably those guided by the old men, became more and more like evergreens and less like spring flowers. They did not die when wounded, but took a wound, and survived with a scar. *The Odyssey,* which remembers all that men and women have learned about the Great Father and the Great Mother during a hundred thousand years, amounts to an announcement that this sort of man is now in the world.

Moreover, the leg wound that the King's men gave has created, according to the fantasy human beings have carried for centuries, a womb inside the male body. No one gets to adulthood without a wound that goes to the core. And the boy in our story does not become King without that wound.

The old tradition says that women have two hearts: one heart in their chest and another heart in their womb. They are doublehearted.

The old initiators then make the young man, through the wound given in ritual space, double-hearted. Now the man has the physical heart he has always had, but also a compassionate heart. He has a double heart. We'll see from the story how that comes about.

The Story: Asking for the Bride

The King's daughter the next day inquired to the gardener about his boy. "He's back at work in the garden. That strange coot went to the festival yesterday, and only got back last night. He showed my children, by the way, three golden apples he had won."

The King called the young man in, and he appeared with his tarboosh back on his head. The King's daughter, however, went up to him and pulled it off, and his golden hair fell down over his shoulders; his beauty was so great that everyone was astounded.

The King said, "Are you the knight who appeared

each day at the festival with a different color horse, and each day caught the golden apple?"

"I am," he said, "and the apples are here." Taking the apples from his pocket, he handed them to the King. "If you need more evidence, you can look at the wound that your men gave me when they were chasing me. What's more, I am also the knight who helped defeat the enemy."

"If you can perform feats of that magnitude, you are obviously not a gardener's boy. Who is your father, may I ask?"

"My father is a notable King, and I have a great deal of gold, as much as I will ever need."

"It's clear," the King said, "that I am in debt to you. Whatever I have in my power that would please you, I will give."

"Well," the young man said, "I'd suggest that you give me your daughter as my wife."

Then the King's daughter laughed and said, "I like the way he doesn't beat around the bush; I already knew he was no gardener's boy from his golden hair." And so she walked over and kissed him.

The young man called in by the King knows that the time of golden hair has come. His golden hair fell down around his shoulders when he was wounded, and now it falls down once more as he stands in the King's presence. It's all right because the holy moment has come. Whatever happens in that moment is right.

The young man repeatedly has put the covering back on his head, following the principle: hide your gold when you are young. We recall that he gave away the gold coins; he declined the public praise after his victory over the King's invaders; he refused the public acknowledgment each time the golden apple went to him. Why is it all right now for him to let the hair flow, show the golden apples, accept reward for saving the kingdom?

A connection with the feminine is also right. The young man's walk on an exlusively masculine path has now ended. The Wild Man, who is a **god** of nature, has guided the young man's initiation. Iron John's teaching never aimed at masculine separation, or separatism anyway, and we will soon see how deeply and in how many different ways the progress of our story involves partnership with the feminine principle. In nature, the yang and the yin interweave everywhere; nature is inconceivable without the incessant and joyful intermingling of receptivity and initiative, curiously mingled in all snail shells and oak trees, all tigers, all mountains, all bees.

Time moves more swiftly in a fairy tale than with us; and the man in earth time would be about fifty years old now, or older. Some flower has finally unfolded and blossomed; the golden salmon have laid their eggs; the young man has received through his descent a grounding that allows him to reconnect with some creativity that would have frightened him when he was younger.

Fairy tales say that we each bring with us at birth certain golden rings or spindles or memories of glory that assure us we have a transcendent or grand side. But life in a family takes that assurance out of one fast; and each of us goes through a shaming time or deprivation time. Men and women during this time live depressed, know nothing of golden thoughts, get trampled by horses, run over by large semis, are thoroughly parted from esteem. The crown is put away, locked in a chest, lost in the cellar, stolen by thieves, gone. "We are the hollow men, alas."

But all during that time, if we are lucky, the bridge is being rebuilt. Who has the design, who the architect is, who makes the bricks or the steel beams, no one knows for sure, and it is different for each person anyway. But, eventually, at fifty or fifty-five, we feel a golden ring on the finger again.

Most psychological systems don't want any expression of masculine grandeur. All talk of grandeur is inflation, and all crowns are to be left in the dust. Our story carries from its outset a different view. It holds that human self-esteem is a delicate matter, and not to be dismissed as infantile grandiosity. Our "mirrored greatness" as Heinz Kohut calls it, needs to be carefully honored, neither inflated nor crushed. If a man's or a woman's "mirrored greatness" is entirely dismissed, he or she will be crippled, and a candidate for all sorts of invasions by the group mind.

Kabir says:

Inside this clay jug there are canyons and pine mountains
And the maker of canyons and pine mountains.
All seven oceans are inside,
And hundreds of millions of stars.
  Translated by R.B.

The young man in our story has become a friend of the Wild Man and has received a drink of that luminous water. He has not lost his connection to the King. The Warrior has offered him a cup. Hermes has given him a sip from time to time.

All of this rebuilding of the bridge, all of this honoring of the great self, all of this distribution of the waters that satisfy thirst, has been, in our story, under the Wild Man's guidance. Perhaps now it is time to ask, "Who is this Wild Man?"

The Wild Man and His Qualities

Western man's connection with the Wild Man has been disturbed or interrupted for centuries now, and a lot of fear has built up. "Every angel is dangerous," Rilke says, so some fear is appropriate. But knowing nothing is not appropriate.

Rather than looking outside for a Wild Man, though, we could look at the traces that remain inside us. One trace of the Wild Man is the spontaneity we have preserved from childhood. No matter how many family reunions we have participated in, or how many committee meetings we have attended, funny little motions of the shoulders and weird cries are waiting inside us. When we are in a boring conversation, we could, instead of saying something boring, give a cry. We can never predict what will come out; and once it is out, we leave it to the others to interpret, no apologies or explanations. Little dances are helpful in the middle of an argument as are completely incomprehensible haikus spoken loudly while in church or while buying furniture. Rudeness and sarcasm may be savage, but the unexpected is not savage.

When the Wild Man has been preserved inside, a man also feels a genuine friendliness toward the wildness in nature. A Concord woman set down a description of Emerson, Hawthorne, and Thoreau ice skating. Emerson leaned forward as if breasting the wind, Hawthorne skated like an immensely calm statue, and Thoreau gave little leaps and pirouettes constantly. Gerard Manley Hopkins, always making unexpected sounds, said:

> *What would the world be, once bereft*
> *Of wet and of wilderness? Let them be left,*
> *O let them be left, wildness and wet;*
> *Long live the weeds and the wilderness yet.*

Thoreau said, "In literature it is only the wild that attracts us." It is the Wild Man who is protecting the Spotted Owl. The Wild Man is the male protector of the earth.

I think we are remembering the Wild Man now—and women are remembering the Wild Woman and other Invigorators—because men and women need now, more than ever in history, to protect the earth, its creatures, the waters, the air, the mountains, the trees, the wilderness. Moreover, when we develop the inner Wild Man, he keeps track of the wild animals inside us, and warns us when they are liable to become extinct. The Wild One in you is that one which is willing to leave the busy life, and able to be called away.

> *The strong leaves of the box-elder tree,*
> *Plunging in the wind, call us to disappear*
> *Into the wilds of the universe,*
> *Where we shall sit at the foot of a plant,*
> *And live forever, like the dust.*

The Wild Man, we could also say, represents the positive side of male sexuality. The hair that covers his whole body is natural like a deer's or a mammoth's. He has not been clean shaven out of shame, and his instincts have not been so suppressed as to produce the rage that humiliates women. The Wild Man's sexuality does not feed on the feminine or pictures of the feminine; it resonates also to hills, clouds, and ocean. The native American has much Wild Man in him, and it comes out in love of ordinary things. Lame Deer mentions over and over in his autobiography that the Indian experiences the divine in a bit of animal hide, in mist or steam, and in ordinary events of the day. A Chippewa wild woman wrote this little poem:

Sometimes I go about pitying myself,
And all the time
I am being carried on great winds across the sky.

The Wild Man is the door to the wildness in nature, but we could also say the Wild Man is nature itself. The same has to be said of the Wild Woman. Hermes, Apollo, the Virgin may be above nature, but the Wild Man *is* nature.

The Wild Man encourages and amounts to a trust in what is below. The Wild Man encourages a trust of the lower half of our body, our genitals, our legs and ankles, our inadequacies, the "soles" of our feet, the animal ancestors, the earth itself, the treasures in the earth, the dead long buried there, the stubborn richness to which we descend. "Water prefers low places," the Tao Te Ching says, which is a true Wild Man book.

That attention to what is below encourages us to follow our own desires, which we know are not restricted to sexual desire, but include desires for the infinite, for the Woman at the Edge of the World, for the Firebird, for the treasure at the bottom of the sea, desires entirely superfluous. James Hillman praises this paragraph by William James as great words about desire.

Man's chief difference from the brutes lies in the exuberant excess of his subjective propensities. His preeminence over them lies simply and solely in the number and in the fantastic and unnecessary character of his wants, physical, moral, aesthetic and intellectual. Had his whole life not been a quest for the superfluous, he would never have established himself so inexpungeably in the necessary. And from the consciousness of this, he should draw the lesson that his wants are to be trusted, that even when their gratification seems furthest off, the uneasiness they occasion is still the best guide of his life, and will lead him to issues entirely beyond his present powers of reckoning. Prune down his extravagances, sober him, and you undo him.

—from *The Will to Believe*

We need to build a body, not on the parallel bars, but an activated, emotional body strong enough to contain our own superfluous desires. The Wild Man can only come to full life inside when the man has gone through the serious disciplines suggested by taking the first wound, doing kitchen and ashes work, creating a garden, bringing wild flowers to the Holy Woman, experiencing the warrior, riding the red, the white, and the black horses, learning to create art, and receiving the second heart.

The Wild Man doesn't come to full life through being "natural," going with the flow, smoking weed, reading nothing, and being generally groovy. Ecstasy amounts to living within reach of the high voltage of the golden gifts. The ecstasy comes after thought, after discipline imposed on ourselves, after grief.

> *I am content to follow to its source*
> *Every event in action or in thought;*
> *Measure the lot; forgive myself the lot!*
> *When such as I cast out remorse*
> *So great a sweetness flows into the breast*
> *We must laugh and we must sing,*
> *We are blest by everything,*
> *Everything we look upon is blessed.*
>
> —from "A Dialogue of Self and Soul"
> by W. B. Yeats

The Wild Man, then, through his disciplines, prepares an emotional body that can receive grief, ecstasy, and spirit. He prepares matter. Sophia descended from the upper Aeons down onto this planet, the story says, and got caught here in matter. As a result we can find Sophia in every piece of bark and every stone or feather. The Wild Man is a friend of Sophia. "Everyone who is calm and sensible is insane," says Rumi.

Finally, the Wild Man's energy is that energy which is conscious of a wound. His face, which we see in medieval carvings, and his body, which we see in the small basalt statue from 4000 B.C., contains grief, knows grief, shares grief with nature. The hard survivor in us survived to adulthood. But the Wild Man leads the return we eventually have to make as adults back to the place of childhood abuse and abandonment. The Wild Man is a better guide in some ways to that pain than our inner child is, precisely because he is not a child. Because he is not a child, he knows stories, and can lead us into the personal suffering and through it.

The Wild Man's qualities, among them love of spontaneity, association with wilderness, honoring of grief, and respect for riskiness, frightens many people. Some men, as soon as they receive the first impulses to riskiness and recognize its link with what we've called the Wild Man, become frightened, stop all wildness, and recommend timidity and collective behavior to others. Some of these men become high school principals, some sociologists, some businessmen, Protestant ministers, bureaucrats, therapists; some become poets and artists.

But if a man doesn't descend to the kitchen, he won't know ashes. Some men are open to ashes, and they are as diverse as Richard Pryor, John Cassavetes, James Baldwin, Reshad Field, C. Everett Koop, Woody Allen, the recent Jimmy Carter, Cesar Chavez, and so on. All advise the path that involves intensity, awareness of the wound, alertness to impulse, the possibility of a fall.

The Russians are now taking into their hands the ashes of incompetent industry, collectivized farming, lies, Stalinist paranoia, military machoism, the Gulags, Leninist madness, and so on. We have to respect that; perhaps because they handle ashes they have ideas.

It's sad that the United States still stubbornly refuses to pick up the ashes we have created in the last four decades. Our agricultural policy is ashes, our schools are ashes, the treatment of blacks is all ashes, the trade deficit is ashes, the environmental policy is ashes, the poverty of women and children is ashes.

When the descent begins in a person or a nation, we experience a fall, an agreed-on tumble out of respectability and obedience into the dark underbelly of the whale, "down and out in Paris and London," a dive to the bottom, feeling the weight of the car fall on you.

Blake and Yeats are for readers of poetry the masters of the Wild Man path. Blake takes his imagined god Orc, who lives in flames, as his image; Yeats takes Cuchulain as his image of the Wild Man, and the two grand women, Emer and Crazy Jane, as his images of the Wild Woman.

Cuchulain and Crazy Jane do not want the ordinary life; they prefer the possibility of intensity, even though it entails risk of failure or insanity, preferring it to the "even-tempered life promised to the good servant." Crazy Jane and Cuchulain are the risk takers, those who would rather go to Hell if it were lively than to live comfortably in Heaven.

The aim is not to *be* the Wild Man, but to be *in touch with* the Wild Man. No sane man in Greece would say, "I want to be Zeus," but in American culture, past and present, we find people who want to be the Wild Man—writers as intelligent as Kerouac fail to make the distinction between being, and being in touch with. Trying to be the Wild Man ends in early death, and confusion for everyone.

The Community Inside the Psyche

The Wild Man is part of a company or a community in a man's psyche, and it would be just as foolish to concentrate on him exclusively as to concentrate on the Warrior exclusively. Just as the man in our story exists as a companion to feminine energy, sometimes following its lead, sometimes not, so the Wild Man lives in complicated interchanges with the other interior beings. A whole community of beings is what is called a grown man.

I see seven of these beings so far. In this book, we've spoken at length about the being we've called the King, and paid much attention to the Warrior as well. One of the greatest figures in the male psyche is the Lover, and we talked of him when we spoke of the garden. The Wild Man of course energizes this whole story. Here I will comment briefly on the three others not spoken of so far.

The Trickster we'll call the fifth being. It was an American scholar, Paul Radin, who did the fundamental description in his book, *The Trickster,* drawing from the great Winnebago trickster cycle. More trickster energy seems to be stored in the North American soil than in any continent in the world. Native Americans have developed outrageous coyote stories, and Sitting Bull was a "heyoka" all his life. Melville's *Confidence Man* picks up all the nineteenth-century men in whom it was wise to have no confidence.

The Trickster does not "go with the flow," but his job is to reverse it, as soon as he sees in what direction it is flowing, so that the larger energy continues to move. Anyone who has watched the American comic Cary Oates has seen the Trickster in a wonderfully pure form. The Hermes elegance we've spoken of here, such as the introduction of the Princess to the boy through bouncing sunlight, belongs to the Trickster. Shakespeare always brings the clown or jester in to balance the King; he loves that set of opposites. During *King Lear,* written late in his career, he honors the Trickster more than ever before.. As King Lear, toward the close to the play, finds a hut in the storm, Lear says to the jester: "You go in first."

The sixth being I call the Mythologist or the Cook. He knows how long cooking should go on, and how to move from one stage to another. Robert Moore, who has written well about him, calls him the Magician or the Magus. At the highest level he is a shaman. He deals with energies in the invisible world, and for that reason one could say that mathematicians are also magicians.

Sometimes even when a man's emotional body is severely crippled in childhood, the Magician or Cook may survive. That pure intellectual energy, not as damaged as the emotions, figures things out and ascends to keep sane. Perhaps the Magician's wise ascension is the way the naïve man gets born. The Mythologist, the Cook, or the Magician then is a great blessing. He moves behind the screen of our story invisibly, sending the young man on to the garden, for example, no matter what the King says.

The seventh being I call the Grief Man. I believe there is a special figure in men who leads them down into one of their great strengths—the power to grieve. There is a grief in men that has no cause. We can feel it in Bach, Rembrandt, Goya, Homer. I don't mean that women do not feel grief; but a man's grief has a separate tone to it. Yet in our culture a man gets very little permission to grieve.

> *Well, on the day I was born,*
> *God was sick.*
>> —César Vallejo

> *It is still beautiful to feel the heart beat,*
> *but often the shadow seems more real than the body.*
> *The samurai looks insignificant*
> *Besides his armor of black dragon scales.*
>> —from "After a Death" by Tomas Transtromer

> *How can I live without you?*
> *Come up to me, love,*
> *Out of the river, or I will*
> *Come down to you.*
>> —from "To the Muse" by James Wright

As a man gets older, he gives himself more permission to go down.

> *All our life we keep our longing to go down.*
> *Now the ground knows when it is time to fall.*

The community of seven beings just mentioned makes a structure that we could imagine as a crystalline underpinning to the soul water. The upper fifty feet or so of water in the male soul is, as we all know, very roiled and turbid these days. So many roles that men have depended on for hundreds of years have dissolved or vanished. Certain activities, such as hunting or pirating, no one wants him to do anymore. The Industrial Revolution has separated man from nature and from his family. The only jobs he can get are liable to harm the earth and the atmosphere; in general he doesn't know whether to be ashamed of being a man or not.

And yet the structure at the bottom of the male psyche is still as firm as it was twenty thousand years ago. A contemporary man simply has very little help in getting down to it.

This underlying structure which I see is made by the interlacing or interlocking of the old familiar energies, the seven figures or beings or luminous powers. A man finds one or two strong in him as a gift; then he has to develop the others.

We know that the waters of the woman's soul are also highly disturbed now. And I believe the structure of the woman's psyche also involves a firm interweaving of beings, some of which she is charged with in common with men; some are private to her.

Teachers and therapists often have a strong Cook, Mythologist, or Magician inside. But if a teacher has not developed the Wild Man or Wild Woman, that person becomes the strange being we call an "academic," whose love of standards is admirable in every way, but who somehow filters the wildness out of Thoreau or Emily Dickinson or D. H. Lawrence even as he or she teaches them. Not all teachers do that, thank God, but universities shelter a lot of them.

If a therapist doesn't dive down to meet the Wild Man or Wild Woman, he or she will try to heal with words. The healing energy stored in waterfalls, trees, clay, horses, dogs, porcupines, llamas, otters belong to the domain of the Wild People. Therapists will have understood this when they insist on doing therapy with a cow in the room.

The Grief Man without the Wild Man can become lost in the labyrinth of childhood. The Grief Man can fall in love with metaphor and symbol, as Coleridge did, and not make the connection with mountains, rocks, and flowers that Wordsworth insisted on and fed from.

When a man inherits great warrior energy but does not incorporate the Wild Man or Wild Woman, he may sacrifice others but not know to whom he is to be sacrificed. He may fight for the State but not the Cosmos, using the terms John Weir Perry brought forward.

When the Wild Man is not a strong part of the Trickster, the Trickster may reverse all flows but have none of his own. We know what he isn't, but we don't know where his depth is. He shoots arrows from behind a tree, so to speak, but doesn't himself present a landscape.

If a Lover lacks the Wild Man, he may not give enough wild flowers. He may make love indoors too much, be too respectable, lack what Yeats called "folly," the willingness to throw away house or land for a woman. Grania, as we recall, drove a knife into Diarmud's thigh when she became angry with him, and he left it there. Refusing to pull the knife out was an unconventional expression of his love, and it was convincing to her.

A King without enough Wild Man will be a king for human beings, but animals, ocean, and trees will have no representation in his Senate. We sense that was true of President Truman. And Reagan, we recall, said, "If you've seen one redwood, you've seen them all."

Bishops and Popes have traditionally been lacking in the Wild Man; they take church doctrine seriously but not the ecology of the earth.

The Story: The Wedding Feast

We are ready now to turn to the last scene of our story, in which the masculine and feminine come together at last. The original father and mother are present as well. It is a wedding ceremony, interrupted by a strange event.

> The young man's father and mother were among those invited to the wedding, and they came; they were in

great joy because they had given up hope that they would ever see their dear son again.

While all the guests were sitting at the table for the marriage feast, the music broke off all at once, the great doors swung open, and a baronial King entered, accompanied in procession by many attendants.

He walked up to the young groom and embraced him. The guest said: "I am Iron John, who through an enchantment became turned into a Wild Man. You have freed me from that enchantment. All the treasure that I own will from now on belong to you."

As we look back at the story, we realize that the Wild Man has been slowly ascending step by step in harmony with the young man's slow descent.

In one Swedish version of our story, the main character, the initiator, is actually an animal, called the "ugly animal." He escapes, gives the boy horses, et cetera. When it's time for the wedding he arrives, but crawls underneath the table where the bride and groom are sitting, and from there, tells the young man what to do. At the right moment, the groom touches the "ugly animal" with a rusty sword, and the animal changes into a king missing in that area for a long time. Placing the animal underneath the table is a gorgeous variation on the theme: the despised and lowly becomes honored, the being that is apparently primitive becomes a king.

We have become used to seeing the Wild Man as wet, moist, foresty, ignorant, leafy, and all at once he is related to holy intellect and sun radiance—he is a King.

The energy that is hidden by water, dark, lying on its back among reeds, becomes a luminous power. As we watch, the great doors of the wedding hall open, and a baronial king enters with many well-dressed attendants.

As we hear or read this last scene, we say in some shock: "Whose story was this?" We assumed it was the boy's story; but we see it may be the Wild Man's story. And there is something we were ignorant of. Some invisible force that we know nothing about has put the sophisticated energy of this being into a primitive form and shape, as if into a cage.

Our work then as men and women is not only to free ourselves from family cages and collective mind sets, but to release transcendent beings from imprisonment and trance. That's what the story says in the end.

I think we have said as much as is proper here about the Wild Man. Some people dislike the very phrase "Wild Man." It is rather inflammatory, and I am not fond of it myself. On first hearing, it promises too much. Moreover, I am afraid of how-to-do-it books on the Wild Man. "I ate a bran muffin and I found the Wild Man." "I did mythological thinking for ten minutes, and the Wild Man leapt through the window."

We need delicacy around both the Wild Man and the Wild Woman, so that we brush them with the wingtip of our minds. It would be disastrous to throw a net over either, or to tranquilize them with jargon, and take them home to our private zoo.

In ordinary life, a mentor can guide a young man through various disciplines, helping to bring him out of boyhood into manhood; and that in turn is associated not with body building, but with building an emotional body capable of containing more than one sort of ecstasy.

We know, moreover, that such initiation does not take place at any one moment or only once. It happens over and over. An Australian aborigine said something to this effect: "I've been doing this initiatory work with young men for forty years now, and I think I'm beginning to get it myself."

The initiatory road in our story includes eight segments, but another story may offer the same stages but in a different order, or entirely different stages. I admire the order of teachings in "Iron John," but I don't think there is any one right order of initiation. We go through the round of experiences over and over—at first lightly, then as we get older, more deeply.

A stage that we imagine we have missed may have taken place, even though we weren't conscious of it. The leg wound, for example, that gave us a second or compassionate heart may have happened, and what we need is more imagination in order to grasp how and when it did.

Male initiation goes on, female initiation, and human initiation. Men and women share a complicated initiation into human warmth that has no relation to gender. Our story doesn't talk about that directly. Certain initiations belong in essence to the human, some in essence to the feminine, some in essence to the masculine. It's important to be able to say the word *masculine* without imagining that we are saying a sexist word.

Geneticists have discovered recently that the genetic difference in DNA between men and women amounts to just over three percent. That isn't much. However the difference exists in every cell of the body.

We know that many contemporary men have become ashamed of their three percent. Some feel shame over the historical past, over oppressive patriarchies, insane wars, rigidities long imposed. Other men who have seen their fathers fail to be true to the masculine and its values don't want to be men. But they are. I think that for this century and this moment it is important to emphasize the three percent difference that makes a person masculine, while not losing sight of the ninety-seven percent that men and women have in common.

Some say, "Well, let's just be human, and not talk about masculine or feminine at all." People who say that imagine they are occupying the moral high ground. I say that we have to be a little gentle here, and allow the word *masculine* and the word *feminine* to be spoken, and not be afraid that some moral carpenter will make boxes of those words and imprison us in them. We are all afraid of boxes, and rightly so.

Many men say to me they literally don't know what the word *man* means, nor whether they are grown men or not. When an older man riskily names some masculine qualities which he sees, then the younger man can see how far he is from that spot, in what direction it lies, and whether he wants to go in that direction at all. Simply naming *human* attributes doesn't help such a man.

I've mentioned that certain contemporary female psychologists believe in naming womanly attributes as well, so that a woman can become a conscious woman instead of an unconscious one. All naming of qualities is dangerous, because the naming can be made into boxes. But we have to hope to do better than in the past.

I don't believe that this attention to initiation of men will make men and women grow farther apart. A man whose Warrior or Lover has been crushed (and he remains unaware of it) is already farthest from women. He couldn't be farther.

Some people believe that "men's work" is important only for some men, the "sensitive ones." "Well, all this mythology stuff is fine for the sensitive men; they probably need it. But I see construction workers eating their lunch with other men—they don't have any problem with their masculinity. They don't even think about it. They are the real men. . . . "

But do the twenty-six-year-old journalists, men and women, who say this truly believe that blue-collar workers do not feel shame about being men? Do they imagine that the childhood homes of these "men's men" were not also messed-up? Whenever a man makes insulting remarks to women going by he is usually doubly insecure in that he remains unaware of the shame.

Dividing men that way into "sensitive men" and "construction workers" makes no sense anyway. The blue-collar workers and woodsmen who have participated in the conferences that I have experienced are just as thoughtful and sensitive as any professors, CEOs or therapists. So I think we have to say that the shame over the three percent and the pride over the three percent belong to all contemporary men, not just to some.

Our obligation—and I include in "our" all the women and men writing about gender—is to describe *masculine* in such a way that it does not exclude the masculine in women, and yet hits a resonant string in the man's heart. No one says there aren't resonating strings in a woman's heart too—but in the man's heart there is a low string that makes his whole chest tremble when the qualities of the masculine are spoken of in the right way.

Our obligation is to describe the *feminine* in a way that does not exclude the feminine in men but makes a large string resonate in the woman's heart. Some string in the man's heart will resonate as well, but I suspect that in the woman's heart there is a low string that makes her whole chest tremble when the qualities of the feminine are spoken of in the right way.

At the same time, we all know that there are in reality besides these two states, "feminine" and "masculine," all sorts of degrees, intermediate states, unions, combinations, special cases, genius exceptions, and so on.

For the time being, it is the men and women who have passed through the grief door into their own childhood to whom the story we've retold will speak best. They will be able to use the story and others like it, blessedly preserved by the memory culture that our ancestors lived in up till the time of writing.

We all recognize certain holy moments, when outer and inner worlds cross, when vertical and horizontal time intersect. That moment occurred when the King's men wounded the rider. Even though he remained on his horse, his helmet fell off, and the golden hair tumbled down. In that moment, his true identity can be revealed, and soon after, the true identity of the Wild Man. Rumi said:

> It's important to pay attention to the name the
> Holy One has for things.
> We name everything according to the number of
> legs it has
> But the Holy One names it according to what is
> inside.
> Moses had a rod. He thought its name was "staff";
> But inside its name was "dragonish snake."
> We thought the name "Omar" meant agitator
> against priests,
> But in eternity his name was "The One Who
> Believes."
> No one knows our name until our last breath goes
> out.
> *Version by R.B.*

The young man in our story descended from courtyard to ashes, from ashes to earth, then to horses under the earth, and so on. The Wild Man passes him on the way up, having ascended from under the water to the courtyard, then to his own sacred spring, then to the Master of Horses, and finally to the state of kingship.

The Wild Man part of each man that was once in touch with wilderness and wild animals has sunk down below the water of the mind, out of sight, below human memory. Covered with hair now, it looks as if it were an animal itself. The Wild Man in our wedding scene says in effect: "A strong power forced me by enchantment to live under the water until a young man appeared who was ready to undergo the discipline and go through the suffering that you have gone through. Now that you have done that, I can appear as I am—a Lord."

The Wild Man in
Ancient Religion, Literature,
and Folk Life

The Hunting Era

The imaginative leap that led to the vision of the Lord of Animals, part human, part god, part animal, we can rightly think of as a great religious event. Ancient women, in a distinct and parallel event, saw with their inner eyes a compassionate, nourishing, abundant, ruthless being, a Birth Mother and Grave Mother, who gleamed behind the confusing spectacle of aging seals, bright-eyed infants, buds and dry leaves, minnows and whales, girls and crones.

In each case the ancient men and the ancient women see through a veil to a firm, invisible being on the other side of the screen of nature.

The Lord of Animals or the Releaser of Animals, in the time before time, crossed the line from the animals' side of things to the human side, and back. Tales of the Lord of Animals or the Master of the Hunt are everywhere present in Mediterranean, African, Siberian, aboriginal, Chinese, North European, and American Indian cultures. The Blackfeet, for example, recount an early time of starvation when an old man appealed to the buffalo. The buffalo chief responds by requesting a human bride. The old man's daughter moves to the buffalo camp, and in response dozens of buffalo gallop over the cliff to feed the tribe. The father, visiting the buffalo camp sometime later to see his daughter, is found out and trampled to death. His daughter eventually reconstitutes him from a single vertebra. But it's clear that both father and daughter have now felt the impersonal power of the buffalo realm, and some sort of contract has been worked out that the intellect cannot completely understand.

This story, and hundreds like it, suggests that a compact was made sometime in the past between the human realm and the animal realm, and that agreement seems to be a tough one, providing obligations and rights on each side. Moreover, we gather that the eaten buffalo gallops up the ravine the next year; the buffalo sacrificed is soon reborn. And a human being crosses to their side when one of them crosses to ours.

By the Stone Age the Releaser of Animals appears as the Master of Creatures in full glory dancing on the walls of the Dordogne caves. The "sorcerer" painted high on the walls of the Trois Frères sanctuary is believed to be this Lord. Many scholars of the Paleolithic period now believe, as John Pfeiffer reports in his book *The Creative Explosion*, that the caves, which date to around 12,000 B.C., were not solely places for fertility or hunting rituals, but chambers for the initiation of young men.

If that is so, the Wild Man, or the Lord of Animals, has been associated with the initiation of young men for at least fourteen thousand years. Through the Wild Man's initiation, men learn to worship the animal soul, and that ancient worship to this day calls up from the busy adult man the sorrow of animal life, the grief of all nature, "the tears of things," the consciousness that is betwixt and between; and finally, it awakens in the shaman the ability to step over into the consciousness possessed by mountains, rocks, waters, trees, and demons. Above all, the devotion to animals that die calls up the knowledge of sacrifice, and what sacrifice can possibly mean.

When animals die in the presence of a hunter, does a willing sacrifice take place, or is it all a dream? We ask that question when a holy man sacrifices himself or when a holy woman sacrifices herself. The question and the answer belong to the knowledge domain of the Master of the Hunt.

This is not the place for a long essay on Paleolithic mysteries. All we want to do here is affirm that the hairy man, who appears under the water as our story starts, has another place in the upper realm populated by the gods. He is the god of depth, wounds, and sacrifice. Mircea Eliade has said that he regards the Master of the Hunt as "the most divine figure in all prehistory," and so the prototype of all subsequent gods. In our industrial system, we ignore the Great Mother, and we ignore the Lord of the Animals also. We are some of the first people in history who have tried to live without honoring him and his depth, his woundedness, and his knowledge of appropriate sacrifice. As a result, our sacrifices have become unconscious, regressive, pointless, indiscriminate, self-destructive, and massive.

The Agricultural Era

What happened to the Lord of Animals when human beings moved from the hunter culture to hunter-gatherer, and then to agricultural society? No accurate statement can ever be made about the transformation of gods, for the gods include one another, trade back and forth, make bewildering unions that leave mythologers far behind.

Having stated that qualification, we can also state confidently that in the Indian subcontinent the Lord of Animals transforms in such a way as to become Shiva.

The Dravidian culture of southern India, which was prior to the Hindu culture, gave the name Pashupati to the Master of Animals and gave the name Parvati to his companion, the Lady of the Mountains. Scholars have traced this pair back to the Old Bronze Age and the Neolithic period. The immense philosophical and religious movement around the Lord of the Animals and the Lady enters classic Indian culture as Shivaism, which merged with the earlier animism, and from whose source many later religions flow. The Dravidian language of southern India is the main carrier of Shivaite energy, and Alain Danielou notes in his book *Shiva and Dionysus* that it shares many words with the Sumerian, Basque, and Georgian languages. *The Dance of Shiva* by Ananda Coomaraswamy gives beautiful details on the religion of Shiva; and Gary

Snyder mentions that Shiva is still the god with the most living worshippers on this planet.

Shiva is a blossoming or development of the Wild Man, immensely articulated. Shiva keeps the wild aspect—his followers go naked and do not cut their hair—but also has an ascetic aspect, a husbandly side, and the enraged or Bhairava side.

The Lord of Animals in the area around the Caucasus, Thessaly, Greece, and Crete expands and elaborates into the god called Zagreus, Zan, or, in Crete, Zeus.

The ancient Cretan culture named the Lord of Animals Zagreus and the Lady of the Mountains Cybele. The bull, the snake, and the phallus speak for Zagreus or Zan or Zeus, and the tiger and the lion speak for Cybele. As Cretan culture developed, the birth rituals of the baby Zeus on Mount Ida and Mount Dicte began to merge with the rituals around the baby Dionysus. We recall that Dionysus came directly from the thigh of Zeus.

After the Mediterranean peoples became farmers and wine growers, Dionysus steps forward to carry the old Animal Lord energy, and the Lady of the Mountains becomes Ariadne, which means simply the Holy Woman. The rituals around Dionysus show clearly how, as mankind moves toward the mystery of plants, the Lord of Animals can change while still keeping his sacrificial essence. Dionysus, as we said before, is the clump of grapes which, when torn apart, trampled, and enclosed in the darkness of an ox hide, gives to everyone in the community an ecstasy, that is to say, a wine. And the Sufis can tell us how subtle that wine can be. "Nothing can be sole or whole / That has not been rent."

The Master of Animals' continuation in the form of Dionysus brought tremendous gifts to our own culture, in the shape of Greek tragic theater, and the entire concept of tragedy. The word tragedy means the song of the (sacrificed) goat. The Dionysian inheritance also gives us what respect we have for the beneath darkness, the sun under the earth, the ecstasy of wine, and the silence that lies inside the grief-knowing man. Dionysus carries knowledge that comes to the soul when it broods on tearing and being torn.

The Wild Man continues his existence throughout the Celtic

societies of ancient Europe, where he appears under the name Cernunnos, or Cornely, or Cornelius, the root syllable emphasizing the stag horns. In some Celtic lands he is known as Herne the Hunter, whose hunting dogs are white with red ears.

A fine visualization of Cernunnos has survived, saved on a cauldron found in Jutland, known as the Gundestrup Cauldron and dating from the first century B.C. Cernunnos is seen sitting in the yoga posture, holding a serpent in one hand and the Lady's neck ring or "torc" in the other hand, allowing stag horns and leaves to rise from his head. All around him is a company made up of dolphin, gazelle, lion, and dog. The Celtic Arthurian cycle, which surfaced in the twelfth and thirteenth centuries, keeps memories of him, for example, in *Yvain*, where he is named as Lord of the Animals and Guardian of the Fountain. Cernunnos' female companion has many names, among them Artio—whose root she shares with Arthur—meaning "female bear."

The Wild Man, then, which seems to be a silly phrase when we first hear it, and which is so easily confused with irresponsible man or churlish man, carries inside an enormous amount of historical information.

When we look into the past, holding the Wild Man telescope to our eyes, many fuzzy images come into focus, among them John the Baptist, the wild man who baptized Christ, and Mary Magdalene. Mary Magdalene carries some of the feeling of light hidden in darkness, which we associate also with Sophia. Both Sophia and Dionysus contain in their legends the secret of a sun that does not shine from the sun down, but rather a sun deep in earth which shines up toward us.

The Old Stone Age Master of Animals, then, as he transforms into Pashupati, Shiva, Dionysus, and Cernunnos, retains and elaborates the original energy. He is placed inside vast religious and mythological gardens where he blossoms. But the gardens end in the West. It is sad to note that the development of the Forest Lord stops dead around A.D. 1100; of course, it's possible that one should set the date earlier, in the first century B.C., when Caesar invaded Gaul. However one understands all this, it's clear that the Lord of

Animals does not contribute his moistness and energy to our religions. As the Wild Man, he is remembered of course in literature and in folk imagination.

The Wild Man in Ancient Literature

We first see the Lord of Animals as a fully developed epic character in the Sumerian epic *Gilgamesh*, which was written down around 700 B.C. but draws from much earlier material. The great city-states are already in place. When a young king, Gilgamesh, golden, inflated, greedy for pleasure, begins to cause trouble, the elders say the only solution is to bring him in touch with the man called Enkidu.

> The whole of his body was hairy and his locks were like a woman's, or like the hair of the goddess of grain. Moreover, he knew nothing of settled fields or of human beings, and was clothed like a deity of flocks. He ate grass with the gazelles, jostled the wild beasts at the watering hole, and was content with the animals there. . . . When Gilgamesh was apprised of the marvel, "Go, my hunter," he said; "take along with you a temple prostitute, and when he comes to the watering hole, with the beasts, let her throw off her clothes, disclose her nakedness, and when he sees, he will approach her; and the beasts thereafter will desert him, which grew up with him on his plain."
>
> The hunter and temple prostitute set forth, and three days later reached the watering place. One day they sat; two days; and on the next the beasts arrived, Enkidu among them, feeding on the grass with the gazelles. . . .
>
> The woman did as told: made bare her breasts, revealed her nakedness. Enkidu came and took possession. She was not afraid, but, having put aside her clothes, welcomed his ardor; and for six days and seven nights Enkidu remained mating with that temple maid's abun-

dance—after which he turned his face and made a move toward the beasts. But on seeing him, they ran off, and Enkidu was amazed. His body stiffened, his knees froze—the animals were gone. It was not as before.

Enkidu returned to the woman and, sitting at her feet, gazed up into her face; and, as she spoke, his ears gave heed. "You are beautiful, Enkidu, like a very god," she said to him. "Why do you run with the beasts of the plain? Come, I will take you to the ramparts of Uruk, the holy temple city of Anu and Ishtar, where Gilgamesh dwells, unmatched in might, who, like a wild bull, wields power over men." And as he heard, his heart grew light. He yearned for a friend. "Very well!" he said. "And I shall challenge him.

Enkidu then travels to the city and meets Gilgamesh; the two wrestle, Enkidu wins, and the two become inseparable friends. Enkidu appears here as the hairy shadow of the new civilized city king.

Readers of the Old Testament recall Esau, the hairy man in Semitic legends, who brought wild goat meat to his blind father, Isaac, as a gift. We already know that the wily farmers will replace the religious hunters all over the Middle East, and we are not surprised when Jacob, faking animal hair on the back of his hands, wins the father's blessing that rightfully belonged to Esau. So it goes in the agricultural world. The tale of Esau implies that at a certain point in Near Eastern history the hairy man was exiled or disenfranchised.

The Wild Man in the European Middle Ages

The Wild Man takes a very vivid part in the fantasy and folk life of the Europeans during the Middle Ages. Yearly pageants or folk plays, in which he was the central character, took place in Germany, Austria, Holland, and neighboring countries. Scenes from those pageants became a favorite of northern European artists.

An example is Pieter Breughel, the Elder, who painted a scene from a Flemish pageant, which was then copied in 1566 as a woodcut by an anonymous artist. That woodcut has survived. We see the village square at the moment the Wild Man enters from the forest. The village players have earlier gone out into the forest, dressed a young man in a sort of fish-scale costume, and given him vine tendrils entangled in hair and beard. Other tendrils are tied around his waist, and he carries a club that resembles the club belonging to the Cerne Abbas giant carved into the Dorset hillsides in England. Three actors representing established or civilized powers meet him in the square. An actor representing the Holy Roman Church and the Emperor shows him the globe surmounted by a cross in order to remind the Wild Man that his time is over. The military man carries an armed crossbow, which he aims at the forest man. The third personage, a woman, wears, in several depictions of this pageant, the same curiously conical hat. In her dress she resembles a nun, and holds out to him a golden ring. The ring would appear to be the holy ring of sexual union, which the Temple priestess offered him in Sumeria 2,200 years earlier. The Metropolitan Museum of Art a few years ago published a book called *The Wild Man in Medieval Myth and Symbolism*, which reproduces this woodcut. The editor, Timothy Husband, sums up the priestess's offer this way: "Symbolizing union with a woman, the ring tempts the Wild Man into the holy and legal bond of matrimony from which he is barred. The soldier and emperor, with his sword drawn in the painting Breughel did, stalk the Wild Man, ready to strike him down for his transgression against man's civilized order."

The Wild Man disregards all these threats and refuses all these offers to come in; he refuses to give up his forest life. The woodcut indicates that dancing and wild celebrations have begun the moment the Wild Man enters the town, and this seems to be the start of Mardi Gras. He leaves the town to the cheers of the young men and the exuberant dancing of the lovers.

But the pageant apparently ended with a more ominous event. A mile or so out of town, townspeople meet him. They put the Wild Man costume on a straw man, and then throw the straw man into a lake or pond, and he is ritually executed. That detail is

fascinating in relation to our own story, because it explains mythologically how the Wild Man got to be at the bottom of the pond
in the first place. We can also see in this ritual event vestiges of an
actual execution, which was probably carried out in earlier times.

Timothy Husband reproduces as well a manuscript illumi-
nation that shows Alexander the Great separating a Wild Man
from his wild wife, and then throwing him in the fire. In other
paintings we see the Wild Man being brought up before ecclesi-
astical authorities for judgment. The burning of the Wild Man
preceded the burning of the witches by several centuries, and it
proceeded from the same fear and anger.

The Wild Man also played other roles in Middle Ages fantasy:
he was known to be the friend of lovers. The courtly love tradition
incorporated the Wild Man. Some stained glass windows from
family chapels, for example, show Wild Men climbing castle walls.
They have replaced the courtly knights "storming the Castle of
Love." Husband remarks,

> The maidens in the castle are winsomely seductive crea-
> tures who seem to toss their flowers more to encourage
> than to repel their attackers. The young wild men, aware
> of the true nature of their business, have abandoned
> weaponry and armor. The wild man's legendary sexual
> prowess, combined with the willing attitude of the maid-
> ens, produces an image of pure wantonness. No longer
> a bulwark of purity, the castle becomes a seat of sen-
> suality, and the storming of the castle is equated with
> the satisfaction of physical desire.

The German artist, Schweiger, created about 1515 a marvelous
ink drawing of Mary Magdalene as a Wild Woman. He draws her
the way artists traditionally drew wild women: covered with hair
everywhere on the body except for nipples, elbows, and knees.
Three draped angels and one feathered angel are carrying her to
heaven. The drawing shows considerable affection for the Wild
Woman.

The Wild Man and Wild Woman, then, occupy a complicated
place in folk and aristocratic imagination of the Middle Ages.

Sometimes the figures are praised for their spontaneity and sexual energy but more often punished or exiled or killed for them.

We have to admire Middle Ages culture for keeping the Wild Man in consciousness. It's clear that the Mardi Gras in New Orleans, for example, descends from the village pageants, but it has forgotten the personage of the Wild Man. Basel still preserves that connection, and their Fastnacht, enacted every year, remains true to the mood, and many Wild Man masks are part of the celebration.

The Threat of the Wild Man in Europe

We might ask why northern Europe felt so threatened by the Wild Man. I don't think the answer would be surprising. The Wild Man is a relative, perhaps an uncle, of Pan, the Greek god whose name means "everything," and which, by indirection, suggests nature itself. Pan had hairy legs, which, one could say, belonged to the very same goat Esau loved so much, and which the Church later slandered by giving the legs to Satan.

The ascetic attitudes, or the popular longing to repress the libido, which grew so strong at the end of the pagan era, joined in Roman culture with fears of the libertine emphases of the Great Mother to form an antisexual front.

A friend once told of his visit to the ancient monastery of Mount Athos in Greece, whose traditions date from the earliest days of Christianity. He sat one evening for several hours side by side with an old monk, looking out over the mountains and sea. He knew no Greek, but longed for a conversation about spiritual matters with the old man. The old monk must have sensed it, and said at last in English the sentence: "Women are evil." That was it. The idea implies that all sexuality is evil. We can sense the dark side of medieval culture in that story, and we can deduce from this instant in the monastery how little support the ascetic wing of Christianity, Islam, or the Sikh would give to a hairy Magdalene or a Wild Man.

Powerful sociological and religious forces have acted in the

West to favor the trimmed, the sleek, the cerebral, the noninstinctive, and the bald. Blake said:

Priests in black gowns are walking their rounds,
And binding with briars my joys and desires.

Women's sexuality has suffered tremendously and still suffers from this tyranny of the bald, ascetic, and cerebral. The goddess Aphrodite, alive inside the female body, is insulted day after day.

The same forces have doomed male sexuality to the banal and the profane and the hideously practical. By contrast the Wild Man's elaboration through Indian imagination into Shiva honors sexual energy. We see statues of Shiva in great sexual glory sitting next to Parvati, whose sexual energy radiates from every inch of her body. Jesus had no wife or children, and the reason for his association with Mary Magdalene does not survive the Gospels. In Christianity, it was Paul who laid the ground for the hatred of sexuality, saying in the First Epistle to the Corinthians, "Let those who have wives live as though they had none." Origen performed the castration operation on himself. Justin reports that Christian men in his time, the second century A.D., implored surgeons to remove their testicles; many monks of Mount Athos accepted castration at that time, and later, Gregory of Nyssa said, "Marriage, then, is the last stage of our separation from the life that was led in Paradise; marriage therefore, if it's an ellipsis, is the first thing to be left behind." Augustine said, "A man by his very nature is ashamed of sexual desire," and he, though he acted as a libertine in his youth, changed when he became Christian. Later in life, his sexual member rose, he said, whether he wanted it to or not. He called this "a movement of disobedience" which shows that "mankind since Adam has been entirely corrupt." The Wild Man would take that event to be a charming evidence of spontaneity.

We know that inside Christianity, as inside Judaism and Islam, there have been and still remain contrary currents of opinion that defend sexual love. Among the Christian groups we know of the Brotherhood of Love, the Cathars, the troubadours, and the Brethren of the Free Spirit, for whom Bosch painted his altar pieces. But these sensible movements could not alter the institutionalized drive of Christianity, which is toward the idea that sexuality inhibits spiritual growth.

I am going over this ground not in order to attack asceticism, which has its own dignity, but to remind us of the complicated feelings the villagers in Europe would have when they saw the Wild Man being led off for ritual execution.

With thinkers of Augustine's quality on our side, it's amazing that men can make love at all. Young men in contemporary culture conclude quickly that their sexual instinct is troublesome, intrusive, weird, and hostile to spirit.

Permissive attitudes of the sort favored by *Playboy* editors miss the battle entirely, because *Playboy* assumes that male sexuality is secular, a sort of play, proper for a playboy.

When the Church and the culture as a whole dropped the gods who spoke for the divine element in male sexual energy— Pan, Dionysus, Hermes, the Wild Man—into oblivion, we as men lost a great deal. The medieval Western imagination did not carry the Lord of Animals or the Wild Man on into a well-developed Shiva or Dionysus, and the erotic energy of men lost its ability to move, as they say in music, to the next octave.

We will bring this brief history of the Wild Man's place in religion, literature, and folk imagination to a close here. I once heard Marie-Louise von Franz lecture on the Wild Man, and she chose a historical wild man in medieval Switzerland, who went into the forest for many years and whose advice was much sought by both rulers and common people. She remarked that she has noticed in dreams of both men and women in recent decades a figure who is spiritual but also covered with hair, a sort of hairy Christ. She believes that what the psyche is asking for now is a new figure, a religious figure but a hairy one, in touch with God and sexuality, with spirit and earth.

The Story of Iron John

There was, once upon a time, a King, who had near his castle an enormous forest, in which wild animals of all sorts lived. One day he dispatched a hunter into those woods to take a deer, but the hunter did not return. "Something went wrong out there," said the King, and the next day he sent two more hunters out to search for the first, but they did not return either. On the third day, he called all his huntsmen in, and said, "Scour that entire forest, and stay at it until you've found all three of them."

Not a one of those hunters ever returned, and moreover, the pack of dogs that went out with them never came back either.

No one after that dared to enter the forest, and let it be in its deep stillness and solitude. Only now and then an eagle or a hawk flew over it.

This situation went on for years, and then one day a strange hunter appeared who wanted some work to do, and he offered to set foot in the dangerous woods.

The King however refused to consent, saying, "It is not safe in there. I have the feeling that you will end up like the others, and this is the last we'll see of you." The hunter replied: "Sire, I'm well aware of the risk, and fear is something I pay no attention to."

The hunter took his dog with him, and walked into the forest. It wasn't long before the dog picked up the scent of game and went in pursuit; but he had hardly run three steps before he stood at the edge of a deep pool and could not go farther. A naked arm reached out of the water, grabbed hold of him, and pulled him down.

When the hunter saw that, he went back to the castle, got three men, who came with pails, and they bucketed out the water. When they got down to the ground, they saw a Wild Man lying there, whose body was as brown as rusty iron. His hair hung down from his head over his face and all the way to his knees. They tied him with cords and led him back to the castle.

At the castle there was great astonishment over this Wild Man; and the King had him locked up in an iron cage that he had placed in the courtyard, and he forbade anyone, on pain of death, to open the locked door. He gave the key into the keeping of the Queen. Once that had been done, people could go safely into the forest once more.

The King had an eight-year-old son, who one day was playing in the courtyard, and during that play his golden ball fell down into the cage. The boy ran to the cage and said, "Give me my golden ball." "Not until you've opened the door for me," the man answered. "Oh no," said the boy, "I can't do it, the King won't let me," and he ran away. The next day the boy returned and asked for his ball again. The Wild Man said, "If you open the door," but the boy would not. On the third day, while the King was out hunting, the boy came once again, and said, "Even if I wanted to, I couldn't open the lock because I don't have the key." The Wild Man said, "The key is under your mother's pillow; you can retrieve it."

The boy, who really did want his ball back, threw caution to the winds, went into the castle, and got the key. The cage door was not easy to open, and the boy pinched his finger. When the door stood open, the Wild Man walked through it, gave the boy the golden ball, and hurried away.

The boy suddenly felt great fear. He shouted and cried out after him, "Wild Man, if you go away, they will beat me!" The Wild Man wheeled around, lifted the boy onto his shoulders, and walked with brisk steps into the forest.

When the King returned, he noticed the empty cage, and inquired of the Queen how the Wild Man had gotten loose. She knew nothing about it, went to check the key, and found it gone. She called the boy, but got no answer. The King sent a search party out into the fields, but they did not find the boy. It wasn't difficult to guess what had happened; and great grief and mourning settled on the royal house.

(2)

When the Wild Man had reached the dark forest once more, he took the boy from his shoulders, put him down on the earth, and said, "You will never see your mother and father again, but I will keep you with me, for you have set me free, and I feel compassion for you. If you do everything as I tell you, all will go well. I have much gold and treasure, more than anyone else in the world."

The Wild Man prepared a bed of moss for the boy to sleep on, and in the morning took him to a spring. "Do you see this golden spring? It is clear as crystal, and full of light. I want you to sit beside it and make sure that nothing falls into it, because if that happens, it will wrong the spring. I'll return each evening to see if you've obeyed my order."

The boy sat down at the spring's edge. Occasionally he glimpsed a golden fish or a gold snake, and he took care to let nothing fall in. But as he sat there, his wounded finger was so painful that, without intending to, he dipped it into the water. He pulled it out instantly, but he saw that the finger had turned to gold, and no matter how much he washed it, the washing did no good.

Iron John came back that evening and said, "Anything happen with the spring today?"

The boy held his finger behind his back to keep Iron John from seeing it, and said, "No, nothing at all."

"Ah, you've dipped your finger in the spring!" said the Wild Man. "We can let it pass this once, but don't let that happen again."

Early the next morning, the boy sat again at the spring watching over it. His finger still hurt and after a while, he ran his hand up through his hair. One hair, alas, came loose from his head and fell into the spring. He immediately reached down and pulled it out, but the hair had already turned to gold.

The moment Iron John returned, he knew what had happened, "You've let a hair fall into the spring. I'll allow it this time, but if it happens a third time it will dishonor the spring, and you will not be able to stay with me any longer."

The third day, as the boy sat by the spring, he was determined, no matter how much his finger hurt him, not to let it move. Time passed slowly, and he began gazing at the reflection of his face in the water. He got the desire to look straight into his own eyes, and in doing this, he leaned over farther and farther. All at once his long hair fell down over his forehead and into the water. He threw his head back but now all his hair, every bit, had turned gold, and it shone as if it were the sun itself. Now the boy was frightened! He took out a kerchief and covered his head so that the Wild Man wouldn't know what had happened. But when Iron John arrived home, he knew immediately. "Take the kerchief off your head," he said. The golden hair then came tumbling down over the boy's shoulders, and the boy had to be silent.

"You can't stay here any longer because you didn't make it through the trial. Go out into the world now and there you will learn what poverty is. I see no evil in your heart, however, and I wish you well, so I'll give you this gift: whenever you are in trouble, come to the edge of the forest and shout, 'Iron John, Iron John!' I'll come to the edge of the forest and help you. My power is great, greater than you believe, and I have gold and silver in abundance."

(3)

Then the King's son left the forest, and walked by beaten and unbeaten paths ever onwards until at length he reached a great city. There he looked for work, but could find none, and he had learnt nothing by which he could help himself. At length, he went to the palace, and asked if they would take him in. The people about court did not at all know what use they could make of him, but they liked him, and told him to stay. At length the cook took him into his service, and said he might carry wood and water, and rake the cinders together.

(4)

Once when it happened that no one else was at hand, the cook ordered the boy to carry the food to the royal table, but because the boy did not want his golden hair to be seen, he kept his tarboosh on. Such a thing as that had never happened in the King's presence, and he said, "When you come to the royal table you must take your cap off." He answered: "Ah, Lord, I cannot; I have a sore place on my head." The King called the cook up, scolded him, and demanded how he could have taken such a boy as that into his service; and told him to fire the boy and get him out of the castle.

(5)

The cook, however, had pity on the youngster and exchanged him for the gardener's boy.

Now the boy had to set out plants in the garden, and water them, chop with hoe and spade, and let wind and bad weather do what they wished.

Once in summer, when he was working in the garden by himself, it got so hot that he pulled his head covering off, so that the breeze would cool his head. When the sun touched his head, his hair glowed and blazed out so brightly that beams of sunlight went all the way into the bedroom of the King's daughter, and she leapt up to see what that could be. She spied the boy outside, and called to him, "Boy, bring me a batch of flowers!"

He quickly put his tarboosh back on, picked some wild flowers for her, and tied them in a bunch. As he started up the stairs with them, the gardener met him, and said, "What are you doing bringing the King's daughter such ordinary flowers? Get moving and pick another bouquet, the best we have and the most beautiful."

"No, no," the boy answered, "the wild flowers have stronger fragrance and they will please her more."

When the boy walked into her room, the King's daughter

said, "Take your headthing off; it isn't proper for you to wear it in my presence."

He replied, "I don't dare do that. I have the mange, you know."

She however grabbed the tarboosh and yanked it off; his golden hair tumbled down around his shoulders, and it was magnificent to look at. He started out the door at a run, but she held him by the arm and gave him a handful of gold coins. He took them and left, but put no stock in them; in fact he brought the coins to the gardener and said, "I'm giving these to your children—they can use them to play with."

The next day the King's daughter again called the boy to her and told him to bring her some more wild flowers. When he walked in with them, she reached for his little hat and would have torn it away, but he held on to it with both hands. Once more she gave him a handful of gold coins, but he refused to keep them and gave them to the gardener as playthings for his children.

The third day things went the same way: she couldn't manage to get his hat off, and he wouldn't accept the gold coins.

(6)

Not long after, the country was swept up in war. The King gathered his forces and was not positive that he could succeed against the enemy, who was powerful and retained a large army. The gardener's boy said: "I am quite grown now, and I will go to war, if you'll just give me a horse." The other men laughed and declared: "When we've gone, you go look in the stable—we'll certainly leave a horse behind for you."

When they had all gone, the boy went into the barn and led a horse out; it was lame in one leg, and walked hippity, hoppity. He climbed on it and rode to the dark forest.

When he came to its edge, he called three times: "Iron John," so loud that it echoed through the trees.

In a moment the Wild Man arrived and said, "What is it you want?"

"I want a strong war-horse because I intend to go to the war."

"You will receive that, and more than you have asked for as well."

The Wild Man turned then and went back into the woods, and not long afterwards, a stableboy came out of the trees leading a war-horse that blew air through its nostrils and was not easy to hold in. Running along after the horse came a large band of warriors, entirely clothed in iron, with their swords shining in the sun. The boy turned his three-legged nag over to the stableboy, mounted the new horse, and rode out at the head of the soldiers. By the time he neared the battlefield, a large part of the King's men had already been killed, and not much more was needed to bring them to total defeat.

The boy and his iron band rode there at full speed, galloped on the enemy like a hurricane, and struck down every one that opposed them. The enemy turned to flee, but the boy kept after them and pursued them to the last man. Then, however, instead of returning to the King, the boy took his band a roundabout way back to the forest, and called Iron John out.

"What do you want?" the Wild Man asked.

"You can take your horse and your men back, and give me again the three-legged nag."

So it all happened as he requested, and he rode the hoppity hop back home.

When the King returned to his castle, his daughter went to him and congratulated him on his victory.

"It wasn't me," he said, "who managed that, but a strange knight and his warrior band who arrived to help."

The daughter asked who this strange knight was, but the King didn't know, and added: "He galloped off in pursuit of the enemy, and that's the last I saw of him." The girl applied to the gardener and inquired about his boy, but he laughed and said, "He is just now arrived home on his three-legged nag. The farm help made fun of him, shouting: 'Guess who's here? Moopygoop.' Then they said, 'You've been under a lilac bush, eh? How was it?' He said back to them, 'I fought very well; if I hadn't been there, who knows what would have happened?' They all fell over themselves laughing."

(7)

The King said to his daughter: "I'll arrange a great festival that will last three days, and you will be the one who throws out the golden apple. Perhaps the mysterious knight will appear."

After the announcement of the festival had been made, the young man rode to the forest's edge and called for Iron John.

"What do you need?" he asked.

"I want to catch the golden apple the King's daughter is going to throw."

"There's no problem: you virtually have it in your hands right now," Iron John replied. "I'll provide you more: red armor for the occasion, and a powerful chestnut horse."

The young man galloped to the field at the proper time, rode in among the other knights, and no one recognized him. The King's daughter stepped forward, and she threw a golden apple into the group of men; and he was the man who caught it. However, having caught it, he galloped off and was gone.

When the second day arrived, Iron John had him fitted out with white armor, and provided for him a white horse. This time also the apple fell into his hands; once more he did not pause for even an instant, but galloped off.

That made the King angry, and the King said, "This behavior is not allowed; he is supposed to ride over to me and report his name."

"If he catches the apple the third time, and gallops off again," he told his men, "chase him. What's more, if he refuses to return, give him a blow; use your sword."

For the third day of the festival, Iron John gave the young man black armor and a black horse. That afternoon the young man caught the apple also. But this time, when he rode away with it, the King's men galloped after him, and one got close enough to give him a leg wound with the end of his sword. The young man escaped; but his horse made such a powerful leap to do so that the young man's helmet fell off, and everyone could see that he had golden hair. The King's men rode home and told the King everything that had happened.

(8)

The King's daughter the next day inquired to the gardener about his boy. "He's back at work in the garden. The strange coot went to the festival yesterday, and only got back last night. He showed my children, by the way, three golden apples he had won."

The King called the young man in, and he appeared with his tarboosh back on his head. The King's daughter, however, went up to him and pulled it off, and his golden hair fell down over his shoulders; his beauty was so great that everyone was astounded.

The King said, "Are you the knight who appeared each day at the festival with a different color horse, and each day caught the golden apple?"

"I am," he said, "and the apples are here." Taking the apples from his pocket, he handed them to the King. "If you need more evidence, you can look at the wound that your men gave me when they were chasing me. What's more, I am also the knight who helped defeat the enemy."

"If you can perform feats of that magnitude, you are obviously not a gardener's boy. Who is your father, may I ask?"

"My father is a notable King, and I have a great deal of gold, as much as I will ever need."

"It's clear," the King said, "that I am in debt to you. Whatever I have in my power that would please you, I will give."

"Well," the young man said, "I'd suggest that you give me your daughter as my wife."

Then the King's daughter laughed and said, "I like the way he doesn't beat around the bush; I already knew he was no gardener's boy from his golden hair." And so she walked over and kissed him.

The young man's father and mother were among those invited to the wedding, and they came; they were in great joy because they had given up hope that they would ever see their dear son again.

While all the guests were sitting at the table for the marriage feast, the music broke off all at once, the great doors swung open, and a baronial King entered, accompanied in procession by many attendants.

He walked up to the young groom and embraced him. The guest said: "I am Iron John, who through an enchantment became turned into a Wild Man. You have freed me from that enchantment. All the treasure that I own will from now on belong to you."

Translation by Robert Bly of the story by Jacob and Wilhelm Grimm in Grimms Märchen *(Zurich: Manesse Verlag, 1946)*

Parts of this translation may be found in the chapters noted in parentheses.

Notes

CHAPTER ONE

P. 13   Alice Miller, *For Your Own Good* (New York: Farrar, Straus & Giroux, 1983).

P. 19   D. H. Lawrence, *The Portable D. H. Lawrence,* ed. Diana Trilling (New York: Viking Penguin, 1955), p. 623.

P. 20   D. H. Lawrence, *Sons and Lovers* (New York: Viking Penguin, 1958).

P. 21   "Finding the Father," from Robert Bly, *Selected Poems* (New York: Harper & Row, 1986), p. 132.

P. 21   Alexander Mitscherlich, *Society Without the Father* (London: Tavistock, 1969).

P. 26   "A Meditation on Philosophy," from Bly, *Selected Poems,* p. 162.

CHAPTER TWO

P. 28   Mircea Eliade, *Rites and Symbols of Initiation* (New York: Harper & Row, 1975).

P. 31   Robert Moore, *Rediscovering Masculine Potentials* (Wilmette, Ill.: Chiron, 1988, four cassette tapes).

P. 33   Alice Miller, *Drama of the Gifted Child* (New York: Basic Books, 1981).

P. 35   Philippe Aries, *Centuries of Childhood* (New York: Knopf, 1962).

P. 35   James Hillman, "The Great Mother, Her Son, Her Hero, and the Puer," in *Fathers and Mothers* (Dallas: Spring Publications, 1990).

P. 38   Geoffrey of Monmouth, *Vita Merlini* (Life of Merlin) (Cardiff, 1973).

P. 38   Aries, *Centuries of Childhood.*

P. 38   Eliade, *Rites and Symbols.*

P. 38   "Fifty Males Sitting Together," from Robert Bly, *Selected Poems* (New York: Harper & Row, 1986).

P. 40   Robert Bly, trans., *The Kabir Book* (Boston: Beacon Press, 1977).

P. 43   Libby and Arthur Coleman, *The Father* (Wilmette, Ill.: Chiron, 1988).

P. 44   Alexander Mitscherlich, *Society Without the Father* (London: Tavistock, 1969).

P. 47   "Four Ways of Knowledge," from Bly, *Selected Poems.*

P. 48   "The Three Beggars," from W. B. Yeats, *The Poems of W. B. Yeats,* ed. Richard J. Finneran (New York: Macmillan, 1983), p. 111.

P. 51   "Moral Proverbs and Folk Songs," from Antonio Machado, *Times Alone,* trans. Robert Bly (Middletown, Conn.: Wesleyan University Press, 1983), p. 147.

P. 51   Juan Ramón Jiménez from *Lorca and Jiménez: Selected Poems,* trans. Robert Bly (Boston: Beacon Press, 1973), p. 77.

P. 52   "Guardian Angel," from Rolf Jacobsen, *Twenty Poems,* trans. Robert Bly (Madison, Minn.: Seventies Press, 1976).

P. 52   "The Marriage of Heaven and Hell," from William Blake, *The Portable Blake,* ed. Alfred Kazin (New York: Viking, 1946).

CHAPTER THREE

P. 57   "Science," from Robinson Jeffers, *Selected Poetry* (New York: Random House, 1953).

P. 57   Marie-Louise von Franz, *Puer Aeternus* (Boston: Sigo Press, 1981).

P. 62   Maggy Scarf, *Intimate Partners* (New York: Random House, 1987).

P. 69   George Orwell, *Down and Out in Paris and London* (New York: Viking Penguin, 1962).

P. 71   "every mark of his former art and life." From "The Thirty-Three Ring Circus," John Logan, *Collected Poems* (Brockport, N.Y.: BOA Editions, 1989), p. 133.

P. 71   Sandra Gilbert and Susan Gubar, *The Madwoman in the Attic:*

A Study of Women and the Literary Imagination in the Nineteenth Century (New Haven, Conn.: Yale University Press, 1979).

P. 72 "The Spider" by César Vallejo, from *Neruda and Vallejo, Selected Poems,* trans. Robert Bly and James Wright (Boston: Beacon Press, 1971).

P. 73 "Have You Anything to Say in Your Defense?" by César Vallejo, from *Neruda and Vallejo.*

P. 75 "Standing Up" by Tomas Transtromer, from *Friends, You Drank Some Darkness: Three Swedish Poets,* trans. Robert Bly (Boston: Beacon Press, 1975).

P. 75 "Fourteen Poems," from Antonio Machado, *Times Alone,* trans. Robert Bly (Middletown, Conn.: Wesleyan University Press, 1983), p. 113.

P. 76 "Healing," from D. H. Lawrence, *The Complete Poems of D. H. Lawrence,* vol. 3 (New York: Viking Penguin, 1971), p. 50.

P. 78 Charlotte Guest, trans., *The Mabinogion* (Chicago: Academy Chicago Publishers, 1978).

P. 79 R. Keyser, *Private Life of the Old Northmen* (London: Chapman and Hall, 1868).

P. 82 "The Oven Bird," from Robert Frost, *The Poetry of Robert Frost,* ed. Edward C. Lathem (New York: Henry Holt, 1979).

P. 83 "Brussels" by Pablo Neruda, from *Neruda and Vallejo.*

P. 84 Murray Stein, *In MidLife* (Dallas: Spring Publications, 1983).

P. 86 Gilbert H. Herdt, ed., *Rituals of Manhood: Male Initiation in Papua New Guinea* (Berkeley and Los Angeles: University of California Press, 1982), p. 121.

P. 89 Joseph Campbell, *Occidental Mythology* (New York: Viking, 1964), p. 14.

CHAPTER FOUR

P. 92 Geoffrey Gorer, *The American People* (New York: W. W. Norton, 1964).

P. 93 Bruno Bettelheim, *Symbolic Wounds* (Glencoe, N.Y.: The Free Press, 1954).

P. 95 Alexander Mitscherlich, *Society Without the Father* (London: Tavistock, 1969).

P. 98 D. H. Lawrence, *Apocalypse* (London: Penguin, 1978), p. 21.

P. 100 James Hillman, "The Great Mother, Her Son, Her Hero, and the Puer," in *Fathers and Mothers* (Dallas: Spring Publications, 1990).

P. 100 Marie-Louise von Franz, *Puer Aeternus* (Boston: Sigo Press, 1981).

P. 105   Edward Edinger, *Anatomy of the Psyche* (LaSalle, Ill.: Open Court, 1985), p. 211.

P. 107   John Weir Perry, *Lord of the Four Quarters: Myths of the Royal Father* (New York: Braziller, 1966).

P. 108   Robert Moore and Douglas Gillette, *King, Warrior, Magician, Lover: Rediscovering the Archetypes of the Mature Masculine* (New York: Harper & Row, 1990).

P. 112   William Stafford, "The End of the Golden String," in *Writing the Australian Crawl* (Ann Arbor: University of Michigan Press, 1978).

P. 115   Franz Kafka, *Metamorphosis* (New York: Schocken, 1968).

P. 115   Franz Kafka, *The Complete Stories* (New York: Schocken, 1983).

P. 121   John Layard, "On Psychic Consciousness," in *The Virgin Archetype* (Zurich: Spring Publications, 1972).

CHAPTER FIVE

P. 123   Charlotte Guest, trans., *The Mabinogion* (Chicago: Academy Chicago Publishers, 1978).

P. 124   John Cheever, "The Chaste Clarissa," in *The Stories of John Cheever* (New York: Knopf, 1978).

P. 126   "Little Infinite Poem" by Federico García Lorca, from *Lorca and Jiménez: Selected Poems,* trans. Robert Bly (Boston: Beacon Press, 1973).

P. 129   "Heaven-Haven," from Gerard Manley Hopkins, *Poems and Prose,* ed. W. H. Gardner (New York: Viking Penguin, 1953).

P. 129   "I am too alone in the world," from Rainer Maria Rilke, *Selected Poems of Rainer Maria Rilke,* trans. Robert Bly (New York: Harper & Row, 1981).

P. 130   "Little Infinite Poem" by Federico García Lorca, from *Lorca and Jiménez: Selected Poems.*

P. 131   "The Minimal," from Theodore Roethke, *The Collected Poems* (New York: Doubleday, 1975).

P. 131   "Someone Digging in the Garden," from Rumi, *Open Secret,* trans. John Moyne and Coleman Barks (Putney, Vt.: Threshold Books, 1984).

P. 132   "The Mole" by Al-Muntafil, from Robert Bly, ed., *The Sea and the Honeycomb* (Boston: Beacon Press, 1971).

P. 132   "The meeting" by Ibn Hazm, from Bly, ed., *The Sea and the Honeycomb.*

P. 133   "When we are in love," from Robert Bly, *Silence in the Snowy Fields* (Middletown, Conn.: Wesleyan University Press, 1962).

P. 133 "It was among ferns," from Robert Bly, *Loving a Woman in Two Worlds* (New York: Doubleday, 1985).

P. 134 "Come to the Garden in Spring," from Rumi, *Open Secret*.

P. 134 Marian Woodman, *Addiction to Perfection* (Toronto: Inner City Books, 1982).

P. 134 "I have many brothers in the South," from Rilke, *Selected Poems*.

P. 138 "A Dream of an Afternoon with a Woman I Did Not Know," from Robert Bly, *This Tree Will Be Here for a Thousand Years* (New York: Harper & Row, 1979).

P. 138 "The woman I worship" by Dante, trans. Robert Bly, unpublished. The original can be found in *Vita Nuova*.

P. 139 "Memory," from W. B. Yeats, *The Poems of W. B. Yeats,* ed. Richard J. Finneran (New York: Macmillan, 1983), p. 149.

P. 140 "Poem #4," from Robert Bly, trans., *The Kabir Book* (Boston: Beacon Press, 1977).

P. 141 "The Scholars," from W. B. Yeats, *The Poems,* p. 140.

P. 141 John Layard, "On Psychic Consciousness," in *The Virgin Archetype* (Zurich: Spring Publications, 1972).

P. 142 "Close to the road," from Antonio Machado, *Times Alone,* trans. Robert Bly (Middletown, Conn.: Wesleyan University Press, 1983).

P. 143 Rafael López-Pedraza, *Hermes and His Children* (Zurich: Spring Publications, 1977).

CHAPTER SIX

P. 147 Gershen Kauffman, *Shame* (Cambridge, Mass.: Schenkman Books, 1980).

P. 147 Merle Fossum and Marilyn Mason, *Facing Shame* (New York: W. W. Norton, 1986).

P. 148 "Snow Geese," from Robert Bly, *Selected Poems* (New York: Harper & Row, 1986).

P. 149 Georges Dumézil, *The Destiny of the Warrior,* trans. Alf Hiltebeitel (Chicago: University of Chicago Press, 1971).

P. 150 Robert Moore, *Rediscovering Masculine Potentials* (Wilmette, Ill.: Chiron, 1988, four cassette tapes).

P. 152 Neil Forsythe, *The Old Enemy: Satan and the Combat Myth* (Princeton, N.J.: Princeton University Press, 1987).

P. 152 About Marduk and Tiamat, see Joseph Campbell, *Occidental Mythology* (New York: Viking, 1964), pp. 74–84.

P. 155   Jean de Breuil quote from Norbert Elias, *The Civilizing Process* (New York: Urizen Books, 1978).

P. 159   "Defeated," from Bly, *Selected Poems,* p. 19.

P. 160   "And what if after so many words" by César Vallejo, from *Neruda and Vallejo, Selected Poems,* trans. Robert Bly and James Wright (Boston: Beacon Press, 1971).

P. 163   Henri Corbin, *Spiritual Body and Celestial Earth,* trans. Nancy Pearson (Princeton, N.J.: Princeton University Press, 1977), pp. 171–175.

P. 164   José Ortega y Gasset, *Meditations on Quixote* (New York: W. W. Norton, 1969).

P. 166   C. G. Jung, "Seven Sermons to the Dead," Chapter 11 in *Psychology and Religion* (Princeton, N.J.: Princeton University Press, 1958).

P. 168   Marie-Louise von Franz, private communication.

P. 168   Marian Woodman, *The Ravaged Bridegroom* (Toronto: Inner City Books, 1990).

P. 172   Anton Chekhov, "The Darling," from *Tales of Chekhov: The Darling,* vol. 1 (New York: Ecco Press, 1984).

P. 173   "Home Burial," from Robert Frost, *The Poetry of Robert Frost,* ed. Edward C. Lathem (New York: Henry Holt, 1979).

P. 176   "Parable," from Richard Wilbur, *Ceremony and Other Poems* (New York: Harcourt Brace, 1950).

P. 176   "The Wild Old Wicked Man," from W. B. Yeats, *The Poems of W. B. Yeats,* ed. Richard J. Finneran (New York: Macmillan, 1983), p. 310.

P. 177   Edward Edinger, *Anatomy of the Psyche* (LaSalle, Ill.: Open Court, 1985), p. 195.

CHAPTER SEVEN

P. 180   Michael Ventura, "The Age of Endarkenment," *Whole Earth Review,* Winter 1989.

P. 183   Marian Woodman, *The Ravaged Bridegroom* (Toronto: Inner City Books, 1990).

P. 183   Charlotte Guest, trans., *The Mabinogion* (Chicago: Academy Chicago Publishers, 1978).

P. 183   Aleksandr Afanas'ev, comp., *Russian Fairy Tales* (New York: Pantheon, 1975).

P. 184   Marian Woodman, private communication.

P. 185   Mari Sandoz, *These Were the Sioux* (Lincoln, Nebr.: University of Nebraska Press, 1985).

P. 194   Victor Turner, *Ritual Process* (Ithaca, N.Y.: Cornell University Press, 1977).

P. 195   Morris Berman, *The Enchantment of the World* (Ithaca, N.Y.: Cornell University Press, 1981).

P. 199   "How sweet to weigh the line" by Robert Bly, unpublished poem.

P. 199   "Snow White," in Ralph Manheim, trans., *Grimm's Tales for Young and Old* (New York: Doubleday, 1983).

P. 200   Turner, *Ritual Process.*

P. 200   Victor Turner, *A Forest of Symbols* (Ithaca, N.Y.: Cornell University Press, 1970).

P. 201   Turner, *Forest of Symbols.*

P. 201   Barbara Walker, *The Crone* (New York: Harper & Row, 1985).

P. 202   Carl G. Jung; see Edward Edinger, *Anatomy of the Psyche* (LaSalle, Ill.: Open Court, 1985).

P. 202   J. S. La Fontaine, *Initiation* (New York: Viking Penguin, 1985), pp. 154–159.

P. 203   Afanas'ev, comp., *Russian Fairy Tales.*

P. 203   Wolfram von Eschenbach, *Parzival* (New York: Vintage Books, 1961).

P. 206   "The Draft Horse," from Robert Frost, *The Poetry of Robert Frost,* ed. Edward C. Lathem (New York: Henry Holt, 1979).

CHAPTER EIGHT

P. 207   Chretien de Troyes, *Perceval,* from Laura H. Loomis and Roger S. Loomis, eds., *Medieval Romances* (New York: Random House, 1965).

P. 210   Sir James Frazer, *The Golden Bough* (New York: Macmillan, 1907).

P. 211   Ad de Vries, *Dictionary of Symbols and Imagery* (New York: American Elsevier, 1976).

P. 211   Robert Graves, *The Greek Myths* (New York: Viking Penguin, 1955).

P. 212   John Layard, *The Stone Age Men of Malekula* (London, 1942).

P. 212   Ovid, *Metamorphoses,* trans. Rolfe Humphries (Bloomington, Ind.: Indiana University Press, 1955).

P. 213   Margaret Walker, *Encyclopedia of Women's Myths and Secrets* (New York: Harper & Row, 1983).

P. 213   Bruno Bettelheim, *Symbolic Wounds* (Glencoe, N.Y.: The Free Press, 1954).

P. 214   Robert Fitzgerald, trans., *The Odyssey* (New York: Doubleday, 1961).

P. 216   André Leroi-Gourhan, *Treasures of Prehistoric Art* (New York: Abrams, 1967).

P. 217   William Shakespeare, "Venus and Adonis."

P. 218   "Crazy Jane Talks with the Bishop," from W. B. Yeats, *The Poems of W. B. Yeats,* ed. Richard J. Finneran (New York: Macmillan, 1983), p. 259.

P. 221   Heinz Kohut, *Self Psychology and the Humanities,* ed. Charles B. Strozier (New York: W. W. Norton, 1985).

P. 223   "Heaven-Haven," from Gerard Manley Hopkins, *Poems and Prose,* ed. W. H. Gardner (New York: Viking Penguin, 1953).

P. 223   "The strong leaves of the box-elder tree" from "Poem in Three Parts," from Robert Bly, *Silence in the Snowy Fields* (Middletown, Conn.: Wesleyan University Press, 1962).

P. 224   "Sometimes I go about pitying myself," from Robert Bly, *News of the Universe* (San Francisco: Sierra Club Books, 1981).

P. 224   William James, *The Will to Believe* (Cambridge: Harvard University Press, 1979).

P. 226   Rumi, *Open Secret,* trans. John Moyne and Coleman Barks (Putney, Vt.: Threshold Books, 1984).

P. 228   Paul Radin, *The Trickster* (New York: Schocken, 1972).

P. 228   Robert Moore, *Rediscovering Masculine Potentials* (Wilmette, Ill.: Chiron, 1988, four cassette tapes).

P. 229   "Have You Anything to Say in Your Defense?" by César Vallejo, from *Neruda and Vallejo, Selected Poems,* trans. Robert Bly and James Wright (Boston: Beacon Press, 1971).

P. 229   "After a Death" by Tomas Transtromer, from *Friends, You Drank Some Darkness: Three Swedish Poets,* trans. Robert Bly (Boston: Beacon Press, 1975).

P. 229   "To the Muse," from James Wright, *Collected Poems* (Middletown, Conn.: Wesleyan University Press, 1981).

P. 236   "It's important to pay attention," from Rumi, *When Grapes Turn to Wine,* trans. Robert Bly (Cambridge, Mass.: Yellow Moon Press, 1986).

EPILOGUE

P. 239   John Pfeiffer, *The Creative Explosion: An Inquiry into the Origins of Art and Religion* (Ithaca, N.Y.: Cornell University Press, 1985).

P. 240   Mircea Eliade, in *The Creative Explosion*.

P. 240   Alain Danielou, *Shiva and Dionysus* (London: East-West Publications, 1982).

P. 240   Ananda Coomaraswamy, *The Dance of Siva: Essays on Indian Art and Culture* (New York: Dover, 1985).

P. 242   Chretien de Troyes, *Yvain, the Knight of the Lion,* trans. Burton Raffel (New Haven: Yale University Press, 1987).

P. 243   *Gilgamesh:* see Joseph Campbell, *Occidental Mythology* (New York: Viking, 1964), pp. 88–92.

P. 245   Timothy Husband, *The Wild Man in Medieval Myth and Symbolism* (New York: Metropolitan Museum of Art, 1980).

P. 248   William Blake, *The Portable Blake,* ed. Alfred Kazin (New York: Viking, 1946).

P. 248   For Gregory of Nyssa and Augustine: see Elaine Pagels, *Adam, Eve, and the Serpent* (New York: Random House, 1988), pp. 79–80, 110–III.